ACROSS THE ATLANTIC

THE ADAMOWICZ BROTHERS

POLISH AVIATION PIONEERS

Across the Atlantic
The Adamowicz Brothers
Polish Aviation Pioneers

by

Zofia Reklewska-Braun

and

Kazimierz Braun

Los Angeles, 2015

Across the Atlantic: The Adamowicz Brothers, Polish Aviation Pioneers
By Zofia Reklewska-Braun and Kazimierz Braun

This book is a publication of **Moonrise Press**
P.O. Box 4288, Los Angeles – Sunland, CA 91041-4288
info@moonrisepress.com
www.moonrisepress.com; moonrisepress.blogspot.com

© Copyright 2015 by Moonrise Press and the authors, Zofia Reklewska-Braun and Kazimierz Braun

This is an expanded and revised edition of a book first published in Polish: Zofia Reklewska-Braun and Kazimierz Braun, *Bracia Adamowiczowie Emigranci – lotnicy; Pierwsi polscy zdobywcy północnego Atlantyku. Z archiwum pisarza*, Rzeszów, Poland: Wydawnictwo Uniwersytetu Rzeszowskiego. 2011. ISBN 978-83-7338-656-3. A different English version, edited by Dr. Mary Anne Rokitka, was published as *The Adamowicz Brothers. Immigrants--Aviators. First Polish Conquerors of the North Atlantic*. Buffalo, NY: Polish Cultural Foundation, 2011.

All Rights Reserved
No part of this book may be reproduced or utilized in any form or by any means, electronic or mechanical, including photocopying and recording, or by any information storage and retrieval system, without permission in writing from the publisher.

Book design and layout by Maja Trochimczyk using fonts: Times New Roman and Tahoma. Cover design by Maja Trochimczyk.

MANUFACTURED IN THE UNITED STATES OF AMERICA

The Library of Congress Publication Data:

Zofia Reklewska-Braun (1939–) and Kazimierz Braun (1936–)
Across the Atlantic: The Adamowicz Brothers, Polish Aviation Pioneers
    pp. xxii+218, 15.2 x 22.9 cm.
    Includes 56 illustrations and portraits, bibliography, and an index.

ISBN 978-0-9963981-2-1 (paperback)
ISBN 978-0-9963981-3-8 (eBook – EPUB format)

10 9 8 7 6 5 4 3 2 1

TABLE OF CONTENTS

List of Illustrations (vii)

Introduction (xii)

Acknowledgments (xvi)

Chapter 1: Genealogy (3)

Chapter 2: On the New Continent (16)

Chapter 3: Work and Leisure (22)

Chapter 4: The Brothers in Business (27)

Chapter 5: Planting Roots in America (31)

Chapter 6: Soda Water and Soda Pop (38)

Chapter 7: First Flights (45)

Chapter 8: Air Conquest of the Atlantic (51)

Chapter 9: Bellanca (64)

Chapter 10: A "Trial Flight" Across the Ocean (76)

Chapter 11: Being a Pole in America (81)

Chapter 12: Learning to Fly and Navigate (85)

Chapter 13: Heading for Poland (92)

Chapter 14: Across the Atlantic (98)

Chapter 15: In Europe (110)

Chapter 16: In Poland (116)

Chapter 17: In Warsaw (119)

Chapter 18: A Royal Reception (130)

Chapter 19: The Tour of Poland (140)

Chapter 20: Polonia Congress in Warsaw (151)

Chapter 21: In Their Birthplace (158)

Chapter 22: A "Little Man" Above the Atlantic (162)

Chapter 23: Return to America (168)

Chapter 24: Facing American Justice (173)

Chapter 25: The First Trial (177)

Chapter 26: The Second Trial (181)

Chapter 27: Imprisonment (187)

Chapter 28: Bankruptcy (191)

Chapter 29: Adamowicz Brothers Pass Away (194)

Postscript (199)

Selected Bibliography (203)

About the Authors (207)

Index (210)

LIST OF ILLUSTRATIONS

NOTE: The following abbreviations are used to indicate sources of illustrations:
- *BFRC – photographs and illustrations from the Braun Family Research Collection. Used by Permission.*
- *BJA – Photographs from the Adamowiczes' book, Przez Atlantyk, 1934, edited by Stanisław Strumph-Wojtkiewicz. Public Domain.*
- *MMMC - photographs and illustrations from the Maureen Mroczek Morris Collection. Used by Permission.*

Figure 1: "Leliwa" coat of arms from Wojciech Wiiuk Kojałowicz, *Herbarz szlachty Wielkiego Księstwa Litewskiego zwany Nomenclator* [The Armorial of the Nobility of the Grand Duchy of Lithuania, known as Nomenclator]. 1658. Reprinted in Kraków, 1905.

Figure 2: Map fragment of "The Partition of Russia in Europe" with borders from 1914. The area that the Adamowicz family comes from is near the borders of Poland, White Russia and Lithuania to the west of the center of the map. Maja Trochimczyk's Collection.

Figure 3: Handwritten Manifest of Passengers from a ship arriving in 1905, The name of Osip Adamowicz is second from the bottom. Courtesy of American Family Immigration History Center at Ellis Island.

Figure 4: Document from the Immigration Office at Ellis Island in New York stating Bronisław Adamowicz's entry to the United States, April 5, 1911. Courtesy of American Family Immigration History Center at Ellis Island.

Figure 5: The Adamowicz brothers' apartment building. Three brothers occupied apartments on the first floor. Photo by Monika Braun.

Figure 6 a, b: Joseph Adamowicz's application for American naturalization dated December 16, 1925. He was naturalized on March 23, 1926. Courtesy of the U.S. Department of Labor.

Figure 7 a, b: Benjamin Adamowicz's application for a passport for a travel to Poland. The passport was issued June 14, 1933. It is one of the proofs that Ben and Joe planned to fly to Poland in 1933 r. Courtesy of the U.S. State Department.

Figure 8: The Adamowicz "soda water factory" in 2010. The bottling plant was on the first floor and the "Speak Easy" hall on the second floor. Photo by Monika Braun.

Figure 9: The factory and the apartment building (seen in 2010). Photo by Monika Braun.

Figure 10: Charles Lindbergh's historical plane, The Spirit of St. Louis, in the National Air and Space Museum, Washington, D.C. Photo by Raul654, May 7, 2005. Wikimedia Commons.

Figure 11: Bellanca WB-2 Columbia, 1927 Transatlantic flight 4-6 June 1927 from New York to Eisleben in Germany. Wikimedia Commons. Photograph from RAF Museum, UK: www.rafmuseum.com/milestones-of-flight/world/1927.html.

Figure 12: Major Stanisław Skarżyński, 1934 portrait by Willem van de Poll. Dutch National Archives, The Hague, Fotocollectie Algemeen Nederlands Persbureau (ANeFo), 1945-1989, Nummer toegang 2.24.14.02 Bestanddeelnummer 190-1343. Wikimedia Commons.

Figure 13: Majors Idzikowski and Kubala in a French plane Amiot 123 named *Marszalek Pilsudski,* in an attempted transatlantic flight in 1926. Wikimedia Commons.

Figure 14: A Lithuanian banknote for 10 litu, commemorating the flight of Darius and Girenas. Wikimedia Commons.

Figure 15: Bellanca "Warsaw" before its flight on August 8, 1934 from Floyd Bennett Field in New York to Harbour Grace in Newfoundland, Canada. *Lotnictwo z Szachownicą* 31.

Figure 16: A 1927 press report about Bellanca's 1930 victory in a flight competition, the National Air Tour.

Figure 17: Bellanca's 1934 press add emphasizing the aircraft's safety.

Figure 18: A Press Report about Bellanca's Win in Cleveland. *Aviation,* October 5, 1929.

Figure 19: The Adamowicz's Bellanca stored in an air hangar in Poland, airport Katowice-Muchowiec, 1937. *Lotnictwo z Szachownicą* 31.

Figure 20: Bellanca at the start of the last stage of their flight around Poland, from Toruń to Warsaw, July 2, 1934, at 4 p.m. *Lotnictwo z Szachownicą* 31.

Figure 21: Bellanca at the Warsaw airport. BJA.

Figure 22: Press clipping of the pilots with their family (Ben with his wife and Joe with their sister) before departure from the Floyd Bonnet Airport, New York. *Indiana Evening Gazette*, 29 June 1934.

Figure 23: The farewell ceremony on June 28, 1934 at 7:30a.m. at the Floyd Bennett Field, New York. *Lotnictwo z Szachownicą* 31.

Figure 24: From the flight log. The Atlantic flight is recorded as start to Warsaw. BJA.

Figure 25: Bellanca in Harbour Grace, Newfoundland, on 28 June 1934, 12 hours before departure. Standing, L to R: Otto Hillig, former owner of the plane and Ben Adamowicz. *Lotnictwo z Szachownicą* 31.

Figure 26: A flight log page with a prayer "God, have mercy on us." BJA.

Figure 27: Photo of the Brothers and onlookers before their departure from Chessay, France. BJA.

Figure 28: Bellanca in Paris. In front of the aircraft from the left: Polish Ambassador Afred Chłapowski, Ben Adamowicz, Joseph Adamowicz. *Skrzydlata Polska* 6.

Figure 29: The plane and the onlookers after the landing in Nedlitz Thiemenberg, Germany. BJA.

Figure 30: Refueling of Bellanca at the Torun airport, July 2, 1934. *Lotnictwo z Szachownicą* 31.

Figure 31: Welcoming crowds at Warsaw's Pola Mokotowskie airport. *Polska Lotnicza*, 1937.

Figure 32: Photo of a triumphant passage through Warsaw from the airport the City Hall. BJA.

Figure 33: Ben and Joe with the American Ambassador John Cudahy at the Warsaw's City Hall just after their arrival. Wikimedia Commons.

Figure 34: Brothers Adamowicz received by the President of Poland Ignacy Mościcki. L to R: Capt. Henryk Dąbrowski (official chaperon of the brothers in Poland) Ben, Joseph, President Mościcki, Ambassador John Cudahy. BJA.

Figure 35: Joseph, Prince Janusz Radziwiłł (President of the Polish Aero Club), Ben, Ambassador John Cudahy, Major Stanisław Skarżyński. BJA.

Figure 36: Ben and Joseph decorated with the CDYDOLHU Cross of the Order of the "Polonia Restituta" by the Minister of Transportation. Michał Butkiewicz (first from the left). BJA.

Figure 37: The brothers' crosses, given to Lanny Kemmis; photo from L. Kemmis sent to Maureen Mroczek Morris.

Figure 38: Bolesław Adamowicz with wife Elizabeth. BJA.

Figure 39: The brothers visiting the PKO Bank in Warsaw. BJA.

Figure 40: Bellanca before takeoff from Warsaw to Inowrocław.

Figure 41: The Adamowicz brothers with Major Stanisław Skarżyński, the first Polish pilot to cross the Atlantic in a solo flight. *Polska Lotnicza*, 1937.

Figure 42: The brothers are driven through the streets of Grudziądz. On the back seat – Ben, Elizabeth, and Joseph. BFRC.

Figure 43: The brothers with their Bellanca. *Lotnictwo z Szachownicą* 31.

Figure 44: The Adamowicz brothers with their Bellanca. BRFC.

Figure 45: Greetings from the pilots to the Polish children, published in the Polish children's magazine *Płomyczek* [Little Flame], Warsaw, 9 July 1934.

Figure 46: The Adamowicz brothers with their plane in Warsaw. BFRC.

Figure 47: A Polish cartoon of "Adamowiczes, the only brothers that flew across the Atlantic." MMMC.

Figure 48: Stamped mail envelope commemorating the transatlantic flight, with American and Polish stamps. The brothers took with them several dozens of such envelopes on their flight to Warsaw. Maja Trochimczyk Collection. Used by Permission.

Figure 49: Response from the U.S. Department of Justice to a query about the incarceration of the brothers Adamowicz: Benjamin, Bronisław and Joseph. MMMC.

Figure 50: General view of the United States Federal Penitentiary, Lewisburg.

Figure 51: United States Federal Penitentiary, Lewisburg.

Figure 52: Map of St. John Cemetery in Brooklyn with the location of the Adamowicz brothers' tombs.

Figure 53: The Adamowicz brothers' tombstone, with the following inscription: Joseph (1893–1970), Benjamin (1896–). St. John's Cemetery, Middle Village, New York. Photo by Adolfina Tymczyszyn.

Figure 54 a, b: Bruno Adamowicz's Death Certificate. Courtesy of Bureau of Records, Department of Health, Borough of Brooklyn. Used by permission.

INTRODUCTION

In this volume, we present our readers with the very first, comprehensive history of the lives and deeds of the Adamowicz brothers, Polish-American aviation pioneers. *Across the Atlantic* is the only comprehensive history of the lives and deeds of Joe and Ben Adamowicz – aviation heroes forgotten by time and the *first amateurs*, to have crossed the Atlantic by air. We examine their victories and defeats, years of hard work, crowning achievements, short-lived celebrity, and their illicit business ventures leading to imprisonment and bankruptcy.[1] At the time, in Europe Hitler rose to power and was mobilizing to invade Poland. In America, Prohibition had only recently been revoked.

During the summer of 1934, two Polish amateur-pilots, Joseph (Józef) and Benjamin (Bolesław) Adamowicz, who immigrated to the United States of America more than twenty years earlier, accomplished an extraordinary feat. While using exclusively their own resources, skills, brains, cleverness, and diligence, and while taking an enormous risk, they flew over the North Atlantic on a single-engine Bellanca aircraft. Their trip took them from New York to Warsaw.

Their arrival incited euphoria in Poland. Enthusiastic crowds shouting their names met them as they landed at Warsaw's airport, and then dozens of times during their triumphant tour of their native land. The highest dignitaries of the Republic of

---

[1] This book is a translation of Zofia Reklewska-Braun and Kazimierz Braun (*Bracia Adamowiczowie Emigranci – lotnicy; Pierwsi polscy zdobywcy północnego Atlantyku Z archiwum pisarza*, v. 2. Wydawnictwo Uniwersytetu Rzeszowskiego. Rzeszów 2011 (in Polish). ISBN 978-83-7338-656-3. An English edition was published as *The Adamowicz Brothers. Immigrants--Aviators. First Polish Conquerors of the North Atlantic*. Buffalo, NY: Polish Cultural Foundation, 2011. The present project is a corrected and expanded version of the book.

Poland received them with honors: President Ignacy Mościcki, Prime Minister Leon Kozłowski, members of the government, mayors of the cities, and generals. During theatrical spectacles actors presented tributes that they designed and rehearsed especially for them.

The pilots were amply honored and decorated; both received the "Cavalier Cross of the Order of the Resurrected Poland." The two pilots were transformed into icons of both resilient Polish patriots and successful emigrants. They became instant celebrities, favorites of the journalists, photographers, and the public on both sides of the Atlantic.

The Polish press reported every step they made in Poland and the American press hailed them as heroes. Newspapers all over the world informed about their flight. They recounted their story to a writer, Stanisław Strumph-Wojtkiewicz, who immediately proceeded to print it in installments in a newspaper[2] and soon after publish this exciting story as a book.[3] Furthermore, a variety of commercial memorabilia were marketed and sold, including envelopes with the Adamowicz signatures, as well as postage stamps and commemorative medals with their faces – an assortment of trinkets immortalizing their flight.

"All that jazz," however, lasted only for a blink of an eye. In a few years, the Adamowicz brothers sunk into oblivion. The World War II erased memories about them; it also resulted in the

---

[2] Bolesław and Józef Adamowicz, "Przez Atlantyk [Over the Atlantic]" transcribed from the aviators account and edited by Stanisław Strumph-Wojtkiewicz. Printed in *Ilustrowany Kurier Warszawski*, evening edition, serialized since July 10, 1934, later printed also in the morning edition of the same newspaper. Published as a book under the same title in August 1934.

[3] Adamowicz, Bolesław and Adamowicz, Józef. *Przez Atlantyk.* Spisał z relacji lotników i opracował Stanisław Strumph Wojtkiewicz. „Pod egidą Aeroklubu R.P."[*Across the the Atlantic.* Written down from the reports of flyers and edited by Stanislaw Strumph Wojtkiewicz. Under the aegis of the Aero Club of the Republic of Poland]. Warszaw: Wydawnictwo M. Arcta, 1934

loss of many documents, photographs, newsreels, and paper clippings. Most poignantly, the historical Bellanca aircraft which carried them over the ocean from America back to their homeland was destroyed by the Germans.

After the initial enthusiasm, the Adamowiczes adopted country, the United Stated of America, treated them harshly. As non-professionals in the aviation world, distant from the elite pilots of their times, the flights by these Polish-Americans were not included in the registers of major achievements of American pilots. Similarly, the general history of aviation neglected to include them in its annals. When it did so, the Adamowicz brothers received only marginal recognition and were mentioned in a context diminishing their achievement. Lies distorted their real story and fun was made of them.

In fact, they were treated as a curiosity. Americans ironically looked upon the figures of two brothers, uneducated Poles, speaking in broken English, with a heavy foreign accent. These pilots were inexperienced in giving interviews, lacked manners, and did not know how to boast and brag about their feats. To make things worse, the disgrace which they carelessly brought upon themselves resulted in almost complete absence of coverage of their lives after their transatlantic journey. Many publications as well as internet files end their story just after their successful landing in Warsaw and the ten-week-long visit to Poland. Frequently, these incomplete accounts conclude with a variant of a remark: "Their further fate remains unknown."[4]

In this book, we break the curtain and narrate both the known and the unknown parts of the Adamowicz brothers' story. These events deserve to be recalled. The brothers deserve that their true story be told accurately, with attention paid to the historical detail — not filled with journalistic gibberish,

---

[4] These comments are based on paper clippings collected by the authors in the private Braun Family Collection (BFRC).

unconfirmed gossip, or deliberately fabricated lies.

The Adamowicz brothers accomplished something really significant. They conquered the North Atlantic only seven years after Charles Lindbergh. They were the first Poles to fly over the ocean. They were the very first aviators to fly from New York to Warsaw. It is imperative to give them justice and worthwhile to understand their motives. Why would two simple boys from a small village somewhere in eastern Poland who became laborers in Brooklyn find in their hearts such dedication and summon up enough courage and perseverance to do what they did?

Amelia Earhart, the first woman-pilot, and a professional pilot who made a solo flight over the Atlantic from New York to Ireland in May 1932, was asked why she loves to fly. Her answer was: "And why mount a horse?"

Benjamin and Joseph Adamowicz, first amateur pilots who crossed the Atlantic in the air, when asked why they did it, used to answer: "For the greater glory of Poland!"

~ Zofia Reklewska-Braun and Kazimierz Braun
Wrocław, Buffalo, New York, 2009-2011

ACKNOWLEDGEMENTS

This book is a collaborative work. Both authors, Zofia Reklewska-Braun and Kazimierz Braun, have been studying and documenting the most recent history of Poland for years. They have been fascinated especially with the history of the Polish immigration to America.

The idea of writing this book was conceived by Grzegorz Braun, their son, a filmmaker. He found materials on the Adamowicz brothers and suggested several structural and historical options for a book on them. We are very grateful to Grzegorz for this incentive and for directing us to follow the Adamowicz footprints.

Zofia started to amass documents, sources, press clippings, and information about the brothers she found on the internet. She worked tirelessly for many, long months. She corresponded with many specialists. Eventually she compiled an extensive collection of materials and created a historic, chronological, and coherent narrative which begins in the last years of the 19th century in the eastern territories of Poland and ends in the cemeteries of New York, in the second part of the 20th century.

Kazimierz put together Grzegorz's ideas and Zofia's research. He added results of his own historical studies and penned the final version of the text.

Monika Braun, Zofia and Kazimierz's daughter, helped in the field investigations in Brooklyn and Lewisburg. She also took pictures of the old properties of the Adamowiczes.

Invaluable partner and companion of this journey into both Poland and America's past and the history of aviation was Maureen Mroczek Morris, an American researcher of Polish descent, a specialist in computer inquiries. She very significantly contributed to this project with her energy, inquisitiveness, ingenuity, and hard work. We thank Maureen wholeheartedly for her efforts and help, as well as kindness and patience with which she answered our never ending questions. It was Maureen who found and shared much of the corroborating data, specifically the genealogy data, including marriage and death certificates, passport applications, passenger records, news reels, and prisoner records. Maureen collected numerous newspaper articles and photographs. She also located the brothers' graves, traced living relatives and friends of the brothers, and established contact with some members of their family. Her contributions are invaluable.

We received important guidance from David Newman, President of the Polish Genealogical Society in Buffalo, New York. Adoflina Tymczyszyn took photographs of tombstones of Adamowicz brothers we used while working on our narrative. We sincerely thank both of them.

Michalina Byra, an adviser at the National Library in Warsaw, was Kazimierz's experienced guide when he was searching for materials. The National Library's manager, Dr. Tomasz Makowski, provided Kazimierz with favorable conditions for his work in the Library. We are very grateful to both the management and the staff of the National Library. Also Danuta Bromowicz from the Library of the Jagiellonian University in Kraków, Poland, sent us many important bibliographical data. We offer her our heartfelt gratitude.

We obtained help from our friend, an excellent historian, Janina Hera-Asłanowicz, who sent us a variety of materials from Polish archives. We thank her with our whole hearts.

We are very grateful to Cono Savino, who is presently the manager of "Savino's Quality Pasta," an establishment producing pizza and other Italian goods which occupies the building of the former Adamowiczes' soda factory, located at 111 Conselyea Street in Brooklyn, New York. Mr. Cono Savino, his father Frank (the owner of the establishment) and his mother Josephine shared with us many pieces of information about this important site, that was truly special for the Adamowicz brothers.

We are enormously grateful to Rzeszów University and its publishing house (Wydawnictwo Uniwersytetu Rzeszowskiego). In particular, Prof. Dr. Marek Stanisz supported and recommendded the publication of this book in Polish, with the scholarly backing of Prof. Dr. Andrzej Olejko, who evaluated the text. Ms. Krystyna Strycharz put a lot of hard editorial work preparing the book for print in Polish language. "Wspólnota Polska" in Rzeszów, with its head Mariusz Grudzień, partially sponsored the publication.

An active participant in our work was – of course indirectly – Stanisław Strumph-Wojtkiewicz (1898-1986), a noted novelist, poet, and journalist. Just after Adamowiczes' landing in Warsaw, he transcribed their accounts and printed them in installments in a newspaper of which he was both the owner and the editor. Soon thereafter, he published the same text in a book, *Across the Atlantic* (1934). We used this valuable source in our rendering of the brothers' story; we often quote it in our book. To simplify, whenever in our narrative a text appears in quotation marks, yet there is no footnote explaining from where it was taken, it means that it is a quote from Strumph-Wojtkiewicz. To spare the reader frequent stumbling on references we are not indicating abbreviations, connections of phrases taken from different sentences, or quotes from foreign sources used by the author. We are very grateful to the late writer for creating such an important and useful document.

We are obliged to many individuals who, and institutions which, put on the web materials, documents, and photographs on the investigated by us subject. We want to acknowledge that many internet sites provide valuable, true, and correct information on the Adamowicz brothers. Unfortunately, there are also many false, misleading, and simply wrong pieces of information disseminated on the web. We are not correcting all of them — there are just too many errors— yet we warn the reader that these partial-truths, half-truths, and un-truths are out there. Let us provide only one example: in the conclusion of the generally correct Wikipedia entry, one can read: "There is information that Adamowicz brothers were active in Polish Air Forces in Division 303 and they died in action during World War II."[5] This is completely wrong.

Generally, we did not want to multiply the footnotes and we inserted references only to the most important sources. The reader may be sure, however, that virtually every sentence of this book is based on sources, information, and data found in books, the period press — many times cross-checked and double-checked. If we were not sure of some facts or we could not find solid information about them, we say so — we say "probably," or "we don't know." On a few occasions, we present different and incongruent versions of a given event, based on different sources.

This book was originally written in Polish. Preparing the English text we did not want to simply translate the Polish original, but rather to write the book anew in English. Dr. Mary Anne Rokitka was so gracious to edit the English version. We are very grateful to her.

Dr. Maja Trochimczyk of Moonrise Press has copy-edited the manuscript and prepared its layout for publication, as well as created the cover design. She found additional photographs, sources, and information, and thus very significantly enriched our book. We appreciate her work and contribution, and we are infinitively grateful for all her support.

---

[5] http://pl.wikipedia.org/wiki/Kategoria:Lotnicy

***

We double-dedicate this book. First, we dedicate it to all brave Polish immigrants to the United States who came from an enslaved country to a free country, found freedom here, and were able to take advantage of the opportunities offered by America. We got to know many such people in "The Land of the Free" and we heard or read about many more.

Second, we dedicate this book to all brave Polish airmen and women who built the foundation and created the early legend of Polish aviation, especially Ludwik Idzikowski, Kazimierz Kubala, Stanisław Skarżyński, Stanisław Wigura, Stefania Wojtulanis-Karpińska, Franciszek Żwirko and so many others, among them Lieutenant Kazimierz Braun (1899-1920,)[6] who belonged to the first generation of Polish aviators and died an aviator's death on December 23, 1920.

***

Brothers Ben and Joe, who piloted the Bellanca over the Atlantic, as well as their older brother, Bruno, were adventurous, colorful, and unusual men. At the same they were average, simple, and typical Polish immigrants to America. Born and reared in Poland, they went to the USA for bread and adventure. They made their way in the new world thanks to their hard work, shrewdness and ingenuity. They used opportunities open for them in America.

Yet, they did it — this must be said at the very beginning of the story — employing both legal and illegal methods. They achieved in America an astonishing success, and they also tasted

---

[6]He was an uncle of the co-author of this book, Kazimierz Braun.

penury, persecution, and humiliation.

Throughout their lives as emigrants they were bound with the Old Country by an unquenched longing and burning love. They ignited, although only for a short while, a hot flame of patriotism and pride in all Poles, on both sides of the ocean. For all these reasons it is good to remember them and to bring their lives back from oblivion.

~ Zofia Reklewska-Braun and Kazimierz Braun

Wrocław, Buffalo, New York, 2009-2015

ACROSS THE ATLANTIC

THE ADAMOWICZ BROTHERS

POLISH AVIATION PIONEERS

CHAPTER 1
GENEALOGY

We start telling the story of the Adamowicz brothers by going back to end of the 19th century and the beginning of the 20th century, to a small hamlet Janowszczyzna near the town of Krajsk in the Wilno region, in the former Polish-Lithuanian Commonwealth.[1] This is where the three brothers were born and raised: Bronisław (known later in America as Bruno; 1885-1948), Józef (Joseph, Joe; 1893-1970), and Bolesław (Benjamin, Ben; 1898-1979). In this book, written for the American reader, we shall use the Americanized forms of their first names, but we note that they are still both known with their Polish first names in Poland. The brothers were the sons of Julian Adamowicz and Anna, née Heyno. They remembered their father's grandfather, Łukasz Adamowicz, who was still alive when they were boys.

Julian and Anna Adamowicz had many children, but it is not known how many. In one interview, Ben recalled that there were eight of them. In American documents we found mentions of two sisters: Emilia (Emma)[2] and Stanisława (Stella), who arrived in the U.S. after being "evicted from her estate by the Bolsheviks"– according to Ben.

Where did they come from? It should be explained that Poland was resurrected after World War I ended in 1918. Its territory had previously been divided into three parts

---

[1] This village is not identical with the current village of Janowszczyzna located in Sokółka County in Podlaskie Voivodeship, north-east of Białystok and near the border of Poland with Belarus. Krajsk or Krojsk, incorporated into Russia after World War I, appears to have ceased to exist or was renamed in the Soviet Union.
[2] In America Emilia became Emma Mathies, using the last name of her husband, Croatian immigrant, Anton Mathies. Stanisława became Stella Gorman when she married.

("partitions") which were under the Russian, Prussian (German), and Austrian rule since the end of the 18th century. The eastern border of the newly independent Poland, established after World War I, was not identical with the border that existed in the 18th century, before the partitions. Thus, the Polish hamlet where the Adamowicz family lived for generations was located after the war within the area controlled by the Soviet Union, ruled by the Bolsheviks. Hence, Maria was "evicted by the Bolsheviks" who ruled in that part of formerly Polish lands after World War I.[3]

According to Ben, both of their parents passed away when he was a child. Talking to Strumph-Wojtkiewicz, he vividly described his mother's death in 1906, when he was just eight years old:

> "She lay white and still. I did not understand what had happened. Father called me and said: 'Go, bring a horse from the meadow.' I brought it. Father ordered a servant to go to Olkowicze and fetch a cross. At that moment, I understood that mother passed away and I began to cry."

His father, Julian, died a few years later, when the three brothers were already in America.

In the passenger records of ships arriving from Europe to New York at the beginning of the 20th century, and in city directories of Brooklyn, we found several listings for "Adamowicz." Some of these were likely cousins of the three brothers. Some might have arrived on the new continent earlier than the heroes of our story. It was a common practice, known since the middle of the 19th century: immigrants who have

---

[3] After World War I, the administrative district of Krajsk was divided between Poland and Russia, with the western portion incorporated into Poland as "gmina Olkowicze" and the eastern portion given to Soviet Union. See Adam Janusz Mielcarek: *Podziały terytorialno - administracyjne II Rzeczypospolitej w zakresie administracji zespolonej.* [Territorial Administrative divisions of the Second Republic in the area of unified administration]. Warszawa: Wydawnictwo Neriton, 2008.

established themselves in America were gradually bringing more and more members of their family or neighbors from the same villages, towns, or neighborhoods, even from the same street. As a result, a large Adamowicz clan was living in Brooklyn in the 1920s and 1930s. There were Heyno relatives as well who joined the Adamowicz brothers in America; Heyno was the maiden name of the brothers' mother.

What is significant for our story is that the three Adamowicz brothers – Bruno, Joe, and Ben–as well as their extended family were a tightly-knit clan. Familial bonds forged in Poland remained strong in America. They supported each other and they loved each other with a simple, healthy and strong love. Both in Poland and in America they were a part of a large community.

All of them came from Janowszczyzna, in the Krajsk County ("powiat"), Olkowicze parish, in Lithuania. The nearest bigger towns were Krajsk and Dołhinów. Wilno (after World War II Vilnius in Lithuania) was located about 50 miles west and Mińsk (now in Belarus) was about 40 miles south. All these localities belonged to the vast eastern territories of the "Republic of Both Nations," as the Polish-Lithuanian Common-wealth had been called since the 16th century.[4] After the partitions at the end of the 18th century these lands were incorporated into Russia. Presently, they are within Belorussian borders. The Adamowicz brothers maintained that they came from the "Wilno country." For them, the city of Wilno, today Vilnius, the capital of Lithuania, was a great Polish metropolis, the center of their universe. They might have visited it occasionally in their youth. After arriving in America, they listed the nearest big town as their place of origin, as other immigrants often did.

---

[4]"The Republic of Both Nations" (Rzeczpospolita Obojga Narodów), was created as union between the Kingdom of Poland and the Grand Duchy of Lithuania in 1569. The king, the parliament, the currency, the foreign and domestic policies were common, while the treasury, the judiciary, the army, and major administrative and military offices were separate.

The root of the name *Adamowicz* (Polish plural "Adamowicze", we will use the form "Adamowiczes" to reduce the successive number of consonants), i.e., the word "Adam," means "man" in Turkish and does not refer to the ancient forefather of humanity. In Polish and Lithuanian genealogy and heraldry the name is associated with the coat of arms "Leliwa."

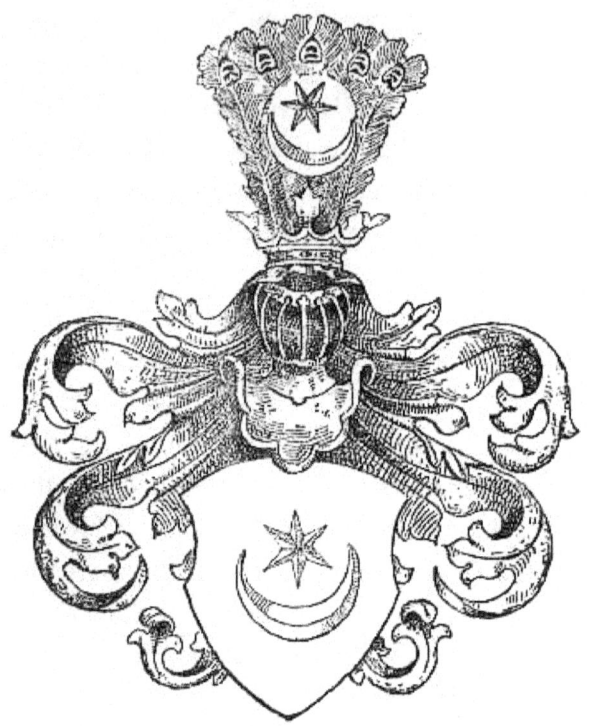

Figure 1: "Leliwa" coat of arms from Wojciech Wiiuk Kojałowicz, *Herbarz szlachty Wielkiego Księstwa Litewskiego zwany Nomenclator* [The Armorial of the Nobility of the Grand Duchy of Lithuania, known as Nomenclator]. 1658. Reprinted in Kraków, 1905.

This coat of arms was used by several hundred *szlachta* families ("szlachta" refers to the petty nobility) during the existence of the Polish-Lithuanian Commonwealth, and remains in use today by the descendants of these families. It is interesting to note that, in addition to the many noble families, the Leliwa became the source of the municipal coat of arms of several cities in eastern and southeastern Poland, including Mińsk Mazowiecki, Siemiatycze, Przeworsk, Tarnów, and Tarnobrzeg; many of these cities were located in the grand estates of the Tarnowski family.[5]

The use of an upward pointing crescent and a star connects this heraldic symbol to the emblems used by Muslims in the Middle Ages. Another version of the star and the crescent pointing to the right was an emblem of the Ottoman Empire, that remained on the Turkish flag after its dissolution in 1918. The star and crescent also appears on many flags of various Islamic nations and organizations. This Muslim connection does not mean that the bearers of the Leliwa coat of arms were necessarily Muslim; some of them were recognized by Polish kings for their achievements in the struggle against the Islamic invaders that attacked the eastern borders of Poland for centuries.

The Adamowicz clan is identified by heraldists as belonging among Lipka Tartars that settled in Poland and Lithuania between the 14th and 17th centuries.[6] The remnant of the great White Horde of Tartars, the Lipka Tartars were granted noble titles and civil protections. In return, they helped the Polish kings defeat the Teutonic Knights during the battle of Grunwald (Grunewald) in 1410 and were rewarded with noble titles and a coat of arms. Again, after the victory of King Jan III Sobieski's army over the Ottoman Empire invaders at Vienna in 1683, a group of Lipka Tartars fighting in the Polish army received land in Lithuania. And rightly so: they saved the life of the King himself! The Lipka Tartar group of Polish-speaking noble Leliwa crest bearers includes the families of: Aksan, Aksanow,

---

[5] Entry on "Leliwa coat of arms" in Wikipedia, http://en.wikipedia.org/wiki/Leliwa_coat_of_arms. Accessed on February 14, 2011.

[6] Tadeusz Gajl, *Herbarz polski od średniowiecza do XX wieku, Ponad 4500 herbów szlacheckich, 37 tysięcy nazwisk, 55 tysięcy rodów* [Armorial of the Polish coats of arms from the Middle Ages to the 20th century. Over 4500 noble coats of arms, 37 thousand names, 55 thousand of noble families], Gdańsk L&L, 2007.

Adamowicz, Abramowicz, Musicz, Illasiewicz and Smolski.[7] Among famous Polish-Lithuanian Lipka Tartar descendants we find also the Nobel Prize winner and writer Henryk Sienkiewicz, the artist Magdalena Abakanowicz and the American actor, Charles Bronson.[8] There are many persons called Adamowicz within the current borders of Poland. One can guess that they are very distant relatives of the three brothers.

The majority of Adamowicz descendants are spread throughout the eastern regions of the former Kingdom of Poland and the Grand Duchy of Lithuania. These multicultural diverse lands were known in Polish history as "Kresy" or Borderlands, and were inhabited by Polish and Lithuanian nobles, Lithuanian and Belarussian peasants, Jewish merchants and artisans, and a small minority of Tartars. Many Poles remained there, and therefore outside of Poland, after the eastern Polish borders were moved westward following World War I, and still further west after World War II, as a result of the Allies' decisions made at the Yalta Conference in 1945.[9] Thus, a large portion of Poland was incorporated into the Soviet Union, i.e., into the Lithuanian, Belarusian, and Ukrainian Soviet Republics; the birthplace of the Adamowicz brothers is now in Belarus.

The countryside of Janowszczyzna was beautiful —slightly hilly, with wide valleys and small dales carved by rivers and creeks. There were fields and woods, and large forests, where wolves and bears roamed freely. The Adamowicz's estate was not big, consisting of about 120 acres. It included farming fields,

---

[7] Jan Tyszkiewicz. *Z dziejów Tatarów polskich: 1794-1944* [From the history of Polish Tartars]. Pułtusk, 2002.
[8] Stanisław Dziadulewicz, *Herbarz rodzin tatarskich w Polsce* [The armorial of Tartar families in Poland]. Wilno, 1929. See also "Lipka Tartars" in Wikipedia, http://en.wikipedia.org/wiki/Lipka_Tatar. Accessed on 14 February 2011.
[9] The Yalta Conference, held on February 4-11, 1945, with the participation of the U.S. President Franklin D. Roosevelt, British Prime Minister Winston Churchill, and the Soviet dictator Joseph Stalin, among other decisions, gave the eastern one-third of the Polish territory to the Soviet Union.

meadows, and two stretches of forest. In the center of the whole property sat the family house, a small mansion. It had a simple ground plan. From the entrance porch a corridor led to the back entrance. A large family room, serving also as bedroom, was at the left. Intermittently, up to ten people would live there: grandfather, parents, and their children.

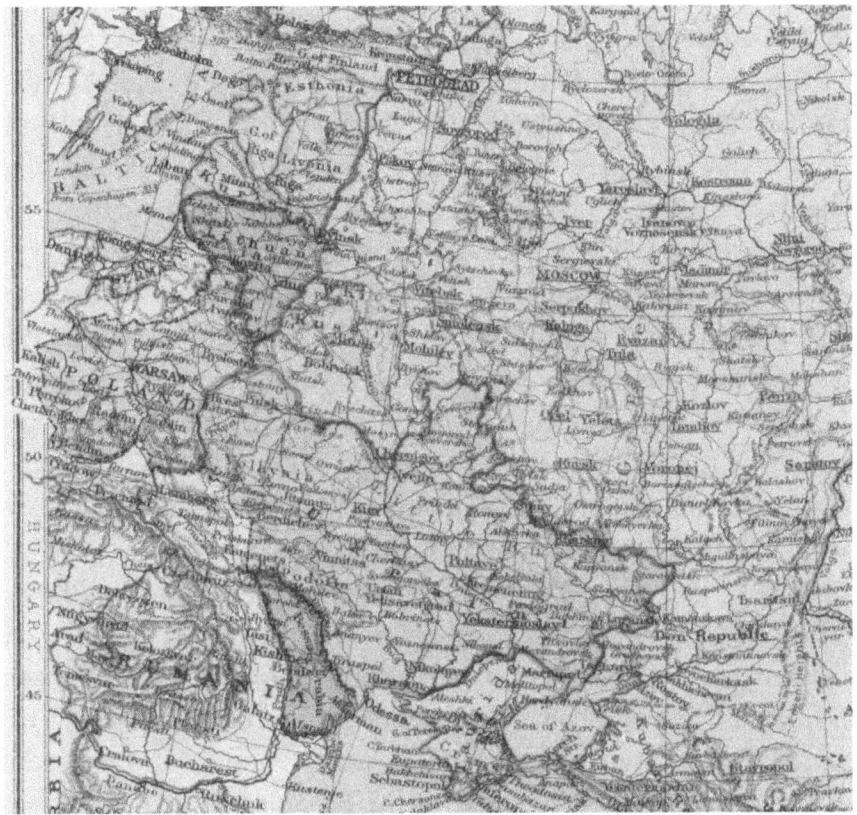

Figure 2: Fragment of the map of "The Partition of Russia in Europe" with borders from 1914. The area that the Adamowicz family comes from is near the borders of Poland, White Russia and Lithuania to the north-west of the center of the map. Maja Trochimczyk's Collection.

(Years later, all these Adamowiczes shared small quarters in Brooklyn. Interestingly, after landing in Warsaw in 1934, Ben and Joe were lodged in two separate spacious apartments in the

Hotel Europejski and they could not fall asleep because they were so accustomed to living all cooped up.)

Let us return to the family estate. To the right of the corridor was a large kitchen with a big table which could seat the whole family and the servants; there was also a tiny room for two maids. Male farmhands slept in the barn in summer or in the stable in winter. For seasonal work more laborers were hired; they lived in their huts in neighboring villages.

Besides the family manor house the property included typical farm buildings: the stable, the barn, the pig-house, and the poultry-house. There was also a small vegetable garden. The livestock inventory consisted of 25 cows, 15 pigs, about 30 sheep and four horses, including a gorgeous stallion, so precious that — as Ben recalls with pride — "the very countess Tyszkiewicz wanted to buy it for 500 Russian rubles." The stallion was kept in a small enclosure at the end of the corridor in the house, in order to guard it from thieves. "One night thieves came and began cutting the padlock, but our dog, its name was Nertchik (Nerczyk) started barking. My father woke up and shot at them from the window. The scoundrels fled."

Thus, we have a picture: A small mansion, farm buildings, 120 acres of land, a few servants, and an old handgun. The Adamowicz were a typical petty-nobility family of the eastern frontier of Poland. They were poor, but not pennilessness. They were Poles and spoke thePolish language at home, but they had to communicate with their servants in Belorussian and in schools they had classes only in Russian.

The oldest son, Bronisław (later: Bruno) Adamowicz was born in 1885. The second Józef (later: Joseph or Joe), in 1893. The third, Bolesław (Benjamin or Ben), in 1898. Bruno occasionally gave as the year of his birth 1888, or 1883. He changed the dates in order to appear older when he was looking for a job. We found that while interacting with authorities or employers, the brothers frequently changed their birthdates; mixed up actual and fictitious Christian names; and impersonated each other in order to trick Russian, and then American officials. This was one of their methods to preserve, as they thought, some measure of privacy and personal freedom.

Bruno graduated from high school, most probably in Krajsk, in 1903, and immediately enrolled in a Russian military school for officers. This indicates that he was born in 1885, after all: he had to be 18-years-old to be admitted. In 1905, after a two-year training period, he received the first rank of junior officer of infantry — Sub-lieutenant. Yet, he did not want to stay in the army and requested to be transferred to the reserves. He was granted the transfer, but soon thereafter he was called to active duty. The Russians needed more troops for their war with Japan.[10] Bruno was afraid of being sent to Manchuria and petitioned the Tsar for a release from service, but it is not known if he received it. Most probably, he did not, because it is known that in the fall of 1905 he left for America in great haste. It appears that he fled the Russian army by escaping beyond the ocean. Ben indirectly confirms this when he recalls his brother coming from America to visit Poland in 1909, and he mentions "an amnesty, which at that time included Bruno."

Among names listed on the *Manifest of Alien Passengers* recording people who arrived in New York from Bremen in Germany on October 1905, we found an "Osip Adamowicz. "The first name Osip was the Russian version of Józef or Joseph, the first name of Bruno's brother, and his own middle name. However, other data clearly indicates that this was no other than Bruno (Bronisław) Adamowicz.[11] The same "Osip" appears

---

[10] The Russo-Japanese war took place between February 8, 1904 and September 5, 1905.

[11] List of *Manifest of Alien Passengers* for the U.S. Immigration Officer at Port of Arrival. October 12, 1905. Such lists were written down by hand, so spelling errors may be common. Source: Ancestry.com

again on the list of passengers of a ship which arrived in New York in April 1914, from Rotterdam, Holland. It seems that in both cases it was Bruno who was erasing his footprints by using a different first name.

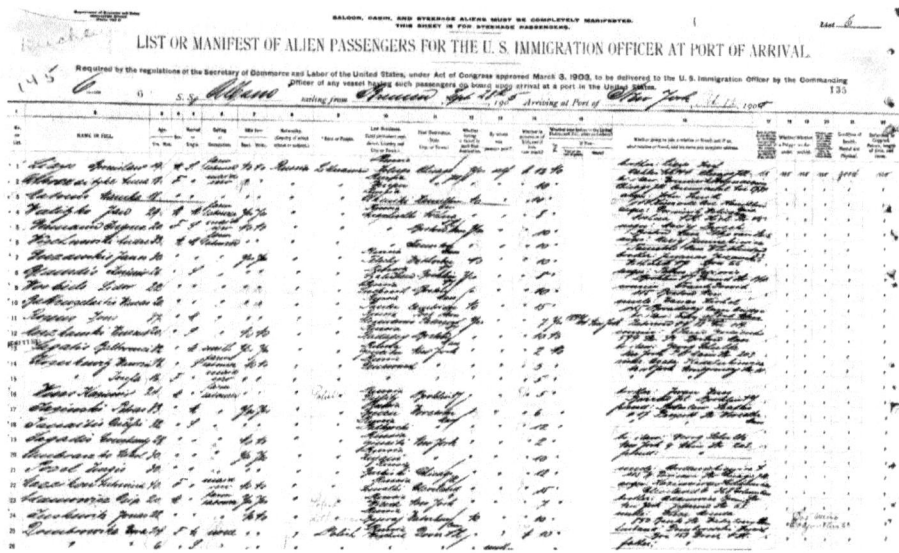

Figure 3: Manifest of Passengers arriving in 1905, Osip Adamowicz is the second from the bottom. Courtesy of American Family Immigration History Center at Ellis Island.

It is worthwhile to remember that at the beginning of the 20th century passports were not yet in use and such changes in dates of birth or names were rather frequent. In any case, we know for sure that Bruno Adamowicz left Poland and arrived in America in 1905. He took up residence at 63 Jefferson Street in Brooklyn, settling in with his acquaintances from Poland who came to America before him. He then found a job in the nearby Abrockler Brothers' sugar factory.

Family documents show that Bruno was married to Anna Skrzetuska. She was born in the village of Olkowicze in 1885 (currently a small village in the Mahilyowskaya Voblast' of

Belarus), and lived in the village of Wróblewszczyzna in the former Polish-Lithuanian Commonwealth. The name "Skrzetuski" ("Skrzetuska" is a feminine form of this name) belonged to minor Polish nobility, immortalized in the fictional character of Jan Skrzetuski, the hero of Henryk Sienkiewicz's famous historical novel, *Ogniem i Mieczem* [*With Fire and Sword*]. The model for Jan was a real nobleman, Mikołaj Skrzetuski (d. 1673), with the coat of arms of Jastrzębiec. He lived in the 17th century and fought in many battles and military campaigns for the King Jan III Sobieski.[12] The connection of Anna Skrzetuska to this branch of a noble family has not been established, beyond sharing an historical name. In any case, she came from the same region where the Adamowiczes lived. It is not clear whether she married Bruno before leaving Poland (probably in 1902) or in New York (possibly in 1906). It is also unknown if they were married legally or, at first fictitiously, declaring marriage only for American immigration officers.

They had two children: Stanley (Stanisław) born in 1907, deceased in 1982,[13] and Anne (Anna) born in 1912, and deceased in 1995. The dates and places of their birth, either in Poland or in America, are different in different documents. It is not the first and not the last time that we encounter ambiguities and prevarications in the Adamowiczes family documentation, created by the Adamowicz brothers themselves, possibly for immigration or tax reasons. Regardless of whether Bruno's marriage was true or false, and regardless of whether he really had a family in Poland or just falsely claimed so, these family

---

[12] Tadeusz Wasilewski, "Kim był Skrzetuski," *Mówią wieki*, 1964, no. 9. Reprinted on the website of the Royal Palace Museum in Wilanów, http://www.wilanow-palac.pl/kim_byl_skrzetuski.html, accessed on February 14, 2011. See also Tadeusz Gajl, *Polski Herbarz*, op. cit.

[13] In Stanley's Application for Social Security Number his date of birth is June 7, 1907. He received SS number 121-22-4262. Anne's data can be found in the family genealogical records.

matters provided him with a reason to travel several times, back and forth, between the two continents, before eventually settling in America.

The second brother Joe (Józef) joined Bruno in Brooklyn in 1907. He was 14 years old at that time. Before leaving Poland he finished four or five years of elementary school in Krajsk. Then he worked as a postman and, as Ben recalled, "he was learning telegraphy." In Brooklyn, certainly upon his older brother's recommendation, he got a job in the sugar factory with Bruno. The dutiful Adamowicz brothers sent money to their relatives at home in Poland, "possibly even a thousand dollars," as Ben recalled. We hear in his account awe and admiration for that magical, omnipotent currency, the American dollar. Both brothers, Bruno and Joe, returned to Poland in the winter of 1909, and they brought with them American dollars and gifts. During long winter nights the Adamowicz family listened with rapt attention to accounts about the wonders and magic of America. Eleven-year-old Bolesław (Ben) was the keenest listener.

After returning from his sojourn in America in 1909, Bruno settled down on the family farm, but Joe was conscripted into the Russian Army (the cavalry) and he was sent to a garrison in Finland that was at the time a part of the Russian Empire. It is not certain if he somehow managed to get a release from the army on the basis that he had "bad teeth" (as Ben recalls) or if he simply fled and went into hiding, while preparing to return to America. In any case, Ben wanted to go with him.

Ben, the youngest of the three brothers, was born in 1898. As did his brothers, he frequently changed biographic data about himself. There are at least three dates of his birth listed in different American documents: 1894, 1896 and 1898. As his birth place he named Krajsk, but we may presume that, similarly to his siblings, he was born in his parents' home, in Janowszczyzna [he lists Janowszczyzna as his birthplace on his 1938 passport application]. He attended an elementary school in Krajsk. It was about three miles from Janowszczyzna and the road led through a forest. Sometimes he would not come back home in the evening for the fear of wolves; on these days he had to stay at school overnight. Like Joe, he finished only four or five years of formal schooling.

As we have seen, none of the brothers advanced far in school. All three remained self-taught, without much formal education, neither general, nor professional. Yet, despite these educational deficiencies, their achievements were considerable. All three brothers became competent businessmen. Moreover, Joe and Ben also turned out to be skillful pilots and dexterous air mechanics.

CHAPTER 2
ON THE NEW CONTINENT

After Bruno and Joe spent two years in Europe, all three brothers left for New York in 1911. First, Joe and Ben departed in April. They were on the ocean for twelve days. Bruno, for some reasons, most likely familial — due to having a young wife and children — stayed behind for a few more months, but he soon joined his brothers. For Joe and Bruno, the trip to America was a return to familiar sites. For Ben everything was new.

A record from Ellis Island reveals that "Bronisław and Bolesław" (Bruno and Ben) Adamowicz arrived in New York from Antwerp on a passenger ship *Finland* on April 5, 1911. In reality they were Joe (Józef) and Ben (Bolesław).[14]

Why did Joe give the immigration authorities the first name of his older brother? Perhaps he wanted to fool the Russian army which might still have been looking for him as a deserter. This could have been the reason why he gave his age as 23, while in reality he was only 18. And it was for sure Joe (Józef) who travelled on the *Finland*, not Bruno (Bronisław) as he stated. At the same time, Ben declared that he was 17 years old while in reality he was only 13 (!). Both Joe and Ben told the immigration officer that their country of residence was Russia and their ethnicity was "Russia, Polish." We have to remind the reader that Poland officially did not exist at that time and the Polish-Lithuanian Commonwealth was dismembered at the end of the 18th century. The brothers were formally Russian citizens. Yet, they acknowledged that they were Poles.

After receiving clearance from the medical officer and paying

---
[14]Manifest of Alien Passengers, US port of arrival, April 5, 1911.

twenty five dollars each, the two brothers took a ferry to the southern tip of Manhattan, and from there a train to Brooklyn. Their destination was 46 Hudson Avenue and an apartment of the Kwiatkowski family from the town of Suwałki (in the Russian partition, the former Grand Duchy of Lithuania, currently in Poland). They were Joe's acquaintances from his previous stay, when Joe lived in Brooklyn with his older brother, Bruno. Now Joe came in the company of his younger sibling, Ben.

Figure 4: Document from the Immigration Office at Ellis Island in New York confirming Bronisław Adamowicz's entry to the United States, April 5, 1911. Courtesy of American Family Immigration History Center at Ellis Island.

In the early 20th century, Brooklyn was a small, yet extremely spread out town. Situated east and south from Manhattan, across the East River, Brooklyn had an appearance of a small town, as it mostly consisted of one or two story houses. Taller apartment buildings, schools, churches, banks, and factories stood out. The streets were narrow, with small stores and small businesses.

Brooklyn was extremely diverse ethnically, with separate neighborhoods created by people of different origins. Usually one or a few blocks were inhabited by people who came from the same corner of the world: Poles, Italians, Germans, Russians, and Jews.

Bruno joined the younger brothers on August 23, 1911. He arrived on board the *Finland*, the same ship which five months earlier brought Joe and Ben. The name of Bruno Adamowicz is recorded on the list of passengers arriving that day. This time it is certainly him, the real Bruno (originally: Bronisław). On the landing documents, he described his status as "Single" ("S") and age as 27. On board of the same ship came his sister, Emilia (Emma) Adamowicz, age 18, also "Single."

American immigration archives show another visit of Bruno to Poland and his return to New York in 1913. We can speculate that previously, in 1909, he came from America to Poland with his wife Anna Skrzetuska and their two children, but then he returned to America in 1911 alone, only with his sister, while Anna and the children stayed in Poland until 29 October 1921 when she arrived in New York. At that time, Bruno lived at 40 Hudson Avenue.

Bruno's marital circumstances are complicated by the fact that a few years after his arrival in 1911 (in 1914), in the office of Kings County, New York, a Bruno Adamowicz married Stanisława Ospalska. It could have been another Bruno, or a fictitious contract of "our" Bruno, which was signed only to help the naturalization of the woman, an illegal procedure frequently used by immigrants then and now.[15] It is possible that Bruno led a double-life: he might have had one wife in the old country and

---

[15] The popularity of this illegal practice resulted in increasing legal strictures and constraints for foreign spouses brought to America by citizens, as the immigration officials were attempting to crack down on the criminal abuse of a humanitarian rule of family re-unification.

another one in America. This bigamous practice also was, and remained a part of immigrant subculture.

In any case, Anna, maiden name Skrzetuska, married Adamowicz (again, we don't know for sure if they married in Poland or America) with two children arrived in New York on *Frederik VIII* from Copenhagen on November 8, 1921. The two children of Anna Skrzetuska and Bruno Adamowicz were: Stanley (born June 7, 1907 in Olkowicze) and Anna (born February 19, 1912, in Olkowicze). In 1936, Bruno and Anna were living on 578 Wythe Avenue and were identified there during the 1940 census.

On the Death Certificate of Bruno Adamowicz, dated in 1941, and signed by his wife, Anna Adamowicz, maiden name Skrzetuska, we found that while answering a question about Bruno, "How many years in America?" she wrote: "28." This would indicate the year 1913 as the year of Bruno's official arrival in the U.S. However, we know that he had lived in America already in 1905-1909, and then he was there since 1911. It is possible that Bruno crossed the Atlantic several times, back and forth. Perhaps he was bringing, smuggled under false names, other members of his family, both men and women?

We write about this in order to pin down the brothers' habits and patterns of conduct: repeated slipperiness, altering documents, falsifying names, dates of birth, and status — once "single," once "married." They impersonated each other and gave to the immigration authorities each other's names. They lived by their wits, invented petty schemes, and frequently cheated. In this way they wanted to outsmart controllers or immigration offices, and to bypass regulations and laws on both sides of the Atlantic. In the future, they were to pay dearly for these practices.

Nonetheless, we have to understand that these habitual behaviors were imprinted on them by their situation from childhood. We have to remember that they were born and lived in a home which was standing in a country enslaved, ruled by foreigners and strangers, a country whose population did not recognize its rulers as legitimate and did not respect its laws. The Russian government of Poland, being a foreign, unwanted government, was seen and felt by the Poles as an alien, occupying hostile presence. Many Poles in the whole of the former Polish-Lithuanian Commonwealth, that is in all three partitions of Poland, ruled respectively by Russia, Prussia (Germany) and Austria, did their best to outsmart, trick, and deceive the authorities. There existed a subculture of approval for conduct that included inventive ways of avoiding or subverting the authority's orders, injunctions, and bans. At the same time, within a nation, a family, or a secret society working against the invaders, the same Poles were utterly loyal, truthful, and supportive of each other. In the familial context, they practiced solidarity very seriously and unequivocally as a virtue and as a way of life.

When the Adamowicz brothers were born, foreign occupation had been lingering for more than a century. Many citizens led double lives; the subculture of deception was widespread. One set of beliefs and values was upheld at home, another, different set of officially approved values and behaviors was practiced at school, at work, and in the army. These distinctions were articulated in language: Polish at home, Russian at school or work. The brothers attended Russian schools and were instructed in Russian; that was the official language of the administration and the judiciary. Similarly, the compulsory military service was in the *Russian* army. However, at home and among intimates, and at church (Roman-Catholic) the brothers spoke Polish (Latin was the official language of the liturgy at church). Russian was required and used everywhere else: it was the language of the foreign occupier.

Living under the yoke of foreign rule produced a culture of

deception, which typified everyday life. Russian, Prussian, or Austrian authorities, institutions, laws, and manners were viewed as illegitimate, nonbinding, and illegal and thus hated, ignored, and resisted. Such attitude was characteristic of large segments of society in Polish lands in the 19th century up until 1918, when the domination by foreigners ended and Poland regained its independence.

Incidentally, the authors would argue that the same "schizophrenic" attitude re-infected the nation during the nearly-50-year domination of the Communist regime post-WW II (1944-1989). Indeed, it was a disease that permeated the realm of Polish politics, economy, and the totality of everyday life. Since the government was perceived as illegitimate, committing fraud against the government's laws and institutions was not seen as criminal. Again, it is hard to understand such an attitude from a law-abiding perspective.

The attitudes and ways of living and doing business brought from the Old Country – a country in bondage – were in conflict with the American way of life and the prevailing American ethos – an ethos of free citizens of a free country. The Adamowicz brothers seemed not to appreciate this difference from the very beginning of their "American way" and they did not grasp it until the very end of their lives.

CHAPTER 3
WORK AND LEISURE

After his return to America in April 1911, Joe Adamowicz went back to the same job he held during his previous stay, that is to the sugar plant of the Abrockler Brothers. Bruno, who arrived later, in August, joined him at the plant. Thirteen-year-old Ben did not start working at once, although he was searching for a job in the neighborhood. At first, people only laughed at him. He was still very much a child: short, of a slight build. He did not look strong. His older brothers provided for him.

A few months later Ben, tirelessly continuing his enquires, found a job in a factory producing bed springs.

"My first American job was to put springs on a steel rod fixing them with a special beater. Each one had to be tested for resistance. During the first two weeks of my work I tested thousands of these springs and finally I received my first pay-day. "Thus, he began to make a living, earning two dollars per week. "I was in heaven. Nobody had to give me anything. I could pay for myself. I remember that I was extremely proud and happy after getting this first pay."

He immediately opened an account in the Savings Bank and he regularly deposited half of his earnings.

After a year, he asked for a raise; instead of getting it, he was immediately fired. One of his colleagues helped him to get another job, in a soap plant. His earnings went up. He was now getting 5 dollars per week. "I had to sit at a large jar, that revolved mechanically; I had to put a cardboard box under a funnel from which a powder was pouring from the machine, close it, and put on the shelf." Ben worked there for a year and half. Next, he moved to a chemical plant, where he got sick inhaling poisonous substances. He decided to organize a strike demanding better work conditions. When the foreman learned about it, he fired Ben at once. He was jobless for weeks. Nobody wanted to hire an impudent worker. Finally, Joe recommended him to the same sugar factory where he was employed.

Ben colorfully recounted how he was hired.

"It was very hard to get a job. In front of the factory gate a thousand men made a long line every morning begging for a job. A man named William, with a dark French beard, was a foreman there. Joe talked to him. He told Joe that I have to stand close to the gate. Joe should point at me when William would come to hire people. I came at night and took a place on a step near the gate. I was short, but the step was high and when a crowd of older and taller men formed a line in the morning I was sticking out, taller than all of them. In this way my brother could clearly show me to William and he gave me the job."

At first Ben had to roll large and heavy barrels. When one of them almost broke his legs, he was moved to sewing bags filled with sugar. He sewed thousands and thousands of them during five years of tedious and monotonous labor.

Bruno and Joe were working at the same factory. Everything was good. But suddenly the whole factory "burnt down to the ground." They had to look for another job. They found it. They enjoyed every earned dollar. They were economizing on everyday living and saving money.

The brothers did not deny themselves, however, small pleasures. At first they rented bicycles by the hour. Then, they bought three used bicycles. Recalls Ben: "We were bicycling to the parks or out of town. In the evenings we would go to a park for a dance. I loved my life. I was earning well and I had my brother always with me. I did not miss my family."

From that time on, we see the two of them always side by side — the brothers, Joe and Ben. The older, Bruno, walked his own way, while his familial bonds with the younger brothers remained strong. All three brothers shared the same values. All three belonged to the same immigrant community. They had common financial dealings. Eventually, they would share imprisonment. But at the beginning, "the time was great. On Sundays we always went with Joe to the old Polish church on Careen Avenue. Only Polish people came there."

It is not the first and not the last utterance on religion in Ben's memoires penned down by Strumph-Wojtkiewicz. Thus, every Sunday the three brothers, as well as other members of their extended family, attended Mass in the Polish church in Brooklyn. But not only there. For example, after the crash of their airplane in Newfoundland in 1933, they went to a church in Halifax, Canada. Similarly, before starting their famous transatlantic flight in 1934, they attended Mass in Harbor Grace in Newfoundland. Then, after crossing the Atlantic, they loudly thanked God after the happy landing on a meadow in French Normandy. Soon after, following their triumphant arrival in Warsaw they planned first of all to go on pilgrimages to Częstochowa's Jasna Góra and to Wilno's Ostra Brama – two national shrines dedicated to the worship of Mary, the Mother of God. They wanted to offer prayers of thanksgiving to her.

An affiliation with the Roman Catholic Church was proudly recalled by Ben many times. In later years, a parish bulletin of Saint Stanislaus Kostka Parish in Brooklyn lists Joseph Adamowicz as a member of its jubilee committee. The faith of brothers Adamowicz was no doubt sincere, simple, and undeviating, as well as strong and stubborn — as stubborn as the three of them. We do not know how they reconciled their faith and religious practices with cheating and law breaking at almost every stage of their lives. They certainly lived by double standards, one for their personal faith and familial relationships and another for the external world.

Their first passion was to ride bicycles (it actually came second to saving money, of course). "Biking was my great joy" — confessed Ben. Soon a new passion followed, as Ben jokingly recalled:

> "We contracted a sickness called motorcycling. We purchased a second-hand, or rather tenth-hand, old motorcycle. An owner of a bike repair shop sold it to us and then he was ready to constantly repair our magnificent vehicle. It was the most expensive bike in the world, because we were spending on it all our earnings, to the point that we were lacking money for food. Additionally, we had accidents that resulted in police tickets and court fines. We were very close to bankruptcy when we finally managed to sell our blood-sucker and return to normal life."

After the United States joined the war in 1917,[16] Bruno, Joe and Ben received summons to civil service. We found Joe and Ben's registration to military service cards, but no record on the registration ever being activated.

> "In the fall of 1918, joyful news came about the armistice in Europe and even more joyful, about Poland's restored independence. Polish émigrés in New York and Brooklyn loved Poland so much that every call for help to the Old Country was met with quick and generous response. Now we were all very happy that Poland is again strong and free."

In such simple and naïve words Ben recalled the historical events of the 1918.

We must strongly emphasize here the intense joy shared at this time by the brothers with the whole Polish diaspora in

---

[16] It was World War I. At that time, it was called the "Great War." Nobody knew that a new war was coming. When it broke out in 1939, it was called World War II.

America: Poland was again a free country! Their love of Poland must be very strongly underlined here. It was the foundation on which Ben and Joe based their decision to fly to Poland. They did not have any other reason for the choice of the destination of their transatlantic flight than love of the Old Country. They did it "For the greater glory of Poland."

CHAPTER 4

THE BROTHERS IN BUSINESS

In 1918, the three Adamowicz brothers decided to begin their "own business," as Ben called it. They wanted to cease working for someone else. Until that time they were employees, simple laborers doing very hard physical work. They started to work on their own. "This business was a very small plant of seltzer and fruit water." Such drink was needed on the market. We have to remember something obvious today: air-conditioning was not used at that time; the need for soft cooling drinks was enormous in the summer and such drinks were popular year round. The harsh New York climate increased demand in the summer — since the early spring until the late fall the temperature remains warm, while for a few weeks in the middle of summer it might be really hot, up to 100 F, or more.

To purchase a small plant, the brothers used money from selling their cash-devouring motorcycle and added their savings accumulated from years of hard work. Joe and Ben became formal owners, with Bruno as a partner with a voice in every operation. When the younger brothers Joe and Ben flew to Poland in 1934, Bruno oversaw the soda-water plant in their absence.

The brothers started beverage production in a "small shed, formerly belonging to the fire-department" between Berry Street and Bedford Avenue. When they had to vacate that location, Bruno found a lot at 111 Conselyea Street in Brooklyn. There were two buildings on this lot, one stone and one wooden. The former was "good for a factory."

This is Ben's version. But documents reveal that the

Adamowiczes purchased an already-functioning soda-water factory from the German-born Wehmhoefer [Wehmhoeffer] brothers. At the time, seltzer water was very popular in America. Coca-Cola appeared on the market in 1886, at first not bottled, but dispensed from fountains in restaurants, bars, diners, and drug-stores. Pepsi-Cola came on the market in 1898. The Adamowiczes' soda-water business competed with other seltzer water manufacturers and the two well-known producers of cola. From the outset they sold their products (carbonated seltzer water and fruit-flavored soda pop) in bottles, not from fountains.

Figure 5: Adamowiczes' apartment building. The three brothers occupied apartments on the first floor. Photo by Monika Braun.

When their plant was up and running, the Adamowiczes built, as Ben recalled, a large apartment building next door to the factory. The factory was on 111 Conselyea Street and the apartment building around the corner on 325 Manhattan Avenue. Joe purchased 325 Manhattan in 1926 for $75,000 as reported in

The Brooklyn Daily Eagle, on September 19, 1926.[17] Several families of the extensive Adamowicz clan moved in, and the remaining apartments were rented.

Here, again, Ben's claim that the brothers built the house does not jive with records found in Brooklyn archives. According to the documents the house was not a new construction in 1920; it was there since 1874. In 1920, the brothers only bought, renovated and refurbished it. In any case, this house became both the Adamowicz family abode and a significant source of rental income, supplementing their earnings from the bottling plant. Both structures, the former factory and the apartment building, stand side by side to this day (the photographs are from 2010 and 2011).

The former factory presently houses *Savino's Quality Pasta*, a small establishment producing pasta, pizza, and other Italian specialties and delicacies. At the front there is a small store and eating area; at the back, the kitchen with necessary appliances. The building is two stories tall. The first floor, which years ago served as the main plant area, has a high ceiling. The second floor's ceiling is lower. The building is 45 feet wide at the front and 125 feet deep. Next to the building is a lot, about 9 feet wide, currently filled with a one-car garage. On the other side of the garage sits the large apartment building. It is constructed solidly, of dark reddish brick; it has four floors. Looking from the front, there is a central entrance leading to a staircase from which, on every level, hallways go to two sides. Originally, the building contained seven large apartments. Now, after a recent remodel, there are twelve apartments, two on each level; each apartment has two bedrooms, each with one window onto the street. A kitchen and a bath are on the back side.

---

[17] $1 of 1920 equals about $10 of 2010. Calculating the price of the house based on 2010 dollar value, the house cost about $750,000. Building it must have taken a substantial loan from a bank.

The story of the acquisition of the property, and enlargement of the lot, as told by Ben, is amusing and moving. The boys' pastor, Father Jarka, evicted them from the small house (a shack, really) where the brothers had first started producing soda water. This story is worth quoting:

> "We established our own business in 1918. Actually, it was Joe who set up the business using money from the sale of his motorcycle. Our business was at first a small plant producing seltzer water and fruit drinks (soda pop). We used a small shack, previously a fire-station, between Berry St. and Bedford Ave. But soon the lot with our shack was acquired by Father Jarka who wanted to build a Polish school there. So just before Christmas 1920, Father Jarka told us: 'Dear children, I pity you, but you have to vacate by January 1st because the old shack will be demolished.' It was a blow. But what could we do? We called a family meeting. There wasn't much time. The plant had to be kept in operation. We had to find a new location."

It was then that Bruno found the building at 111 Conselyea Street and there they moved, proudly affixing on the gate a large sign: "Adamowicz Brothers." But this was not the end of the story: "There was a small smithy next door. A blacksmith was producing iron clamps for house construction and the noise was deafening. We could not hear our telephone orders, and our business was based on phone orders. The owner of the lot agreed to sell it to us for $6,000. We immediately evicted the blacksmith, in the same way that Father Jarka had evicted us."

All the difficulties of establishing a business and developing it are described accurately by Ben, and reflect a not-uncommon experience of many immigrants in America struggling to better their lives.

CHAPTER 5
PLANTING ROOTS IN AMERICA

The eastern Polish border established as a result of the war with the Bolsheviks and delineated at the Riga conference in 1920, moved westward. The Adamowicz family nest, the hamlet of Janowszczyzna, found itself at the Soviet side of the border (and later in Belarus, where it disappeared from the maps). This fact finally sealed the situation of the whole Adamowicz family living in America. Previously, they traveled back and forth between Poland and the U.S.— Bruno a few times, Joe at least twice. They, probably, were not clear where their home was. They had a foothold in both countries. After World War I, they lost the ability to consider Poland their home. Recalled Ben:

> "Since then, we did not have a home in the Old Country. Our home was now America. Our Polish estate was cut off by the new border with the Soviet Union and the Bolsheviks chased out our sister, Stanisława (Stella) from it. Only the parish church in Olkowicze remained on the Polish side of the border."

American administrative and parochial documents indicate that at that time numerous relatives of the Adamowicz siblings arrived in Brooklyn. We also found more Skrzetuskis (the maiden name of Bruno's wife Anna), as well as many cousins named Heyno (sometimes spelled as Hejno) — this was the maiden name of Anna, the mother of our three brothers. For example Jan and Zofia Hejno arrived on August 14, 1923, by ship from the port of Copenhagen and settled down in Brooklyn on the same street, Huston, where the Adamowiczes lived previously.

New immigrants trickled in, to join those already established in America. The whole Adamowicz clan was living in relative proximity in Brooklyn. Upon arrival, newcomers found shelter with their relatives or acquaintances, then looked for apartments or small houses nearby. Several families often lived in the same apartment complex. Many exchanged places, letting relatives rent or buy their small quarters as established families moved to more spacious accommodations. In 1911, Joe and Ben, nearly always living together, resided at 46 Hudson Avenue. Then, they moved to 53 Hudson, then to 40 Hudson, to 87 Russell, and so on. Bruno's first stop in 1911 was with Antoni Kukulski at 38 Hudson Avenue; afterwards he moved many times, but remained within the same neighborhood.

Initially, the brothers used their birth names, but after a few years in America all three switched to Americanized forms of their first names. Thus Bronisław became Bruno (affectionately the family called him Broniś or Bronek), Józef became Joseph or Joe, and Bolesław — Benjamin or Ben.

Taking root in America had serious social dimensions, but also simple and prosaic aspects. These included, for instance, involvement in a street brawl recorded by the police and the press, or a late payment of a loan. Local newspapers documented the tawdry bits of their lives. Let us describe an example. On August 8, 1923, three Poles — Joe and Ben Adamowicz and their colleague Jan Jankowski – while passing by Bielby Place in Brooklyn were attacked by a trio of, apparently, Americans of German descent, listed in the police records as Joseph Bauer, 25, Louis Bracker, 22, and George Denman, 25. Stones started to fly. One struck Jankowski in the head; when the fight was over he was taken to a hospital. Joe, seriously beaten, was lying on the ground; the attackers stole $180 from him.[18]

Another example — we found a note that "J.&B. Adamowicz" are debtors of "F. Hass Motors" in the amount of $137.37, for a

---

[18] *The Daily Star*, 8 August 1923.

late payment for their car.[19]

All three brothers were naturalized American citizens. Bruno, the oldest, received American citizenship first, probably in 1925. Joe applied for naturalization December 16, 1925and became American citizen on March 23, 1926. Ben joined the ranks a year later, in 1927.

Slowly but surely, the Adamowiczes adjusted their self-identities. In the process, an internal change was creeping into their hearts and souls: they were no longer Poles living temporarily in America. They were Americans. Americans of Polish descent, to be sure, nevertheless Americans.

---

[19]*Brooklyn Daily Eagle*, 1924.

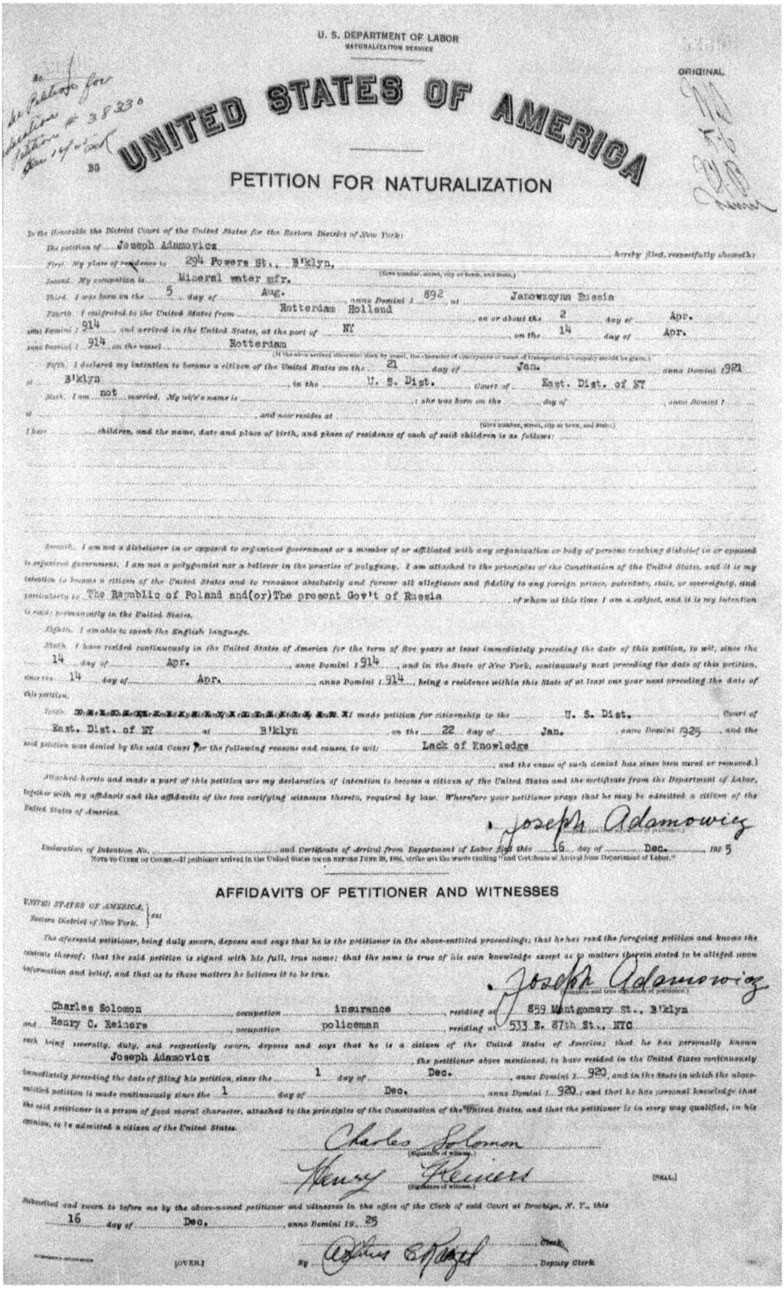

U. S. DEPARTMENT OF LABOR
NATURALIZATION SERVICE

ORIGINAL

UNITED STATES OF AMERICA

PETITION FOR NATURALIZATION

To the Honorable the District Court of the United States for the Eastern District of New York:

The petition of Joseph Adamovicz hereby filed, respectfully showeth:

First. My place of residence is 294 Powers St., B'klyn.

Second. My occupation is Mineral water mfr.

Third. I was born on the 5 day of Aug. anno Domini 1892, at Janowzcyna Russia

Fourth. I emigrated to the United States from Rotterdam Holland, on or about the 2 day of Apr. anno Domini 1914 and arrived in the United States, at the port of NY on the 14 day of Apr. anno Domini 1914, on the vessel Rotterdam

Fifth. I declared my intention to become a citizen of the United States on the 21 day of Jan. anno Domini 1921 at B'klyn in the U. S. Dist. Court of East. Dist. of NY

Sixth. I am not married. My wife's name is ; she was born on the day of , anno Domini 1 at , and now resides at

I have children, and the name, date and place of birth, and place of residence of each of said children is as follows:

Seventh. I am not a disbeliever in or opposed to organized government or a member of or affiliated with any organization or body of persons teaching disbelief in or opposed to organized government. I am not a polygamist nor a believer in the practice of polygamy. I am attached to the principles of the Constitution of the United States, and it is my intention to become a citizen of the United States and to renounce absolutely and forever all allegiance and fidelity to any foreign prince, potentate, state, or sovereignty, and particularly to The Republic of Poland and(or)The present Gov't of Russia of whom at this time I am a subject, and it is my intention to reside permanently in the United States.

Eighth. I am able to speak the English language.

Ninth. I have resided continuously in the United States of America for the term of five years at least immediately preceding the date of this petition, to wit, since the 14 day of Apr., anno Domini 1914, and in the State of New York, continuously next preceding the date of this petition, since the 14 day of Apr., anno Domini 1914, being a residence within this State of at least one year next preceding the date of this petition.

Tenth. I made petition for citizenship to the U. S. Dist. Court of East. Dist. of NY at B'klyn on the 22 day of Jan. anno Domini 1925, and the said petition was denied by the said Court for the following reasons and causes, to wit: Lack of Knowledge, and the cause of such denial has since been cured or removed.)

Attached hereto and made a part of this petition are my declaration of intention to become a citizen of the United States and the certificate from the Department of Labor, together with my affidavit and the affidavits of the two verifying witnesses thereto, required by law. Wherefore your petitioner prays that he may be admitted a citizen of the United States of America.

Joseph Adamowicz

Declaration of Intention No. and Certificate of Arrival from Department of Labor filed this 16 day of Dec. 1925

AFFIDAVITS OF PETITIONER AND WITNESSES

UNITED STATES OF AMERICA, Eastern District of New York. } ss:

The aforesaid petitioner, being duly sworn, deposes and says that he is the petitioner in the above-entitled proceedings; that he has read the foregoing petition and knows the contents thereof; that the said petition is signed with his full, true name; that the same is true of his own knowledge except as to matters therein stated to be alleged upon information and belief, and that as to those matters he believes it to be true.

Joseph Adamowicz

Charles Solomon, occupation insurance, residing at 859 Montgomery St., B'klyn
and Henry C. Reiners, occupation policeman, residing at 533 E. 87th St., NYC

each being severally, duly, and respectively sworn, deposes and says that he is a citizen of the United States of America; that he has personally known Joseph Adamovicz, the petitioner above mentioned, to have resided in the United States continuously immediately preceding the date of filing his petition, since the 1 day of Dec., anno Domini 1920, and in the State in which the above-entitled petition is made continuously since the 1 day of Dec., anno Domini 1920; and that he has personal knowledge that the said petitioner is a person of good moral character, attached to the principles of the Constitution of the United States, and that the petitioner is in every way qualified, in his opinion, to be admitted a citizen of the United States.

Charles Solomon
(Signature of witness.)

Henry Reiners
(Signature of witness.)

[SEAL.]

Subscribed and sworn to before me by the above-named petitioner and witnesses in the office of the Clerk of said Court at Brooklyn, N. Y., this 16 day of Dec., anno Domini 1925

Clerk.

[OVER]

By Arthur C. Ratzel, Deputy Clerk

Figure 6a: Joseph Adamowicz's application for American naturalization dated December 16, 1925. He was naturalized on March 23, 1926

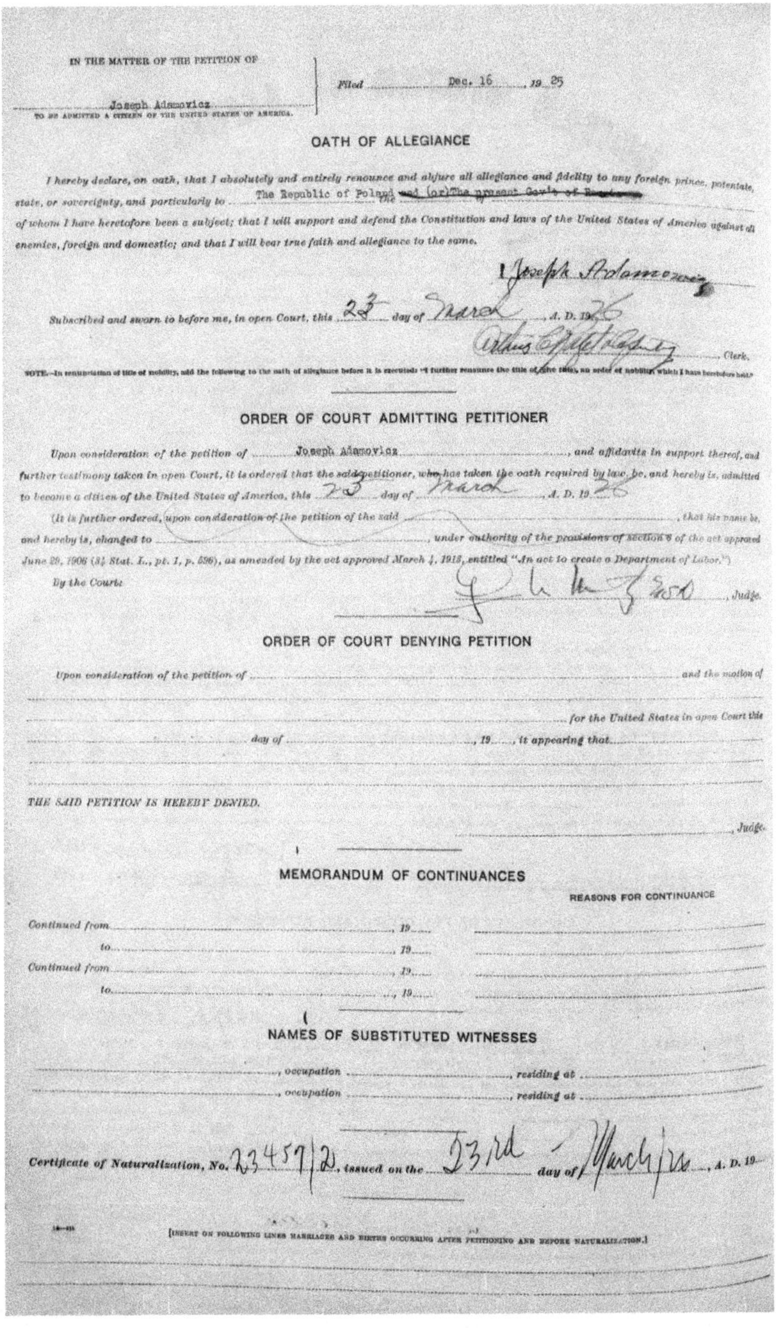

IN THE MATTER OF THE PETITION OF

Joseph Adamovicz

TO BE ADMITTED A CITIZEN OF THE UNITED STATES OF AMERICA.

Filed Dec. 16, 1925

OATH OF ALLEGIANCE

I hereby declare, on oath, that I absolutely and entirely renounce and abjure all allegiance and fidelity to any foreign prince, potentate, state, or sovereignty, and particularly to The Republic of Poland ~~and (or) The present Gov't of~~ *of whom I have heretofore been a subject; that I will support and defend the Constitution and laws of the United States of America against all enemies, foreign and domestic; and that I will bear true faith and allegiance to the same.*

Joseph Adamowicz

Subscribed and sworn to before me, in open Court, this 23 *day of* March, *A. D. 19*26

Clerk.

NOTE.—In renunciation of title of nobility, add the following to the oath of allegiance before it is executed: "I further renounce the title of (give title), an order of nobility, which I have heretofore held."

ORDER OF COURT ADMITTING PETITIONER

Upon consideration of the petition of Joseph Adamovicz *, and affidavits in support thereof, and further testimony taken in open Court, it is ordered that the said petitioner, who has taken the oath required by law, be, and hereby is, admitted to become a citizen of the United States of America, this* 23 *day of* March, *A. D. 19*26

(It is further ordered, upon consideration of the petition of the said ..., that his name be, and hereby is, changed to ..., under authority of the provisions of section 6 of the act approved June 29, 1906 (34 Stat. L., pt. 1, p. 596), as amended by the act approved March 4, 1913, entitled "An act to create a Department of Labor.")

By the Court:

Judge.

ORDER OF COURT DENYING PETITION

Upon consideration of the petition of ... and the motion of ... for the United States in open Court this ... day of ..., 19..., it appearing that ...

THE SAID PETITION IS HEREBY DENIED.

Judge.

MEMORANDUM OF CONTINUANCES

REASONS FOR CONTINUANCE

Continued from ..., 19...
to ..., 19...
Continued from ..., 19...
to ..., 19...

NAMES OF SUBSTITUTED WITNESSES

..., *occupation* ..., *residing at* ...
..., *occupation* ..., *residing at* ...

Certificate of Naturalization, No. 2345712, *issued on the* 23rd *day of* March/26, *A. D. 19*

[INSERT ON FOLLOWING LINES MARRIAGES AND BIRTHS OCCURRING AFTER PETITIONING AND BEFORE NATURALIZATION.]

Figure 6b: Joseph Adamowicz's application for American naturalization dated December 16, 1925, continued.

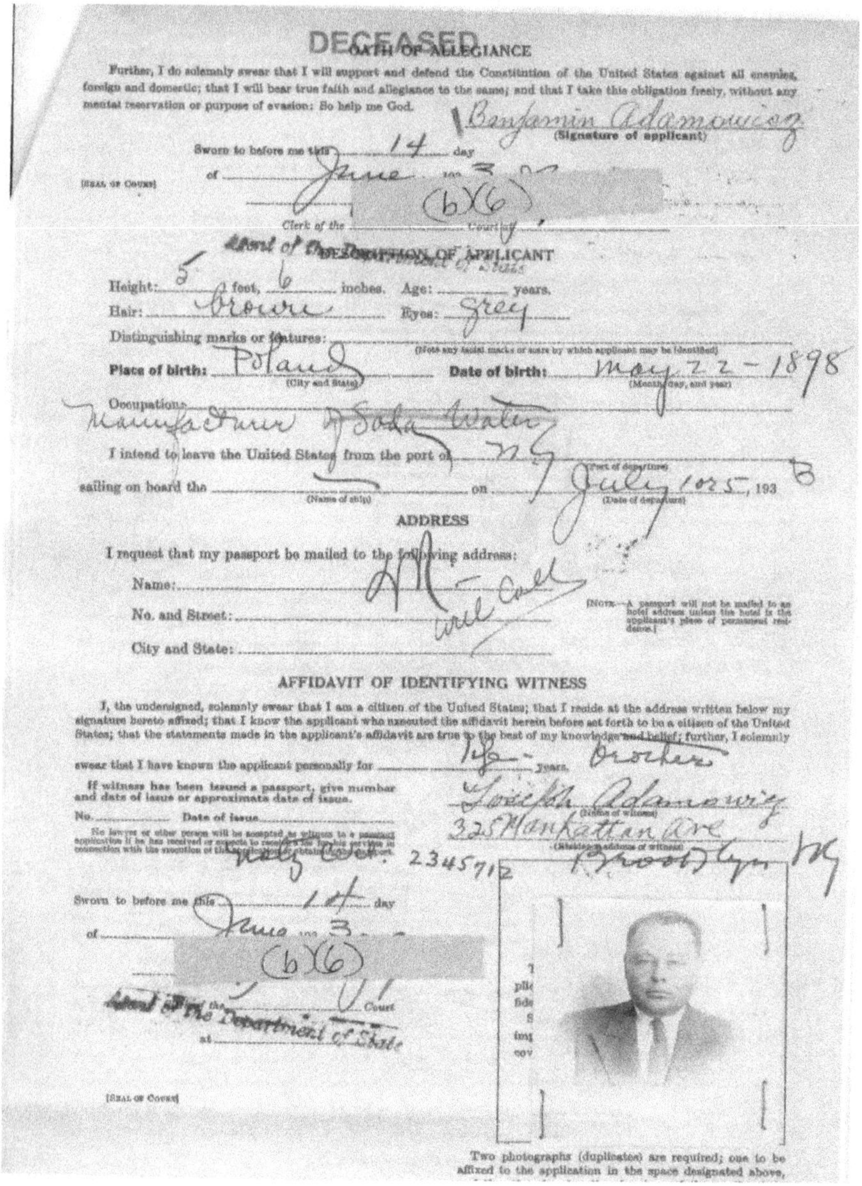

Figure 7a: Benjamin Adamowicz's application for a passport for a travel to Poland. The passport was issued June 14, 1933. It is a proof that Ben and Joe planned to fly to Poland in 1933. Courtesy of the U.S. State Department. Collection of Maureen Mroczek Morris.

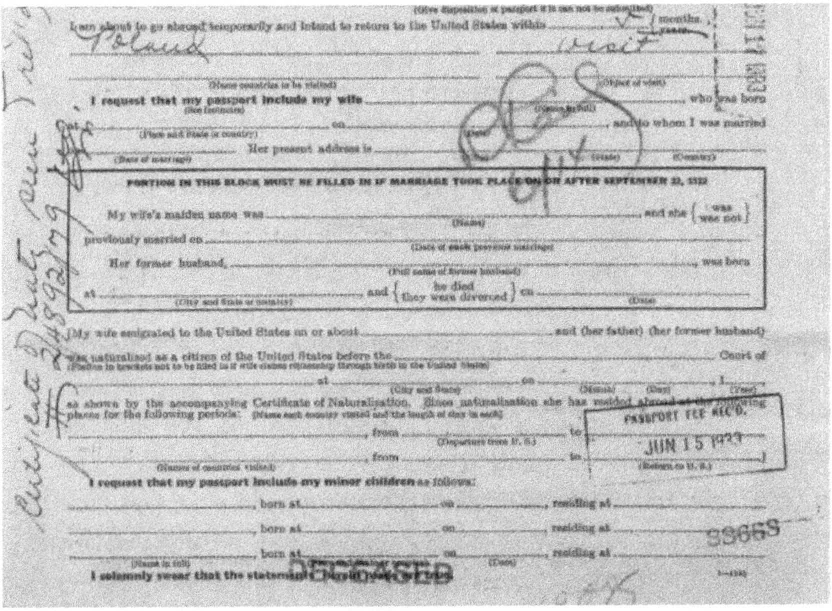

(Give disposition of passport if it is not to be submitted)

I am about to go abroad temporarily and intend to return to the United States within ...... months.

Poland ...... visit

(Name countries to be visited) (Object of visit)

I request that my passport include my wife ...... who was born

(See footnotes) (Name in full)

at ...... on ...... and to whom I was married

(Place and State or country) (Date)

...... Her present address is ......

(Date of marriage) (State) (Country)

PORTION IN THIS BLOCK MUST BE FILLED IN IF MARRIAGE TOOK PLACE ON OR AFTER SEPTEMBER 22, 1922

My wife's maiden name was ...... and she { was / was not }

(Name)

previously married on ......

(Date of each previous marriage)

Her former husband, ... was born

(Full name of former husband)

at ...... and { he died / they were divorced } on ......

(City and State or country) (Date)

[My wife emigrated to the United States on or about ...... and (her father) (her former husband)

was naturalized as a citizen of the United States before the ...... Court of

(Portions in brackets not to be filled in if wife claims citizenship through birth in the United States)

...... at ...... on ...... 1......

(City and State) (Month) (Day) (Year)

as shown by the accompanying Certificate of Naturalization. Since naturalization she has resided abroad at the following places for the following periods: (Name each country visited and the length of stay in each)

......, from ...... to ......

(Departure from U. S.)

......, from ...... to ......

(Names of countries visited) (Return to U. S.)

PASSPORT FEE REC'D.

JUN 15 1933

I request that my passport include my minor children as follows:

......, born at ...... on ......, residing at ......

......, born at ...... on ......, residing at ......

......, born at ...... on ......, residing at ......

(Name in full) (Date)

I solemnly swear that the statements herein are true.

DECEASED

Figure 7b: Benjamin Adamowicz's application for a passport for a travel to Poland. The passport was issued on June 14, 1933. continued.

CHAPTER 6

SODA WATER AND SODA POP

The foundation for their American life was provided by their business. Ben Adamowicz left a very interesting account about the production of the flavored drink:

> "Manufacturing of our 'fruit water' went like this: First, we prepared syrup of sugar and different fruit juices in a big jar; a machine for charging water with carbon dioxide was next to it. Second, the syrup was poured into bottles. Third, the sparkling water was pumped under pressure into the bottles, which were cocked."

Then he added: "People loved us. The business was thriving. Our water had more bubbles than others." Gradually, a sizable factory of the sparkling soda water was created at Conselyea Street. In his account, Ben described in detail the subsequent stages of perfecting the process of adding carbon dioxide to juices and water. He lists expenses for better and better machines. He remembers how Joe went to Poland and from there to Czechoslovakia in 1927, to purchase an apparatus which modernized the production. We suspect, however, that it was not an apparatus for fruit-water but for a much stronger drink, namely, hooch. Yes! They purchased equipment for the distillation of liquor.

Let's discuss this. (A) Prohibition was the law of the land in America at that time and such commercial contraptions were inaccessible. (B) They might be available in Czechoslovakia, an industrialized country. (C) A device for alcohol distillation, imported from abroad, could be easily described as a machine for producing fruit-flavored water. (D) If the brothers were developing an illegal production of alcohol, they certainly did not want to leave any traces in America; purchasing a machine in Czechoslovakia was a convincing camouflage.

Figure 8: Site of the Adamowicz Brothers "soda water factory" seen in 2010. The bottling plant was on the first floor and the "Speak Easy" hall on the second floor. Photo by Monika Braun.

Indeed, Joseph wet to Czechoslovakia and brought back some unusual machinery. The list of passengers arriving in New York from Gdynia on board the Polish liner *Puławski* on March 2, 1927 contains the name of Joseph Adamowicz accompanied by his "wife" Jadwiga (born 1898) and his "son" Witold (born about 1922), all three residing in Warsaw.

We have a few problems here: neither Joseph nor his brothers ever lived in Warsaw. Furthermore, Joseph Adamowicz was described in newspaper reports and on census, passport and other official records including his Death Certificate as "single." Additionally, in many interviews given for years both in America and in Poland about his transatlantic flight, Joseph was always described as single. It is possible that Joseph, out of the goodness of his heart, or maybe for profit, "married" a woman with a son from Poland, both strangers to him. Another possibility pertains to the importation of machinery: a family man would be less likely to come under scrutiny by immigration authorities than a single man, especially a man carrying contraband. Thus, this lie may have been protective subterfuge and Joseph may have paid Jadwiga to be his "wife." [It should be noted that in 1937, Joe placed an ad in the *Brooklyn New York Daily Eagle* searching for his "wife" called Jadwiga Fatina, "missing for 10 years." This action may have been taken for a legal reason, since the "marriage" may have been recorded.]

In any case, about that time — we don't know precisely when — the three brothers embarked on a new endeavor – the production of hooch, or moonshine. They joined the legions of bootleggers profiteering from the Prohibition. There are no historical documents about the start of the Adamowiczes involvement in the illegal distilling and selling of alcohol. The mysterious machine from Czechoslovakia is one indication about this. But there are many other hints and allusions to the presence of vodka in their lives.

In September 1927, Ben had a car accident (drunk driving?) that was reported by several newspapers.[1] In news photographs we see a car that has been dragged from the water – a Studebaker with its back wheels submerged and a crowd of onlookers above. We read that a car driven by Benjamin Adamowicz crashed into another car on the bridge over Newton Creek and breeched the barrier. This creek, more of a canal or drainage ditch full of dirt, toxic waste from factories, and used engine oil, runs between Brooklyn and Queens in an industrial area. It was a miracle that Ben did not drown in the muck. Was he drunk? Or just reckless?

---

[1] These sources included a photograph in the *Brooklyn NY Daily News*, 2 September 1927, as well as an extensive note in *The New York Times* of September 2, 1927.

His car broke through a barrier and fell about 15 feet into water 7 feet deep. Ben was able to extract himself from the sinking car and cried for help. Two people nearby, who happened to be repairing their row boat, rushed to rescue him. He was injured. An ambulance rushed him to St. Catharine's Hospital. After a few hours, he was released.

There were more dodgy dealings: Ben's car was stolen a month later, two days after his driver's license was suspended for reckless driving [*Brooklyn Daily Eagle*, October 6, 1927.] "The police found a 22 caliber revolver and a small dirk in the automobile. Adamowicz... denied knowledge of the weapons." [*Brooklyn Daily Eagle,* October 10, 1927.]

Another indication that something was amiss is Ben's story is recorded by Strumph-Wojtkiewicz and dealing with about an Italian sea captain. This story, dating from 1928, sheds light on the brothers' later travails. (We are going to return to that matter later.) According to Ben, a ship *President Wilson* arrived in the port of New York in 1928. Its captain was "an Italian." He was "an old friend and companion" of the brothers. He invited them for dinner on his ship. After the meal, the brothers reciprocated by inviting him to their factory and treated him with vodka. As Ben explained: "We drove him to our plant. We gave him a lot to drink, and we had plenty of booze, because we had a permit for alcohol. The captain liked it very much." Then, they drove him around the neighborhood and on a new highway on Long Island: "For one dollar one was allowed to drive with a tremendous speed of 50 miles per hour."

The drinking session with an Italian captain, as well as the earlier car accident, could mean that the brothers drank a lot at that time, that they produced alcohol, and served it to their guests, or that they were distributing it on a large scale — "we had lots of booze!" said Ben. But it was still the time of Prohibition, which lasted in the U.S. from 1919 until 1933. Only selected religious institutions were getting "permits for alcohol" — nobody else. Neither for production, nor for possession, nor for serving, nor selling. The brothers' trial in 1934 demonstrated without any doubt that they never had such a permit. (We are going to write about the trial later.) Yet, as Ben said, they had plenty of alcohol in 1928.

Figure 9: The factory and the apartment building (seen in 2010).
Photo by Monika Braun.

The memories of some of the current residents of Conselyea Street in Brooklyn, whom we interviewed, preserved one more astonishing fact: in the main factory building there was a spacious hall on the second floor. In the slang of the time it was called a "Speak Easy." This term denoted a place where people "spoke-easily," because alcohol loosened their tongues. A "Speak Easy" was a bar or a saloon where alcohol was served illegally. In American gangster movies we see many scenes set in such locations where people drank alcohol out of small tea cups or water glasses, the crowd was lively, the music exciting, and everyone had fun, at least until the arrival of the police. The long-term residents of the Conselyea Street apartments remembered that the Adamowicz brothers not only produced alcohol in their factory, but also served it in the room upstairs – of course, only to their chosen guests.

How did it come about? The situation might be reconstructed this way: after the brothers furbished a bottling factory for the production of their soda water, they added the far more lucrative, though illegal, alcohol to their product line. The Adamowiczes already had a space for the production of soda water. They had easy access to sugar. The temptation to flout the law was irresistible; it was part of the brothers' "MO." At first they most likely used a primitive home-made contraption — they certainly knew how to do this from their childhood years. They increased production in 1927 by importing a modern alcohol still from Czechoslovakia. They had bottles readily available. They had a spacious room above the factory to serve as a Speak Easy.

Although impossible to confirm, rumors circulated in Brooklyn that the Adamowicz brothers partnered with the Italian Mafia in the distribution and sale of the alcohol. We don't know for sure whether they entered into a partnership with the Italian mafia for distributing and selling alcohol, yet these rumors appear plausible. Ben's story about the Italian ship captain as their drinking partner seems to confirm the gossip. (We shall return to these matters in the chapters dedicated to the trial of the brothers accused of producing alcohol.)

Another hint of restless discontent appeared in Ben's memoires, when he spoke about Joe's travel to Poland and return on board the Polish ship "Pułaski" in 1927: "I envied Joe a little, that he was seafaring under the Polish flag. I asked him many questions about the Old Country. I, myself, started to think about traveling to Poland, about sailing on a Polish ship. I wanted something new in my life. At that time I didn't know that my yearning would find expression in aviation."

At the beginning of the 1930s the Adamowiczes' business (both legal, and — as we are guessing — illegal) flourished. From many of Ben's statements we can deduce that the brothers' earnings were high. They loved their country of origin, the newly independent Poland; it was still in bondage when they left their ancestral lands for America. At the same time, they considered themselves to be citizens of America, with full rights. Unfortunately, this citizenship did not prohibit them from continually breaking the laws of their new country.

In any case, the brothers were proud of their business and their house. Ben confessed:

> "When eventually everything was nicely painted we felt very happy. For me it was the same feeling that I had when I started to earn my own living and when I got my first paycheck. I don't know how to say it, but with all that I had, I still felt that I was missing something. I looked with great satisfaction at our gorgeous buildings and I didn't know why I wanted more. I had a job that brought in good money. I could work as much as I wished and be merry on Sunday after church. But I wanted more. Something different from a good job, good pay, and leisure time."

Their wealth grew and with it they allowed themselves some extravagances. Soon, a dream about a flight over the Atlantic to Poland would germinate. Something difficult to identify was taking shape. It appeared on the horizon.

The motorcycle craze belonged to the past. Now, new cars, one after the other, appeared in front of the Adamowicz house: an Oldsmobile, a Hudson, a Nash, and a Cadillac — but "we crashed the Cadillac after only three days of driving" recalled Ben. To replace the totaled Cadillac they bought a large, luxury Studebaker (the car that Ben drove over the bridge at Newton Creek in 1927). Next, they bought an airplane.

CHAPTER 7

FIRST FLIGHTS

Joe and Ben boarded an aircraft for the first time in the summer of 1928. Driving to a friend on Staten Island they saw a biplane sitting on a meadow near to the road. They stopped and approached to have a closer look. "The machine seemed to us truly magnificent" — recalled Ben. It turned out that the pilot was offering short rides in the air. Mesmerized, they immediately decided to take advantage of the chance, paying $10 per person. The aircraft was "an old military training machine, no doubt from World War I . It had a landing speed only 15 miles per hour, thus it was good for learning how to pilot a plane." They were in the air for about fifteen minutes. They were enthralled. "The first taking off and going up impressed on me as greatly as the first pay. It's hard for me to articulate this great joy which I felt up there in the sky flying over houses and the city as somebody bigger than ordinary men." Apparently, both brothers caught the "flying" virus. "The plane got to my head and to Joe's head as well. I was thinking it over this for the entire week and felt that I would give my whole money for flying."

After the first experience in the sky, they embarked on their next flying adventure with the Italian captain of *President Wilson*. To crown the day with him — we have already mentioned the dinner on board his ship, drinking in their factory, and automobile speeding — the Adamowiczes treated the captain to a 15-minute flight. Then, they flew again and again, in turns. Each trip was ten dollars per person.

"That memorable Sunday, my brother Joe and I, after having returned from a flight, remained near the aircraft. We asked for the permission to watch. We saw as the passengers were taking seats on board and as the machine was flying wherever its pilot took it. Late night we had a dinner. My heart was burning with jealousy that the pilot flies, not I. I told it Joe. He corrected me at once: no 'not I' — "you should have said 'not us.'"

Again, next Sunday: "We flew one more time for $10, and just after landing we could not stand it anymore." Ben said: "Joe, go and ask how much this plane is?" It was an old model of Waco with eight-cylinder engine Curtiss OX-5. "The pilot told us that it is a good machine and it would cost $3,400."

The pilot offered to help them in purchasing an aircraft. They took a business card from him. They talked it over. They called to tell him that they want to buy an aircraft. He put them in touch with another pilot, Mr. Brown, who promised to acquire such an aircraft from the factory in Detroit and to find for them an instructor who would teach them flying. They had to give him a $500 advance.

Figure 10: Charles Lindbergh's historical plane, *The Spirit of St. Louis*, in the National Air and Space Museum, Washington, D.C. Photo by Raul654, May 7, 2005. Wikimedia Commons.

They did it. They owned a plane. For the transportation of the aircraft from Detroit they had to pay an additional $100. In only a week, the new machine was waiting for the happy buyers in a hangar on the airfield in Garden City near New York. The plane's number was NC 1868. It had two seats in front and one behind. It had two joysticks: one at the left front seat for the student and another one at the back seat for the instructor. "Now we could start conquering the sky"— recalled Ben: "Our hearts and heads were filled only with flying."

From that time on, the two brothers who had always been very close were bonded even stronger by the shared passion for aviation. They formed a team: Ben and Joe. Ben, though younger, gradually took the position of the team leader, as he was more motivated than his brother Joe to start flying. He learned pilotage first. When they flew together, he held the joystick more often, assuming the role of "the first pilot" while Joe was "the second pilot." Bruno remained in the shadows as he did not participate personally in the flying adventure of the younger brothers. Yet, he supported them throughout this time by managing the business and by providing them with sound advice, fraternal care, and unconditional love.

At first, Ben and Joe hired an instructor, a Russian pilot, called Henry Nitry: Ben said that it was "surely a false name." He charged $10 per hour of fight with a student, but, the brothers felt, he was cheating. They were in the air for only 25 minutes, yet they had to pay him $10 each time. For the two of them it was $20 per day. Expensive! So, they decided that only Ben would take the lessons and when he learned how to pilot the plane, he would teach Joe in turn.

Every day after work, the brothers drove 20 miles from their plant to the Roosevelt Field airport and at dusk they took flying lessons. After having taken twenty hours of instruction — at least formally, because Nitry, as we said, was cutting the lessons short

— and after 50 hours of flying solo, Ben received a pilot's diploma. He did not have enough time to teach his brother, so Joe found an instructor for himself, Cecil Corren, and soon he was flying alone.

There was no shortage of dramatic mishaps in this training period which Ben recalls vividly and in detail. The first accident happened to Joe. His instructor criticized him for always landing beyond the indicated point where he should touch the ground. Ben described the incident as follows:

"I was sitting in a tent at the airport, as usual on a Sunday, when I see that our machine virtually stops in the air and begins spinning around. I know that it's very bad and I start running across the airstrip. In the meantime, the aircraft, on the altitude of about a hundred feet, glides on the one side, then on the other, and the very next second it nose-dives and crushes digging into the potato field. I'm getting a chill in my spine and I'm utterly frightened, the more that I see that the instructor gets out of the machine and Joe doesn't. More people come. They pull him out of his seat. One eye opened and the other closed. I feel terribly sorry. An ambulance is called and takes my brother Joe to a nearby National Hospital. Before the ride thy give him a lot of vodka, which obviously does him good."

Let's note: vodka was always handy, and "a lot" of it. Nonetheless, after two weeks in the hospital Joe was fine, but the aircraft fuselage had to be fixed, one wing replaced, a new propeller installed, and the engine sent for a capital repair. The total cost of the accident was more than $2,000.

The next accident happened to Ben: "Immediately after taking off, at the altitude of only about 90 feet, the engine stopped working. I landed with great pain; I had to suddenly make a hairpin turn and I almost brushed the roof of a hangar. Miraculously, I made it safely onto the ground. After one more engine's repair, it functioned without a blemish."

The third accident looked really dangerous. Ben took off just before an approaching storm. When he was already airborne, the wind changed direction by 180 degrees. The pilot did not notice and he attempted to land the plane in the same direction as he took off. He took off, in accordance with the rules, against the wind. But now, after the change of the wind's course, he was ready to land with the wind, and thus contrary to the rules and practices:

> "The landing failed. The machine flew over the runway with a tremendous speed and there was no way to lower it, not even talking about landing at that rapidity. Very surprised, I flew higher and decided to begin the landing from a farther distance. But my machine flew so fast that there was no chance to touch down and arrive on the ground. To make things worse, rain started to pour. Still, I didn't understand what was happening to the machine."

We have to explain that the brothers' airplane, as many at that time, had an open pilot's cabin, with only a small windshield in the front. The pilots were flying in goggles, of course, but these goggles did not help much when there was rain or snow.

> "On the ground people started to wave their hats and coats, but fortunately Joe told them not to, because I could have thought that I lost my landing gear. I should add that at the end of the air strip there were electric wires on tall poles under high voltage. If caught by these wires, both the plane and the pilot would look like a fly which sat on a red-hot kitchen stove. So, I went around one more time and began to make an approach to landing far away from the strip. This time I firmly decided to make a landing at any cost. The rain was blinding me, but I tried to land anyway. Yet, the wind again pushed me over the airfield. I hardly made it above the electric wires. I had enough of all this. Below me was a potato field. I dove, shut the engine, and let it go. The plane dropped from an altitude of about 50 feet into the potatoes, or rather deep mud. The machine hit the ground rather nicely, as a cat on its fours. I

pulled out a blanket over my head and waited until the end of the storm."

In Ben's stories about the training flights, the name of Elisabeth Mattke starts to appear. She was a Prussian German immigrant living in the apartment building at 325 Manhattan Ave. as well as Ben's fiancé and later his wife. Elizabeth ("Lisa or Betty") accompanied the brothers to the airport to watch their not-always-successful antics in the air. Ben married Lisa Mattke on the 21st of September 1930; on the marriage record his age is listed as 23; he was, in fact, about 32 years old.

The training aircraft, exploited without mercy, was soon out of service. The brothers exchanged it for a new one, for a higher price. It was also a Waco, a little bit used, but with a stronger Wright's engine of five cylinders and 165 horsepower. The brothers made new wing-covers and painted on the fuselage a White Eagle, Poland's emblem. Repairs and purchases required thousands of dollars. Ben acknowledged; "Aviation was much more expensive than the previous motorcycling passion."

"We were both flying more and more hours and longer and longer distances. We never had enough. We developed a dream about flying to Poland." When Ben and Joe told Bruno about this dream, he said sternly: "Very well. But don't fly together. In case of an accident, I don't want to lose two brothers at once."

CHAPTER 8

AIR CONQUEST OF THE ATLANTIC

To dream about conquering the North Atlantic in the air was not new in the 1930s, when the idea entered the minds of the Adamowicz brothers. It appeared as early as in the colonial era. Originally, it was the idea of flying over the Atlantic in a balloon filled with gas. A French "aeronaut," Jean Pierre Blanchard (1753-1809), proposed such a means of transportation to the leaders of American Congress in 1793. Of course, nothing came of it. Yet, balloon flights were soon attempted in America. Initially the balloonists flew overland; later—over the ocean. They were of French, German, English and Italian descent: Charles Leroux (1856-1889), William F. Assmann (1862-1920), Thomas Scott Baldwin (1854-1923), Frank George Seyfang (1890-1963), Albert C. Triaca (b. 1875), and many others. However, a transatlantic crossing in a balloon or an airship was not possible because of limitations of the existing technology. Several efforts ended in tragic disasters. In 1910, the airship *America* disappeared over the Atlantic, abandoned by its crew. In 1912, five crewmen died when the airship *Akron* exploded at the start of its planned transatlantic flight. In 1919, the airship called *Wingfoot Air Express* was destroyed in a fire in the air above Chicago. The list goes on and on.

Towards the end of the 19th century various dreamers, bunglers, builders, and daredevils built machines that were heavier than air.[2] Gliders were used, then propellers. The earliest flying device is attributed to a German-American inventor and pilot, Gustave Whitehead. Supposedly, he made a few flights in

---

[2]Tom D. Crouch, *A Dream of Wings: Americans and the Airplane, 1875–1905*. New York: W. W. Norton & Company, 2002.

Bridgeport, Connecticut in 1901. While, there are no photographic records to document this, several eyewitnesses testified under oath that they saw a flying machine in the air. The matter remains controversial. Regardless, other aviation attempts followed soon.

The first well documented and recorded aircraft was built by the Orville brothers and Wilbur Wright. Initially they experimented with gliders. Then they equipped one plane with an engine. On December 17, 1903, Orville flew it for about 120 feet, sustaining the plane in the air for 12 seconds. On the same day he flew again: 852 feet in 59 seconds. This epoch-making event happened on a beach near the town of Kitty Hawk in North Carolina. To commemorate the feat of the Wright brothers, license plates of this state read with pride: "First in Flight."

Since then, the history of aviation began to roll like an avalanche. Airplanes, produced on a mass scale, took an active part in the battles of World War I (1914-1918.) Around the same time flights over the Atlantic were attempted with use of seaplanes, that is, planes with floats, allowing the aviators to take off and land on water. Such machines were built since 1910; less than ten years later, they flew over the Atlantic. A group of American seaplanes flew — with several stops — from Plymouth at the east shores of America to the English coast.[3]

Australian pilot Harry Hawker (1889-1921) with a Scottish navigator Kenneth Mackenzie-Grieve made the very first attempt to conquer the Atlantic with an aircraft. They departed from Newfoundland in the direction of Ireland on May 18, 1919. After fourteen hours of flight their engine broke. They managed to crash-land and float on the water — their machine was not a seaplane — not far from their goal, the western shores of Ireland. They were rescued from their predicament by a Danish ship. Needless to say, they did not make it all the way across the

---

[3] Tom D. Crouch, *A Dream of Wings*.

ocean. Only a few weeks later, two Englishmen, John Alcock and Arthur Whitten-Brown succeeded where the Australians failed. They started from Newfoundland on June 14, 1919, at 1:59 p.m. local time and landed in Ireland on June 15, 1919 in the morning, after 16 hours and 28 minutes in the air. They used a Vickers Vimy bi-plane, bi-engine bomber form World War I, equipped with additional tanks for fuel.

Other transatlantic attempts followed, undertaken from both sides of the ocean. They were frequently encouraged by American entrepreneurs who offered high monetary prizes, envisioning the development of a lucrative air-business in the future. At the beginning of the 1920s, an owner of a hotel chain in New York, Raymond Orteig offered a sum of $25,000 for crossing the Atlantic — a very high sum for the time.[4] An aviators' race began. It was Charles Lindbergh who won this prize in 1927.[5]

Lindbergh flew solo in an aircraft, a one engine high-wing monoplane named the "Spirit of Saint Louis," that was built especially for this flight by the Ryan Company in California. In order to keep the weight of the plane down and allow for additional fuel tanks, he took the risk of flying alone. The gamble paid off. He took off at dawn on May 20, 1927, from the Roosevelt Field airport near New York. He landed at the Le Bourget airport in Paris after over 33 hours in the air. Even though the *Spirit of St. Louis* was "little more than a flying gas tank" (Bryson, p. 49) with wings of cotton covered by metallic paint, the history of aviation entered a new chapter. Lindbergh spent the following years in a whirlwind tour of America, flying from town to town, crisscrossing the continent in his famous, fragile plane. The press followed his every step. With Lindbergh's feat, the intercontinental flight was born, and the

---

[4] About $250,000 in 2010
[5] Bill Bryson, *One Summer: America, 1927* (New York, Doubleday, 2013).

exploration of the intra-continental possibilities of air travel began in earnest.

Soon after Lindbergh, on June 4-6, 1927, Clarence D. Chamberlin and Charles Levine flew a Bellanca plane they called *Columbia* from New York to Eisleben near Berlin in 43 hours and 49 minutes — a flight of an astonishing duration and a proof of Bellanca's excellence. Chamberlin also held the world's aviation endurance record.

Figure 11: Bellanca WB-2 *Columbia*, 1927 Transatlantic flight 4-6 June 1927 from New York to Eisleben in Germany. Wikimedia Commons. From RAF Museum: http://www.rafmuseum.com/milestones-of-flight/world/1927.html

1927 was the year of records. The South Atlantic was conquered the same spring. A Portuguese pilot Jose Sarmento de Beires, navigator Jorge de Castilho, and mechanic Manuel Gouveia, flew a large, metal, bi-engine seaplane Dornier. Theirs was not a non-stop flight. The first stage was their long flight from Europe to Balomain, the Portuguese colony of Guinea (today Guinea-Bissau) on the western tip of Africa. It was marked by many mishaps. In the transatlantic phase of their adventure, they took off from Guinea on April 16, 1927, at 18:06 and after 18 hours and 12 minutes they reached the island of Fernando de Noronha, 200 miles east of the Brazilian coast. In this segment of the itinerary, they covered about 300 miles. They continued their journey with two more stops to Rio de Janeiro.

The late 1920s and early 1930s saw numerous new efforts to conquer the ocean —both successful and failed. Several Poles joined the elite club of aviators that won the struggle with the elements.

Figure 12: Major Stanisław Skarżyński in 1934.[6]

In 1933, a Polish Air Force Captain, Stanisław Skarżyński (1899-1942), crossed the South Atlantic by flying solo in a small Polish-built tourist plane, RWD-5bis. Skarżyński had served in the Piłsudski Legions during World War I. He graduated from the Aviation Academy in Bydgoszcz in 1925, and became a career

---

[6]Major Stanislaw Skarżyński, 1934 portrait by Willem van de Poll. Dutch National Archives, The Hague, Fotocollectie Algemeen Nederlands Persbureau (ANeFo), 1945-1989, Nummer toegang 2.24.14.02 Bestanddeelnummer 190-1343. Wikimedia Commons.

military pilot. During the night of May 7-8, 1933 he crossed the southern Atlantic, remaining in the air above the ocean for 17 hours and 15 minutes; the whole flight lasted for 20 hours and 30 minutes. He flew more than 1,500 miles from St. Louis in Senegal, Africa, to Marcello in Brazil. The flight was a section of his Warsaw to Rio de Janeiro flight that took place between 27 April and 10 May and covered 11,113 miles. Skarżyński was promoted to Major for accomplishing this feat. He then returned to military duties, fought in WWII, and died in action in 1942 as a RAF Commanding Officer of the 305 Polish Bomber Squadron, flying missions against Germany.

Two other Polish Air Force Majors, pilots Ludwik Idzikowski (1891-1929) and Kazimierz Kubala had attempted to cross the Atlantic before Skarżyński. They twice set off from Paris for America in 1928 and 1929. Sadly, both flights, sponsored by the Polish government, ended in disasters. The first plane was named after Poland's Marshall Józef Piłsudski, who was instrumental in restoring Poland's independence and recently had taken over the country in a May 1926 military coup-d'état. The aircraft had a cracked fuel tank and this defect was discovered only half-the-way-through the flight to America. The pilot turned around, returned to Europe, and landed on water after 31 hours in the air. The second transatlantic attempt ended in a tragedy. The plane malfunctioned and Idzikowski was killed in 1929, during a forced landing on the Faial Island in the Azores.

At that time, the Adamowicz brothers were among the crowd of Poles awaiting Idzikowski and Kubala in New York, on July 14, 1929. They had their plane and wanted to be the first to greet the heroes in the air:

> "We were waiting on the airfield and three times we took off to meet them in the skies. There were more than 25,000 Poles, expecting with hope and fear for the arrival of our brothers. When the news came that they crashed we were in despair and precisely

at that moment we made a vow that a Pole must win the ocean. It cannot be that a Pole should be worse than an American, English, French, Dane, or Italian."

That was a turning point in their lives — a truly momentous event with serious consequences.

Figure 13: Idzikowski and Kubala in a French plane Amiot 123 named *Marszałek Piłsudski* and used in an attempted transatlantic flight in 1926. Wikimedia Commons.

In Ben's above-quoted statement (that "a Pole should be [no] worse than an American, English, French, Dane, or Italian"), the "American" was undoubtedly the famous Charles Lindbergh. The "English" probably referred to two English pilots, John William Alcock (1892-1919) and Arthur Whitten-Brown (1886-1948), who, as already mentioned, flew over the Atlantic in 1919. The "French" were most likely Dieudonne Costes (1892-1973) and Maurice Bellonte (1896-1983) who are credited with the first flight from Paris to New York, from east to west, made in 1930. The "Dane" was Holger Hoiriis (1901-1942), a pilot, who along with his passenger, Otto Hilling, an American of German descent and the owner of the Bellanca they flew in, crossed the ocean in 1931.

The "Italian" might refer to a large group of Italian aviators, who, under the command of General Italo Balbo (1896-1940), flew 12 seaplanes Savoia Marchetti S-55, over the South Atlantic in 1930. The Italians, with Balbo – who was, before his untimely death in 1940 the heir apparent to the dictator Benito Mussolini – set to prove the superiority of fascist aviation. They repeated their feat in a group of 24 identical seaplanes that crossed the North Atlantic in 1933.

We have to note that listing "French, Dane, or Italian" in 1929, may be seen as anachronistic, because some of the flights we mentioned happened later, after 1929. However, Ben knew about these aviators and their accomplishments when talking to Strumph-Wojtkiewicz in 1934; the source of the quotation. Therefore, it is highly likely that he put together flights made before 1929, as well as those that postdated that year. His remarks indicate that the Adamowiczes knew the history of transatlantic victories and tragedies; they were aware of aviation's dangers before flying from New York to Warsaw in 1934.

Indeed, we venture to guess that the brothers decided to fly over the ocean exactly when they heard about Idzikowski's death in 1929. We believe that they made such a decision at that time and that they treated it both very seriously and practically – as a realistic and practical goal. This assumption is partly confirmed by our sources. For instance, a press note published at the end of December 1931 informs that "Benjamin and Joseph Adamowicz, two brothers, who plan a non-stop flight from New York to Warsaw next spring, will be guests of honor at the New Year's Eve dinner and dance at 111 Conselyea, the headquarters of 'White Eagle Air Fund', which raises money for their endeavor. Both brothers are described as truly excellent pilots. Ben has 18 years' experience of flying under his belt."[7]

Well, Ben did not have "18 years' experience in flying"— only three years, in fact, but anything goes in publicity. The note stated that a traditional Polish New Year's Eve ball was to be organized in that spacious upper-level room in the factory, known to the Brooklyn neighbors as the "Speak Easy". Though Prohibition was still in full force, alcohol was certainly abundant. As we learned from interviews with Conselyea residents, evenings and nights were frequently filled with drinking and dancing on the premises of the Adamowiczes' business. They were raising money for their aerial adventure by charging an entry fee for the New Year's Eve ball. What matters the most in this press notice, however, is that the brothers clearly were planning their transatlantic flight as early as 1930.

Their decision was reinforced by the news that yet another transatlantic flight attempt failed. This time it was an American of Polish descent, Stanislaus L. Hausner, who tried and failed to cross the ocean. Fortunately, his flight, while not successful, did not end tragically. On June 3, 1932, Hausner left New York on a Bellanca CH Pacemaker plane aiming to reach Warsaw. The first stage, from New York to Halifax, Nova Scotia (Canada) went well. Towards the end of the second stage, from Halifax to Warsaw, an engine failure forced him to perform a sea landing. He was about 500 miles away from the shores of Portugal. He did not fly a seaplane, but he managed to safely put his machine on the waves. For eight long days and nights Hausner drifted on the ocean, sitting astride ("horseback") on the fuselage of his airplane which was kept afloat by a large, empty, leak-proof gas-tank. He was spotted by a passing British tanker and saved.

Hausner's stunt had been wildly announced in the press. The Adamowicz brothers went to see his aircraft at the Bellanca factory in New Castle, Delaware. He was not there at the time, so

---

[7] *Brooklyn Daily Eagle*, December 12, 1931.

they did not have a chance to talk. However, it is highly probable that during that visit they began to think about acquiring this excellent aircraft for use in their own transatlantic adventure.

In 1933, two Lithuanians, Steponas Darius (1896-1933) and Stasys Girenas (1893-1933), attempted to cross the Atlantic from New York to Vilnius, Lithuania. Like Hausner, they flew in a Bellanca; they called their plane *Lituanica* to honor their homeland. Unfortunately, they both died when the plane crashed after having crossed most of Europe, near Soldin (Myśliborz) in Western Pomerania (then in Germany, now in Poland).

Figure 14: A Lithuanian banknote for 10 litu, commemorating the flight of Darius and Girenas. Wikimedia Commons.

By the 1920s women, too, entered into aviation competitions. In 1929, Amelia Earhart (1897-1937) crossed the Atlantic as a passenger – with pilot Wilmer Stultz – on a three-engine Fokker equipped with floats. They departed from Boston, landed in the Canadian province of Nova Scotia and again in Trinity Bay in Newfoundland, and from there they made it to the Irish shores. Earhart then flew over the Atlantic again, this time solo. She commenced her flight in Newfoundland on May 20, 1932, and after 14 hours and 56 minutes in flight she landed in northern Ireland.[8]

It should be noted that in Poland women also began to train and fly, becoming expert pilots, to mention only: Anna Leska, Wanda Modlibowska, Zofia Szczecińska, and Stefania Wojtulanis.[9] None of them attempted to cross the Atlantic.

Several attempts of crossing the Atlantic in the air ended tragically. There are estimates that in the first twenty years of transatlantic aviation (1920-1940), no fewer than 80 people lost their lives. This high mortality rate provides a vivid, if chilling, background for the aerial accomplishments of Ben and Joe Adamowicz. They knew very well the dangers associated with what they were planning to do; they knew the elevated risk and potentially high price of a transatlantic flight.

In 1932, the two brothers, who, let's not forget, were amateur pilots, received a boost for their future rivalry with professionals, all excellent pilots. Many pilots had experience going back to World War I; others, like Lindbergh, were postal-pilots; and still others worked as professional pilots in the rapidly growing airline industry. All the Adamowiczes had was three years of flying lessons and their passion.

On May 30, 1932, the brothers drove – as was their custom on a Sunday morning – to the Floyd Bennett Field airport, where a tourist-aircraft race was being organized. This airport was the first modern and well equipped aviation facility in the New York area. Built in 1930 on the southern tip of Long Island it got its name from an American pilot who first flew over the North Pole

---

[8] This account was compiled from standard aviation histories; including books by Riccardo Niccoli, Adam Przedpelski, Jan Wieroch, David Simons and Thomas Withington, as well as Bill Bryson, listed in the Bibliography at the end of this book.
[9] See M. Berkowicz, *Stefania Wojtulanis-Karpińska. „Aviomama". About a woman who loved to fly.* (Warsaw: ZP Grupa, 2009). In 1939, these women pilots joined Poland's Air Force as members of Eskadra Sztabowa (The Command Division). Izydor Koliński: *Wojsko Polskie: krótki informator historyczny o Wojsku Polskim w latach II wojny światowej.* (Warszawa : Wydawnictwo Ministerstwa Obrony Narodowej, 1978).

in 1926. The airport's construction resulted in joining together several small swampy islands by landfill using sand from the bottom of Jamaica Bay. The official inauguration of the airport took place on May 23, 1931. The did not survive to the present day. Instead, there is a State Park and an Aviation Museum in the vicinity of J. F. Kennedy airport.

After hearing about the race, the brothers decided to enter. The distance was only 11 miles and the planes had to maintain the altitude of 500 feet. The machines flew individually, one by one. Ben and Joe flew the required distance in the shortest time and won. They received a large, glitzy trophy. "We were photographed and our names appeared in the press all over America" — Ben recalled proudly.

Figure 15: Bellanca *Warsaw* before its flight on August 8, 1934 from the Floyd Bennett Field in New York to Harbour Grace in Newfoundland, Canada. *Lotnictwo z Szachownicą*, no. 31.

c/gain BELLANCA WINS
among the single and twin engine
CABIN PLANES
in the National Air Tour

REPEATING its performance of last year, the Bellanca Pacemaker again confirmed its reputation by defeating all cabin planes except two tri-motors, in the National Air Tour. The 4,900-mile course led through varied flying conditions, over the plains of Western Canada, the rugged American North-west, sections of the Rocky Mountains, and the great Middle West. This cross-country speed and efficiency contest was well calculated to determine which make of airplane is superior to the others of its class or typeI

In reporting the results of this year's Tour, an aeronautical critic of The New York Times stated: useveral surprises were evident from the final scores, according to the officials who designed the formula. Chie(among them was George Haldeman in the Bellanca, who led all the cabin planes to the tape with the e;xeeption of the two Ford entries." (The winning

Fords, of course, were trimotors, with only two of their engines counted against them in the efficiency formula). "Haldeman, **. carrying a load in excess of the empty weight of his ship, performed a remarkable feat in averagint 139.1 miles an hour." The second Bellanca was close behind him.

To carry a useful load of 2,310 lbs. in an airplane which, empty, weighs only 2,290 lbs, powered with a 300 h.p.engine, at an average speed of 139.1 miles an hour over the 4,900-mile course of the National Air Tour-tO land on and take off with such a load from airports of all siz.es at all elevations up to 6,150 ft.-to attain at times an altitude of 15,000 ft.in clearing mountains and riding favornble winds— is an accomplishment that speaks for itself. Reduce these facts to terms of an airplane'S earning capacity in business, and you have the reason for Bella.nca succeSs among aH classes of owners.

BELLANCA AIRCRAFT CORPORATION
NEW CASTLE, DBLAWARB
New York Oaice: O.uy ller Buildint
c1tu1i8nI Distri1Illors: B•lla•co Airtrfl/t o/ c411u411.LJd., MuJr•al

The Bellanca Pacemaker is a six-place cabin monoplane powered with 300 h.p. engine, Wright or Pratt & Whitney. Finished in finest automobile coachwork. High speed, 145 m.p.h. Payload with pilot, 1,235 lbs. U. S. Dept. of Commerce Approved Type Certificate No. 129 and No. 328. The Bellanca Skyrocket, of similar specifications, is powered with the 420 h.p. Wasp engine. High speed, 150 m.p.h.

U. S. Dept. of Commerce Approved Type Certificate No. 319. Both types are readily convertible into excellent seaplanes. The Bellanca Airbus is a 12 to 14 place single-engined monoplane, powered with either the Conqueror, Cyclone or Hornet. High speed, 147 m.p.h. Payload, 2,950 lbs. U. S. Dept. of Commerce Approved Type Certificate No. 360.

BELLANCA

Figure 16: A press report (an ad) about Bellanca's 1930 victory in a flight competition, the National Air Tour. *Aero Digest,* November 1930.

CHAPTER 9
BELLANCA

Heartened by their success, the brothers accelerated their preparations for a cross-Atlantic flight to Poland. They were, first of all, looking for an aircraft that could withstand such a challenge. They were aware that they needed a better machine than they had already owned. They tried to raise money among Polish-Americans, but they soon found out how miserly their community was with regard to charitable causes. Thus, according to Ben, the brothers "decided to act on their own and to self-finance the project, that is do it with family's help."

There we go! The family! In the 1930s, the extended family of the Adamowiczes, as well as the Heynos, living in Brooklyn and doing well, supported Ben and Joe in their unusual plans. It is one of the most moving and striking elements of the culture of these families from eastern Poland: their solidarity. Within a family, a house, a clan, or a neighborhood they were bound by unequivocal solidarity. They were loyal to each other beyond reason. They helped each other, they covered for each other, and they were ready to suffer, or to pay one for another. They were motivated to stick together even in the most unfortunate circumstances.

Three Adamowicz brothers speak about themselves and refer to each other always very seriously: "my brother, "the older brother," or "the younger brothers." They reveal in this way the noblest aspects of proper family bonds that are strong, lifelong, and based on mutual respect. The Adamowiczes were connected by an untarnished and simple fraternal love; a love about which no one brags, but everybody practices. They loved each other honestly and strongly. Thus, they decided in a large family circle to share the costs of Ben and Joe's undertaking.

Of course, the solid financial foundation for this generosity was provided by the profits from the prosperous soda water factory. We could also guess that in the early 1930s the illegal alcohol production and sales at the factory and its associate "Speak-Easy" contributed substantial sums of cash toward this purpose.

Even later, when this illegal business was revealed by the police after Ben and Joe's successful conquest of Atlantic and their return from Poland (we shall tell that part of the story soon), the brothers remained univocally loyal to each other, as was the rest of the family loyal to them. They did not start to argue or to cast blame on each other. Instead, all three shared pain, disgrace, and punishment. But that was later. Now, is the time to focus on their long and arduous preparations for the flight, as well as the flight itself, and their triumphant reception – both in Poland and in America – after the record-breaking flight.

First, it was necessary to buy a new aircraft. The choice was a Bellanca. It was an excellent and reliable machine. Chamberlin and Levine flew a Bellanca from America to Europe in 1927. Hoiriis and Hilling flew a Bellanca from Harbour Grace in Newfoundland to Eisleben in Germany in 1930. Hausner flew a Bellanca for 28 hours while trying to cross from America to Europe, before the engine failed. Even then, the waterproof, nearly empty tank saved his life.

Bellanca is the name of a Sicilian family. Five Bellanca brothers arrived in New York form Siacca, Sicily, in 1911, almost at the same time as the Adamowiczes. The oldest of the Bellancas, Giuseppe Mario, born in 1886, was an engineer, a graduate of the Polytechnic University in Milan. In 1909, he designed and built his first aircraft in Italy. He re-created the same model in a garage in Brooklyn, just after his arrival in

America. It was a light, training biplane with two open seats for pilots (or an instructor and a student) one behind the other.

Figure 17: Bellanca's 1934 press ad emphasizing the aircraft's safety.

Soon, however, Bellanca changed the design. He started to build high-wingers with two seats side by side, both equipped with the joystick and all instruments in a closed cabin. This plane was designed for two pilots or an instructor and a student. As early as in 1912, the Bellancas opened an aviation school on Long Island, near Garden City. Giuseppe taught many American pilots there, among them, Fiorello La Guardia, the future hero of the American Air Force during World War I, and later New York's mayor. One of three major airports of the metropolis bears his name.

Bellanca ingeniously answered the growing need for pilots and market for airplanes. He became a well-known designer and manufacturer, one of the leaders of the aviation business. When the brothers were looking for a new machine, Giuseppe Bellanca already headed Bellanca Aircraft Company established in 1927(this was the successor of Columbia Aircraft Company). The firm was based in New Castle, Delaware, with offices in Manhattan. In the same year, 1927, Lindbergh started to negotiate with Bellanca the project of building for him a one-seater for the transatlantic venture. However, Bellanca refused to build an aircraft for only one person to fly solo over the ocean, because he thought such an undertaking to be too dangerous. He did not want to associate his name and the prestige of his planes with an inevitable catastrophe.

Eventually, Lindbergh made his flight on a machine built especially for him by a small firm, Ryan Aeronautical Company in San Diego, California. His plane was called the *Spirit of St. Louis* because a consortium of businessmen from that city sponsored the aircraft and Lindbergh's flight.

On July 4, 1927, *Time* magazine put on its cover the face of Giuseppe Mario Bellanca, the famous engineer, designer and builder of airplanes. It was a testimony to his leading position in the American airplane industry. He manufactured a number of different machines — ranging from small two-seaters to large aircraft, carrying up to twenty passengers with the crew.

Figure 18: A Press report about Bellanca's victory in Cleveland. *Aviation*, Oct. 5, 1929.

All of these machines were light high-wingers, equipped with strong and sturdy Wright's engines. Their speed was about 120 mph at the altitude of 4,500 feet.

In the 1930s, Mussolini tried to attract Bellanca back to Fascist Italy, promising to build for him a whole new aircraft factory. Bellanca visited Italy and entered into negotiations but they were never finalized. Nevertheless, because of these links with Mussolini, the American government refused to grant Bellanca contracts for building war planes during WWII, which was a serious blow to the company. Despite this setback, the company survived and, with a short interlude, it continued to produce airplanes and is still alive today. Presently the company is called Avia Bellanca Aircraft and it is managed by Giuseppe's son, Augusto. The headquarters of the company are located in Annapolis, Maryland.

Ben Adamowicz thus described the purchase:

> "Bellanca offered us a new machine for a price of $19,000 with a trade-in of our old aircraft. It was a huge sum, far over our budget. Yet, we had to go on. We sold our airplane by ourselves for $4,000. We purchased the Bellanca, without a trade-in for $22,000, giving him a down payment of $8,000 at the signing of the contract. It was Bellanca Y300 with Wright's 200-horse-power engine."

Here we have a problem. First of all, according to Bellanca's historical internet files, a new aircraft from the Bellanca Y300 line was substantially cheaper, as it only cost $5,000. This price difference is confirmed by a scene from a film about Lindbergh.[10] When the young pilot negotiates a purchase of a plane with Bellanca, the sum of $15,000 is mentioned – for a machine especially built and equipped for a transatlantic flight. Moreover,

---

[10]*Spirit of St. Louis.* A biographical film about Lindbergh, starring James Stewart, and directed by Billy Wilder, 1957. The same amount, $15,000, is quoted by other sources.

Levine offered his Bellanca to Lindbergh for the same price ($15,000): Levine stated that he paid $25,000 for it, but was ready to sell it for $15,000 to a colleague-aviator. As we have said, Bellanca did not want to build a one-seater for the transatlantic venture. Simultaneously, Lindbergh did not accept Levine's offer. The price of $15,000 was too high for him and his sponsors. Instead, he paid just $6,000 for the plane built for him in San Diego. With an additional sum of $2,500 for the engine, the total cost of the *Spirit of St. Louis* was $8,500.

There is yet another problem with accurately establishing the price of the Adamowiczes' Bellanca. A bill for the aircraft that Bellanca supposedly sold to the Adamowicz brothers surfaced in the 1950s. Its total listed price of $3,000 gives us reasons to sincerely question its authenticity. This bill, among other Adamowiczes' memorabilia, was offered in the 1950s by Christie's auction house in London.

Here one more issue arises, which is even more disturbing. Among the many press articles published after Ben and Joe's transatlantic flight and later in connection with their trial, we found a note about a "a Bellanca aircraft, bought second hand."[11] Other reports by the press confirm that important bit of information. According to one journalist, Ben and Joe flew a used airplane — both used and successfully tested.

Indeed, it appears most likely that the Adamowiczes purchased a used machine, and not a new one, and not from the Bellanca company. In this transaction Giuseppe Bellanca served only as a go-between. The aircraft purchased by the Adamowicz brothers was originally sold in 1931 by Bellanca to Otto Hilling, a businessman and photographer. Hilling bought a brand new plane and hired a professional pilot, Holger Hoiriis. Between June 21 and June 24, 1931, they flew over the Atlantic from New York to Copenhagen, with a stopover in Harbour Grace in

---

[11] *Brooklyn Daily Eagle*, April 20, 1935.

Newfoundland. The aircraft worked perfectly.

It seems most likely that this very machine, the Bellanca already tested over the Atlantic, was purchased by the Adamowiczes directly from Hilling. The Bellanca factory knew about this transaction and made some improvements in response to the brothers' requests — for example the fuel tank was enlarged. These alterations had to cost something and must have increased the total cost of the plane.

According to some press reports from 1933 and 1934, Hillig's Bellanca, already tested over the Atlantic, was purchased by the Adamowiczes for $8,000:

- "Otto... sold the ship... for $8,000" (*The Otsego Farmer and Republican*, November 6, 1934).
- "Miss Liberty Again: Otto Hillig's good plane, 'Miss Liberty' now the 'Warsaw' is off again, this time with Joseph and Benjamin Adamowicz on their way to their native land." (*Birmingham NY Press*, June 29, 1934).
- "The plane is the same one that Holger Hoiriis and Otto Hillig flew to Denmark two years ago" (*New York Herald Statesman* 1933).

This price was more than reasonable. After all, the plane was already three years old and it had been used in a very strenuous, transatlantic flight. There are no records about the cost of the improvements. By calculating all the possible amounts we had earlier considered, we estimated the total price of the Bellanca plane acquired by the Adamowiczes to have been in the vicinity of $10,000 — $12,000.

When Ben was telling the story of the purchase to Strumph-Wojtkiewicz in Poland, after their successful transatlantic flight in 1934 and quoted the much higher cost of the plane, the brothers were negotiating a sale of their machine to the Polish Aero Club. They wanted to get $22,000 for it, so, to justify this sum, they inflated the purchase price and said that they bought it for $22,000. It was a gross overestimate of the value of their Bellanca. In addition, they did not mention, not even once, that the plane was not new when they purchased it and that it had been used to cross the Atlantic. This did not mean that the aircraft was in a worse condition than a new plane would have been; it was, indeed, excellent. Yet, here again we encounter fraudulent statements made by the Adamowicz brothers. Both Ben and Joe repeatedly and publicly stated that they had bought a new machine for their transatlantic flight.

Furthermore, in order to contradict any possible information that could have come to light about the fact that their aircraft had been used, the brothers lied and said that is was "a twin brother" of Hillig's plane and that Giuseppe Bellanca built two identical machines at the same time, one for Hilling and another one for them. It was not so. The Adamowiczes' Bellanca was not a "twin" of Hillig's. It was the same plane. Period.

Let us, then, put aside the facts and speculations about the price and age of the aircraft flown by the Adamowiczes and return to our narrative. Regardless of circumstances, we can simply say that Ben and Joe acquired a Bellanca aircraft in 1932. It was model J-300 Special No. 3003, NR797W. The plane had steel truss ribs and wooden wings, covered by plywood in the front and by linen further back. The framework of the fuselage and the stabilizers were also of plywood and linen. "It was a robust machine, able to fly long distances" — as Ben characterized it.

The basic technical specifications were as follows:
- Aircraft type and model: Bellanca J-300 Pacemaker Special
- Engine: Wright Whirlwind J-6, 300 HP, 9 cylinders, radial setting
- Wing span: 47 feet, 6 in
- Length: 27 feet, 11 in

- Height: 8 feet, 4 in
- Weight — empty: 2,801 lb.
- Weight — full tank: 7,154 lb.
- Main tank: 430 gallons
- Travel speed: 110 mph
- Maximum speed: 130 mph
- Maximum altitude for travel: 15,500 feet
- Maximum altitude: 16,500 feet

Figure 19: The Adamowicz's Bellanca stored in an air hangar in Poland, airport Katowice-Muchowiec, 1937. From *Lotnictwo z Szachownicą*. 31.

How beautiful was this Bellanca! It was a high-winger with the wings supported by wide struts which augmented the lift. The wings, the struts, and the back horizontal stabilizers were painted light blue. The front engine cover and the landing gear were red. The wheels were black: two wheels in the front and a small landing wheel in the back. The fuselage was white, with an enclosed, spacious cabin for two people, and nicely glazed windows in front and on two sides.

The whole structure was well balanced. It conveyed an

impression of both lightness and strength.

The brothers meticulously painted over the former name of the machine, *Miss Liberty*, and gave it the new one: *White Eagle*. In 1933, they attempted to fly to Poland with this name on the fuselage. When this attempt failed, they coated the name *White Eagle* and painted it over with a new moniker: *Warsaw*. This change probably served to erase the fact that the *White Eagle* tried to cross the Atlantic, but did not succeed in doing so. In their subsequent interviews and memoirs, the brothers described the second attempt made in 1934 as the first one, and if they mentioned the *White Eagle* at all, it was only as a "trial flight."

On both sides of the fuselage there was an inscription: "New York — Warsaw," with the Polish emblem, a white eagle on a red background, in the center.[12] Similarly, on both sides under the windows, there was an inscription in small print: "Pilots Adamowicz Brothers." This aircraft had only a simple radio on board; it did not have any sophisticated navigational instruments, just the traditional sextant and a compass. It needs to be said that the brothers were very proud of their aircraft. Ben, when speaking about the Bellanca, used many names: an aircraft, an airplane, an aero-plane, or a "winger." In his stories about the plane one can feel his attachment, confidence, pride, and affection for this flying machine.

The brothers started to fly their Bellanca in the summer of 1932. They first hired a company pilot who introduced them to the new machine and showed them how to fly it. Soon, they were flying independently. Yet, even with all the precautions taken, they did not escape a misfortune. Not long after the purchase, as Ben recalls:

"We had a serious trouble. Our mechanic, who until then was

---

[12] The eagle was not wearing a traditional Polish crown, as on the official state emblem. Polish journalists noted this detail and wrote about this. Probably, the brothers painted the eagle in America without having an actual emblem as a model; they did not know exactly how the Polish emblem should look.

really good, after emptying the engine of the oil forgot about it! He forgot that the engine does not have oil! He started the engine and taxied the machine across the whole airstrip to the hangar. The result was the complete destruction of the engine. I thought that I will go mad. The busted engine was send to the factory and dismantled into the smallest pieces which lay on the tables when we came to see it. It was a heap of junk. The factory very kindly agreed to charge us only $2,750 for a new engine. After a few days we got it."

The brothers installed the new engine in the aircraft themselves. At that time, they were not only skillful pilots, but also good air-mechanics. Let's remember: two boys from a small village, with only a few grades of schooling, without any training in the domains of technique, engineering, or aviation.

Figure 20: Bellanca at the start of the last stage of their flight around Poland, from Torun to Warsaw, July 2, 1934, at 4 p.m. *Lotnictwo z Szachownicą,* 31.

CHAPTER 10
A "TRIAL FLIGHT" ACROSS THE OCEAN

In the summer of 1933, Ben and Joe Adamowicz tried for the first time to conquer the Atlantic Ocean. Much later, they called this first attempt only a "trial flight." Documents and press clippings prove, however, that they planned to fly all the way to Warsaw that summer. They applied for passports. In the passport application there is a question about the purpose of the trip. They wrote: "Visiting Poland."[13] There were also press articles and interviews with the brothers who announced a cross-Atlantic flight to Warsaw. After an accident which cut short the trip, the journalist lamented that the brothers did not make it over the ocean.[14] Notices about the failed attempt were published by both the American and the Polish press.[15] These reports were usually incorrect. In one article, a "crash at the takeoff" was quoted while it was a crash at the landing in Newfoundland that doomed the ambitious undertaking. At the same time the press underlined the fact that the brothers did not give up and decided to renew their efforts. Undoubtedly, while telling his and Joe's story to Strumph-Wojtkiewicz after the successful crossing of 1934, Ben somehow "forgot" about the failure of 1933. He wanted to erase it from his and Joe's biographies.

Ben's version of this first flight was that in the summer of 1933 they only wanted to make it to Newfoundland — in a sort of a reconnaissance flight:

---

[13] Ben's application for a passport, with a date of June 11, 1933, was found by Maureen Mroczek Morris. On the passport, Ben stated that he wanted to travel to Poland.
[14] *Brooklyn Eagle*, July 19, 1933.
[15] *Polska Zachodnia*, vol. 9, no. 54, February 24, 1934.

"We decided to go to Harbour Grace in Newfoundland and come back. We wrote to that locale and the answer was that they did not have an air-strip, and that a piece of land where aircraft had already landed a few times, needed to be put in order. We sent them $100 with a kind request to level the ground, for we were going to arrive soon."

The air-strip at Harbour Grace was particularly dangerous. Actually, it was just a natural, small plateau located between rocky hills, around 180 feet wide and 900 feet long. To land in such a place was difficult indeed. So, the brothers hired an experienced pilot and mechanic, Emile Burgin, to help them. "Eddie," as the man was called, had a good reputation in aviation circles. He offered to land the Bellanca in Harbour Grace. He said that he had done such landings a few times before and he knew the place.

The three of them took off on August 8, 1933, from New York aiming for Harbour Grace. At the time of their landing it was Eddie who was holding the joystick, and Eddie crashed the Bellanca on the rocks and bushes. This was Ben's version. However, American press accounts suggested a different version: Ben was the pilot and he crashed. We think that it was not so. After all, Eddie was hired and paid precisely to fly and safely land the aircraft. He certainly was there. The list of passengers on board of the ship that took the brothers back from Newfoundland to New York also includes Burgin.[16] Why should they have taken him to Newfoundland and, after the crash, why should have paid for his trip back to New York, if they did not have a contract with him to pilot their plane to Newfoundland and land at Harbour Grace?

---

[16] The list of three passengers of a ship *Sana* includes Benjamin Adamowicz, Joseph Adamowicz, and Emile Burgin, with his date of birth: October 17, 1899. There were only three passengers; *Sana* was a commercial, not a passenger, ship. Document retrieved by Maureen Mroczek Morris from Ancestry.com

While reading about Ben's supposed crash-landing we encounter — not for the first time and not for the last — a note of aversion, prejudice, or even hostility of American journalists towards the Adamowicz brothers. Their accomplishments were interpreted as hurting the interests of the closed and exclusive, though still informal, club of American professional flyers. The Adamowiczes were amateurs; they were rough and uneducated immigrants from Eastern Europe. As such, they were considered inferior and were disrespected by Americans of Irish, Italian, German, or Scandinavian descent. At that time, Poles were at the very bottom of the ethnic/racial hierarchy of white immigrants in America. Nonetheless, at least on this occasion they did not lie. While remembering their many different deceptions, this time we believe Ben: it was not Ben who crashed the Bellanca in 1933.

Here's his account:

"At that time, approaching Harbour Grace, Eddie was piloting. When I saw the landing ground, I felt bad. It was a small stretch of a flat terrain surrounded from all sides by rocks. I started to worry for our airplane. I was surprised that instead of flying around and inspecting the place from the air, Eddie lowered the machine as if for immediate landing. To make things worse, we had a back wind. I told Eddie about it. But he did not listen and reduced speed for landing. The plane started to rock in the air. I cried: 'Eddie, don't touch down!' But it was too late. The machine touched the ground and rolled through the stones, pits, and bumps with a high speed. Suddenly it veered to the right. I heard a smack. The right wing hit a bush; immediately afterwards the left wing punched the ground. I gripped the joystick.I did it so firmly that when in the next moment I jumped off the machine, I was still holding the broken joystick in my fist."

Note that the Bellanca had two joysticks, one in front of each of the two seats. Ben's description of what remained of the aircraft is both heartbreaking and hilarious:

"The machine was in a deplorable state. One wing damaged, the other half broken, the landing gear entirely smashed, the propeller bent. I heard Joe's voice calling for help. But this voice was coming not from the inside of the plane but from somewhere outside. I run around the plain and saw a view which in other circumstances would have made me laugh. It was not funny then. As he usually did before every landing, Joe had crawled into the back of the fuselage, to add weight to the tail and make it heavier. He did it this time too. When he felt and heard the crash he understood that it was something very bad and he was afraid that the gas tank could burst in flames. He tried to get out immediately and he broke the linen covering the fuselage exactly in the spot where the White Eagle was painted. He could not move any further. His head was stuck in between two wings of the eagle. We pulled him out. We inspected the damage. It was so extensive that there was no chance to repair the machine there. It was necessary to take it back to the factory."

It is worthwhile to imagine this funny scene in order to realize how fragile these early flying machines truly were: it was possible to pierce the fuselage with one's head! Imagine that heroic transatlantic flights were attempted on such planes.

Both the American and Polish press reported about the breakdown. "The Adamowicz brothers' airplane 'White Eagle' crashed during the landing in Harbour Grace in Newfoundland. The brothers were injured, though not seriously and life threatening. The Polish pilots received medical treatment. The airplane is damaged."[17]

By now, it was necessary to pack all that remained from the machine in boxes and to transport these remnants to Saint John's harbor. By a happy chance, a Norwegian ship *Sana* was ready to sail that very evening to New York. The captain agreed to take the cargo for $100, and charge $35 for each passenger. "I was

---

[17] e.g., a note in *Kurier Bydgoski*, August 10, 1933.

terribly angry paying for Eddie because it was him who crashed the machine" — confessed Ben.

The trip back to New York took one week, with a stop in Halifax, where "because it was a Sunday, we of course went to church." In the port of New York they were met by family, friends, and reporters. Unfortunately, the Floyd Bennett Airport refused to store the damaged remnants of the airplane. "Major Kelly, the airport's manager, told us that he doesn't have room for us. What an unpleasant surprise!" After many efforts, they finally rented the space in a hangar of a Swede, a Mr. Erickson.

This sad return is also yet another proof that while departing from the same airport two weeks earlier the brothers did not plan to return. Most likely, they had terminated the lease of space in the hangar for their Bellanca.

Another circumstantial piece of evidence concerns their living arrangements. After coming back from Newfoundland they lived with their sister; it was probably Emily, who came to the U.S. with Bruno in 1911. This indicates that, in addition to giving up the rental space for the plane, they also ended their apartment lease, not expecting to return to it.

CHAPTER 11
BEING A POLE IN AMERICA

Major Kelly's refusal to allow the Adamowicz brothers to use his hangar at the Floyd Bennett Airport (as they did before departing for Newfoundland) shows again — as if in a magnifying lens —the general unfriendliness of American aviation circles to the Adamowiczes. Why?

They had never become accepted members of the community of American fliers of the time — this elite group included pilots, instructors, mechanics, and businessmen of the air industry. They operated on the outskirts of it. They did not have the experience and connections as military or postal pilots. They did not have support crews. They did the maintenance and the repairs of their machines, as far as possible, by themselves — fixing, mending, gluing...and cutting their costs. They learned flying form the cheapest instructors. They never became true professionals.

Originally farmers from the former Polish-Lithuanian Commonwealth (albeit with noble roots), then common laborers from Brooklyn, the Adamowiczes were lacking in education and manners. They were laughed off by nonchalant reporters and disdainful journalists, who never gave them full credit for their intelligence, imagination, courage, and perseverance — the strong foundation for their accomplishments. These are also the reasons why they were almost completely forgotten by the historians of aviation. Let's talk for a while about this ill-disposition towards Poles in America. Historians of the Polish Diaspora in America say that it has been here forever and that it's hard to point out its exact sources.[18]

---

[18] See entries in James S. Pula, ed., *The Polish American Encyclopedia* (Jefferson, NC: McFarland, 2011). See also William J. Galush, *For More Than Bread: Community and*

During the time of the most intense immigration to the U.S. from Eastern Europe, that is in the last quarter of the 19th century and about the first fifteen years of the 20th century, Poles arriving to America were mostly the poorest among the poor, sometimes illiterate, Polish peasants.[19] Not many immigrants were craftsmen, and even fewer were well-educated. They came from all three parts of Poland, divided at that time between its three neighbors. At the very entrance to America, on Ellis Island, they were confirmed formally as citizens of Russia, Germany or Austria, although they usually identified their Polish nationality as well, even if Poland as a state and political entity did not exist at that time. American immigration officers, usually not well educated in either history or geography, looked at them with scorn. While registering them, the officials twisted and distorted their names and misspelled the locales, villages and townships, from which these poor and illiterate immigrants were coming — these names were typically impossible to render in English.[20]

The vast majority of the Polish immigrants did not know English. They learned it painfully and slowly. A heavy accent marked them as foreigners throughout their whole lives. In terms of their religious denomination, they were mostly Catholics (a sizeable Jewish immigration from the same Polish lands occurred

---

Identity in American Polonia, 1880-1940 (Boulder, Co.: East European Monographs; New York: Distributed by Columbia University Press, 2006); John J. Bukowczyk, ed., *Polish Americans and Their History: Community, Culture and Politics* (University of Pittsburgh Press; 2006).

[19] See John J. Bukowczyk, *A History of the Polish Americans* (Transaction Publishers, 2007). See also Mary Patrice Erdmans, *Opposite Poles: Immigrants and Ethnics in Polish Chicago, 1976-1990* (University Park, Pa.: Pennsylvania State University Press, 1998).

[20] A footnote by Kazimierz Braun: "I was once working in America with an actor whose name was Victor Talmadge. I was searching for the lead in Tadeusz Różewicz's *The Hunger Artist Departs*. During auditions in New York it did not come to me that the actor who impressed me the most and whom I eventually cast in the role was of Polish descent. Later on during rehearsals, sipping a coffee, he told me that he came from a Polish family. His grandfather came from Poland at the beginning of the 20th century — his name was 'Tołmacki.' On the Ellis Island, an immigration officer recorded his name as 'Talmadge.'"

simultaneously). Polish peasants who came to America to leave the abysmal poverty of their villages behind, were accompanied by Polish priests; since the 1880s such priests were also trained in America, in a seminary in Orchard Lake, Michigan. The immigrants built churches and founded Polish parishes, schools and organizations. On American soil, they recreated Polish customs and traditions.

Polish Catholics were confronted in America with two groups. First, the Catholics already living here, the majority of them Irish, or of Irish descent. They had an advantage when arriving since they already spoke English. Early Catholic dioceses in America had mostly Irish clergy, including Irish bishops; some bishops were either Germans or Italians. This led to a schism and the creation of a separate Polish National Catholic Church in 1897, initially led by Father Franciszek Hodur.[21] Second, the mainstream of American religious life was marked not by Catholicism but by Protestantism of different denominations. They practiced their ceremonies; they lived according to their values and culture brought from Britain and northern Europe. In these circumstances, Polish-Catholic immigrants lived on the margins of society. They were perceived as inferior and placed outside of the mainstream of American life.

Instead of integrating, they created their own community. They send their children to Catholic and Polish parish schools that they founded. They published their own newspapers in the Polish language; they created their own, Polish-American literature.[22] They preserved their own customs, often ridiculed by other nationalities. The so-called "Polish jokes" were their

---

[21] Frank S. Mead, "Polish National Catholic Church of America," *Handbook of Denominations in the United States* (10th Edition, Abingdon Press, 1995). Joseph Wieczerzak, *Bishop Francis Hodur: Biographical Essays* (Boulder: East European Monographs; [New York]: Distributed by Columbia University Press, 1998).

[22] Karen Majewski, *Traitors and True Poles: Narrating a Polish-American Identity, 1880-1939* (Athens: Ohio University Press, 2003)

frequent companions. Even their nationality was a subject of fun: instead of Poles they were called "Polacks." A typical icon of such a "Polack" was a "non-educated, narrow-minded, xenophobic Catholic, not understanding the surrounding political, social and cultural environment, yet strong as a bull and stubborn as an ox, drinking a lot of vodka, ready for any work or chore."[23] Press articles about the Adamowicz brothers prove that they were not an exception to these rules.

---

[23] See Danusha V. Goska, *Bieganski: The Brute Polak Stereotype, Its Role in Polish-Jewish Relations and American Popular Culture* (Boston: Academic Studies Press, 2010)

CHAPTER 12
LEARNING TO FLY AND NAVIGATE

We cannot resist a thought that it was actually beneficial to the Adamowiczes and their cause that the Bellanca crashed while landing in Newfoundland in 1933. If the accident did not happen and the Adamowiczes had taken off the next day to fly over the ocean, they most probably would have ended in it. They did not yet have enough experience in piloting the airplane at night or flying in the fog and they did not know even the basics of navigation and meteorology. Their aircraft had no navigation instruments and there was only a basic radio on board, as we have already mentioned. While the brothers were forced to give up their dream of completing a transatlantic flight in 1933, and while they waited for the repair of their aircraft and for better weather in the summer, they used their time for improving their aviation and navigational skills. The setback of a costly accident turned into an opportunity to ensure future success.

"In order to get money for the new machine we had to sell our share of the soda-factory" — Ben claimed, adding that after the return from Harbour Grace both he and Joe were unemployed. As he maintained, they had

> "only a spare engine and a lot of debt for the purchase of aircraft, which increased after making the repairs. Our family helped us. Everybody gave us from their savings to allow us to prepare ourselves without problems for the flight. We lived with our sister's family in Brooklyn; only occasionally we helped Bruno at the factory, managing its operations."

Again, we have to question both statements made by Ben: first, that they were without work and second, that they were without income. Simultaneously, we have to remember that he spoke about their situation in an interview conducted after the successful transatlantic flight. Furthermore, these statements were made for the sake of Polish public opinion – the press, the aviation community, and the authorities. Everything that Ben said in this context was oriented towards impressing his Polish audience. In Poland, the brothers wanted to present themselves as Polish patriots who risked all their resources for "the Greater Glory of Poland," who did not spare money, time, and effort and would not spare their lives in order to achieve this lofty, patriotic goal. We should not forget that, at the same time, they also wanted to facilitate the financial transaction with the Polish Aero Club and sell the Bellanca.

Let us, then, analyze Ben's statements one by one. First, the information that they sold their share in the factory is false, as it was later indicated in the documents presented at their trial. (Again, we promise to write more about the trial later.) As the main co-defendants, they were the co-owners of the factory. Bruno was their partner; he ran the whole operation and worked at the business every day. However, Ben and Joe were working there as well, even if they spent most of their time dealing with their aircraft and getting ready for their dream flight to Poland. Secondly, even if Ben and Joe did not have a steady income, they were still the co-owners of the factory that was consistently bringing a handsome profit. If the business did well (and it did!), they received dividends. We should not forget that the illegal vodka production flourished as well, and brought substantial, though illegal, income. That was not a matter to talk about to the press, of course.

The Adamowiczes spent a lot of time learning navigation and flying in bad weather, or without visibility. A young but experienced pilot, Hubert Huntington, was their teacher. "Only then I realized what a complete stupidity it would have been to fly over the ocean without navigational skills" — confessed Ben. He studied navigation from books and he practiced it by sitting for hours in the plane cabin and learning how to operate the instruments. "Soon I was able to tell my position with longitude and latitude coordinates within ten minutes." And again it makes us think – isn't it a heart-lifting image? A boy with only four or five grades of schooling from an elementary school in a the small, provincial town of Krajsk, a man who never made any educational progress beyond this humble beginning, becomes a specialist-navigator.

The Adamowiczes were studying hard, but did not fly for almost half a year, because their aircraft was being repaired. "It was hard without flying" — recalled Ben. One can only imagine how hard it was for him and his brother, Joe, to live without flying later on, in prison.

Finally, on December 14, 1933, the plane was ready and they could resume their training flights. As Ben admitted, "I somehow got so accustomed to my beloved Bellanca that when I could fly it again I regained both appetite and good mood." Nonetheless, this good mood was somewhat spoiled by the fact that they had to pay installments of $150 for the new engine every month. "The kind and courteous Bellanca told us that we could pay him for the repairs of the fuselage after we make it to Poland."

The brothers practiced flying not only on instruments. This effort significantly improved their navigational expertise. Ben described their progress in the following words:

> "Once we made a long flight at night. We were in the air for nine and half hours and we were not disoriented at all, we perfectly kept the proper direction. This experience made us very merry and this was a good prognostic for our big venture."

They applied in Washington for an official permit to fly over the ocean. A license for flying blind was required. Ben took the exam, held with special strictures by an inspector named Cutrell. "It happened that a few days before, June 13, 1934, an airliner flying from New York to Chicago crashed on top of a mountain. They were searching for a lost machine for two days. High in the mountains, they found only debris and corpses of six passengers. No one survived." It is because of this recent catastrophe that the instructor was so strict.

During the exam, Ben had to pilot an aircraft with covered windows; he had to go down and up relying only on the instruments. He also had to change the direction of the plane and find the airport. At the end, he received the grade: "successful." How could the brothers have imagined making a transatlantic flight a year earlier? It is hard to understand this.

As far as the meteorology was concerned, they had not been paying too much attention to the weather. They were certainly not well prepared for their previous attempt! This time they contacted a specialist, Dr. Campbell,[1] who introduced them to weather patterns and sudden changes over the Atlantic that were common during the summer. He taught them how to find weather-news, broadcast by radio-stations located on land and on ships. He helped them identify the best time to embark upon their flight; he also taught them how to define the optimal altitude and direction.

In particular, Dr. Campbell instructed them to avoid the fog and frost that posed a serious threat over the northern parts of the Atlantic even in July. They were forewarned about the dangers of running into strong storms that move across the southern portion of the ocean. (Here, we only speak about the North Atlantic.) The Adamowiczes decided to choose a golden mean — a route in-between the two dangers, not too far to the north, and not too far to the south.

---

[1] Ben's story does not contain the first name of Dr. Campbell.

There were still formalities to attend to before their flight — they had to register their departure, pay for an official permit to leave the country, and notify other countries about flying in their air space. After formulating a detailed flight plan, they corresponded with different authorities and agencies. They had to obtain passports, visas, and a document from customs stating that "the aircraft is American and should not be subject to the customs fees upon return" — in case that there would be a return flight.

They did not hide their plans. A Polish newspaper carried the following story in the early June of 1934:[2]

> "Polish Flight from New York to Warsaw. Brothers Bolesław and Józef Adamowicz from Brooklyn plan a flight from New York to Warsaw. They have been making preparations for four years. Only recently they were able to accumulate enough money for the purchase of a new airplane, a Bellanca, which is going to bear the name 'White Eagle'. The brothers schedule their flight for June this year."

Figure 21: Bellanca at the Warsaw Pola Mokotowskie airport
From Adamowicz and Adamowicz, *Przez Atlantyk*, 1934.

---

[2]*Polska Zachodnia*, June 6, 1934. There are — as usual — significant inaccuracies in this note.

As we had explained, the *White Eagle* was the name of the Adamowiczes' Bellanca in 1933. After the crash of the *White Eagle* the plane was renamed *Warsaw*.

Because the window of good weather over the Atlantic was rapidly closing, Ben decided not to wait for the final documents to arrive from Washington. He was the moving spirit of the adventure and the informal commander of the aviator duo: "I drew the best route on the maps and June 27 we went to bed slightly earlier than usual."

"In the evening, before I fell asleep, I was thinking about my life and recalling everything in the order as it has happened. So, I am a pilot and I want to fly over the Atlantic to Poland. I could become a pilot because the sparkling water business went well and made profits. Thus, there was money for an aircraft and free time for flying. But that business was good because I worked hard. And everything began with those two dollars, which I put in my account in the Savings Bank years ago. For nine years I kept saving dollars and cents; eventually, I accumulated $2,000. This was the share that I contributed towards buying a lot for the factory. The same was true about Joe. If he had not been saving, we would have remained common workers. It would not have been possible for us to fly to Poland on a fine-looking airplane. I was pleased with myself. With these thoughts, I said a brief prayer and fell asleep for the last time on American soil."

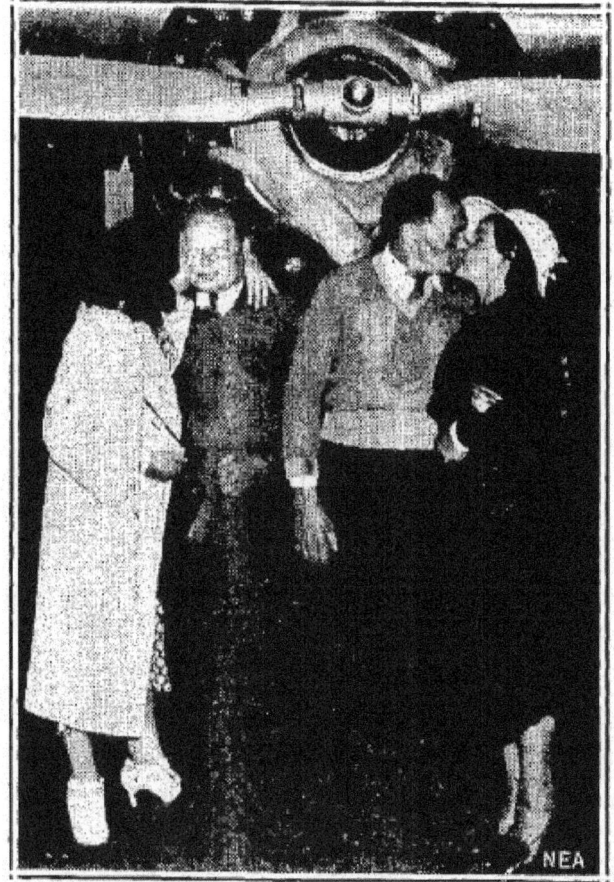

Figure 22: Press clipping of the pilots with their families (Ben with his wife and Joe with their sister) before their departure from the Floyd Bonnet Airport in New York. *Indiana Evening Gazette*, 29 June 1934.

CHAPTER 13

HEADING FOR POLAND

The great adventure began before 6:00 a.m., on June 28, 1934. The brothers' family and friends bade farewell to Ben and Joe Adamowicz at New York's Floyd Bennett Field airport. Representatives of the Polish Consulate, journalists and photojournalists were present as well. Ben noticed, not without vanity, that he, Joe, and the Bellanca were photographed many times. Their faces and captions "New York — Warsaw" and the large inscription of *Warsaw* on Bellanca's fuselage were seen all over the world.

Their aircraft was ready: "We filled the tanks to the brim." Besides the standard Bellanca's fuel tanks, an additional, large tank was installed. All together the plane carried more than 2,500 pounds of special fuel. Heavy!

They did not need to carry so much gasoline on the first stage of their trip, from New York to Newfoundland, because they planned to stop in Harbour Grace. Ever parsimonious and industrious, Ben explained: "We risked a crash at the Newfoundland landing with such a heavy load, but the gasoline was 20 cents cheaper in New York than in Newfoundland. We had to economize. Money was running short."

Obviously, this remark about the lack of money was false. After all, the Adamowiczes had at their disposal the resources created by the prosperous sparkling water factory and by the no-less-thriving illegal vodka business. Prohibition was lifted in 1933, but the brothers did not make their alcohol production official because that would have required them to pay taxes. This part of their business remained underground. While Ben and Joe were getting ready for their grand adventure, Bruno managed both branches of the family enterprise: legal and illegal. It might be interesting here to relate some gossip still shared in the brothers' Brooklyn neighborhood. Present residents of the building on Conselyea Street, where *Savino's Quality Pasta* is now located in the Adamowiczes' former plant, believe that the brothers built their airplane in the back of their factory, kept it in their garage, and used it for illegal smuggling alcohol to Poland.[3] All the elements of this legend are false. We already verified the story of the aircraft's purchase. Furthermore, the Bellanca plane did not have any cargo space for alcohol; all the space it had was used for fuel, including specially constructed additional fuel tanks.

Figure 23: The farewell ceremony on June 28, 1934 at 7:30a.m. at the Floyd Bennett Field in New York. *Lotnictwo z Szachownicą* No 31.

The moment of departure was filled with emotion. Ben, ever down-to-earth, recalled: "I saw that Joe would get emotional any moment, so, when the engine became hot, I immediately began the take-off."

Not so fast, Ben! Did you hold the joystick at that take off? We

---

[3] Based on interviews of June 2010.

are not so sure. A report in the *New York Times*[4] contains information that during the take-off from New York the joystick was held by a professional pilot, Holger Hoiriis, a Dane. According to that report, he piloted the Bellanca on the first leg of the flight, from New York to Harbour Grace. Hoiriis was the experienced pilot who guided the same Bellanca (at that time called *Liberty*) in the transatlantic crossing made with the aircraft's original owner, Otto Hilling.

As we know, the Bellanca had two joysticks in front of each pilot's seat. At the moment of the plane's take-off in New York these seats were occupied by Ben Adamowicz and Holger Hoiriis. Joe must have been lying on a blanket back in the fuselage, a place he preferred for the take-off and the landing. There was no place for him in the cabin because the Adamowiczes' Bellanca had an additional huge fuel tank installed where the second row of two seats would have been. The brothers took Hoiriis with them as a precaution. Previously, in 1933, they also had an experienced pilot, Burgin, that led their aircraft through the dangerous procedures of taking-off in New York and landing in Harbour Grace. These were two especially difficult and dangerous moments and the Polish pilots did not want to risk any mishaps at the outset of their adventure. The start was hard because of the excessive weight of the machine. The landing — because of the exceedingly narrow dimensions of the runway surrounded with rocky hills. The uneventful and safe start from New York can be credited to Hoiriis' skills as well as to the improved conditions of the airport. The runway was recently renovated and paved with concrete.

It was 6:35 a.m. Wind was blowing from the east. They taxied to stop precisely against the wind. Gas. The roar of the engine. Brakes released. A long roll with mounting speed. Off

---

[4]The *New York Times,* June 29, 1934.

the ground! "The takeoff was perfect." They took the course at 64°. Instantly, they were over the ocean. "Finally to Warsaw!" — exclaimed Ben.

They were flying low, at an altitude of about 900 feet, because thick clouds lingered not much higher. When the wind shifted from east to north, it slowed down the aircraft. They veered slightly to the west and flew over Connecticut, then Massachusetts. Ben recalled that he was sorting out his thoughts and feelings at the outset of the transatlantic endeavor: "I was frequently flying over this piece of land during my training flights. But now everything seemed to be different. I tried to think that it was yet another normal flight, as many flights that I did until then. But in spite of myself I felt that this time something completely different was happening. Something that required all my skills. Something which I had to respond to with my absolute best."

Over Maine the weather improved and they could go higher, up to 4,500 feet. Then Canada began to unroll under their wings a carpet of forests, fields and lakes. Above East Point, the eastern tip of Nova Scotia, they again flew over the open ocean. After additional two hours they reached Newfoundland. At 5:00 p.m. they spotted the narrow runway in Harbour Grace. This time, to make sure that the landing was safe, they made two passes above the runway before attempting to touchdown. They landed at 5:40 p.m. Newfoundland time after almost 13 hours in the air, covering about 1,100 miles. It was Hoiriis who succeeded in landing the still very heavy Bellanca on a narrow and short strip of Harbour Grace runway. However, Ben did not mention it in his memoirs. He did not admit that it was Hoiriis who piloted the aircraft from New York to Harbour Grace. He did not mention Hoiriis' presence in the Bellanca's cabin at all!

Many people were waiting for them at the airport, or rather, on the landing field. They were informed by a telegram sent by

Ben just before takeoff from New York. Additionally, people from a few towns over which they flew sent cables to Harbour Grace to notify the airport about the plane's progress. The Adamowiczes anchored the machine with great care, assuring that wind would not knock it over and covered it with a large canvas. Local police promised to guard it overnight. The brothers took a taxi to the town, had coffee and returned to the aircraft. They tanked it full and, additionally, bought 21 five-gallon canisters of gas and one canister of oil. They calculated that they had enough fuel for about 30 to 35 hours of flight, depending on the winds. Thus, they were ready to make it to Warsaw nonstop.

They again took a taxi and went to town for the night. "After paying the taxi driver we found out that we had in our wallets less than $20. But we did not care, for in any case tomorrow was the day which was meant to decide our future. Either we accomplished the plan, or we would drown. Dollars could not help us." — philosophized Ben. He did not hesitate to continue building their legend: a legend of two daredevils and staunch patriots, who bet all they had on a dream.

After a short dinner they went to sleep. A postman with a telegram woke them up in the middle of the night. Doctor Campbell cabled them about the weather patterns over the ocean. The forecast was good. Ben paid the postman his "last $15." Once awake, they could not fall asleep again. At four in the morning they got dressed. Both wore many layers of clothing: warm underwear, pants and shirts with ties, beige sweaters, and on top one-piece flying suits. Of course, they had their pilot helmets lined with fur. This was still not enough clothing for a flight over the North Atlantic at high altitudes — the Bellanca aircraft did not have any heating system and the cabin was not one hundred per cent air-tight.

The brothers had a light breakfast and went to the airstrip. They untied the machine and rolled it to the departure spot. They were ready. Ben was to pilot first.

Here, we have to very firmly and clearly dispose of the lies of the Adamowiczes' enemies that Hoiriis flew with them all the way to Europe, that he kept the joystick during the whole flight. It is an absolute lie. Hoiriis piloted the Bellanca from New York to Harbour Grace — yes, that is true. But he stayed there. The contemporary press reports,[5] eye-witnesses, and dozens of photographs confirm without doubt that only the two Adamowicz brothers made the transatlantic flight in a plane they called *Warsaw*. No one else was on board while the plane was slowly making its way over the ocean, from Harbour Grace to Warsaw. We have to repeat: the Adamowicz brothers crossed the Atlantic in the air by themselves.[6]

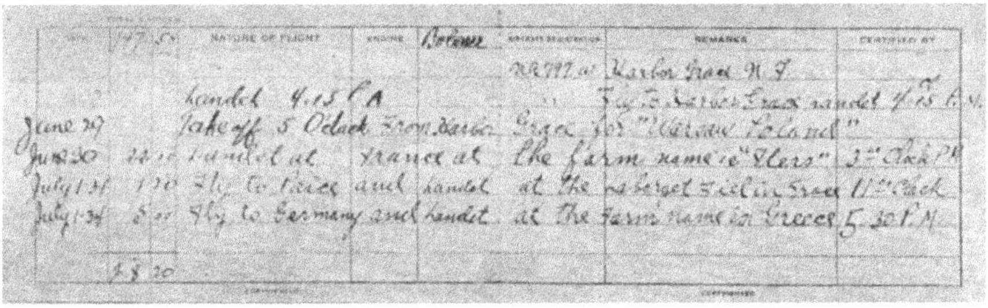

Figure 24: From the flight log. The Atlantic flight is recorded simply as start to Warsaw. From Adamowicz and Adamowicz, *Przez Atlantyk*, 1934.

---

[5] For example: *The Evening Independent*, June 2, 1934.
[6] This lie found its way even to an apparently serious study, F.H. Ellis and E.M. Ellis, *Atlantic Air Conquest. The complete story of all North Atlantic flights and attempts during the pioneer years from 1910 to 1940*. Published by: William Kimbel, London 1963, pages 167-170. We point out this text because it is entirely false. As we explained earlier, we do not debate or denounce the plethora of false information on the Adamowiczes in books, newspapers, and on the internet. It would be a whole thick book. But this one lie is especially vicious and therefore rebuffed here.

CHAPTER 14
ACROSS THE ATLANTIC

The Bellanca Pacemaker aircraft called *Warsaw*, with Ben Adamowicz at the controls, took off from Harbour Grace in Newfoundland, Canada, on Friday, June 29, 1934, at 6:06 a.m.[7] Joe was sitting in his designated place and Ben was the pilot. There were about 300 people bidding them farewell.

Ben and Joe planned to fly to Ireland on the first leg of the whole trip. This part of their flight was to take about eight and a half hours. However, they did not want to land in Ireland, but rather to continue on to Warsaw. They calculated that the whole flight would have spanned the distance of about 4,410 miles. They had more than enough fuel to make it.

Their family and friends from New York gave them food provisions for the journey: sandwiches, oranges, water, and some coffee in a thermos. This coffee turned out to be really bad. "In addition to that, we got a grilled chicken in Harbour Grace" — recalled Ben. "Consul Marchlewski advised us to also take chocolate. He explained that in the case of landing on water chocolate might save us for quite a long time."

Ben's list of provisions and equipment for the flight includes a signaling pistol with 24 rockets, to be used also in the case of

---

[7] The whole transatlantic flight made by the Adamowicz brothers is described in detail by Strumph-Wojtkiewicz in the 1934 book of interviews by the Adamowicz brothers that he transcribed and edited, *Przez Atlantyk* [*Across the Atlantic*] (see Bibliography), based on brothers' narration; it was Ben who spoke about the flight. Both brothers also spoke about the flight in many interviews. The Bellanca's log maintained by Joe, as well as the Book of Flights of the brothers appeared at a Christie's auction in London in 1995. We did not have access to it. If these documents were available we would use them in our book. Auction houses do not reveal the identity of buyers. Perhaps our book will be read by a happy buyer who would contact us through the publisher to clarify additional details.

landing on water, to signal to passing ships. Additionally, the huge main tank was equipped with a special clutch, able to quickly release fuel, and thus lessen the weight of the machine before landing on water. The tank could also serve as a floating device. "We remembered that Hauser was floating on his Bellanca for the whole week thanks to the waterproof tank." The option of splashing down on the waves was quite frankly debated and they were prepared for it.

Figure 25: Bellanca in Harbour Grace, Newfoundland, on 28 June 1934, 12 hours before departure. Standing, L to R: Otto Hillig, former owner of the plane and Ben Adamowicz. *Lotnictwo Z Szachownicą,* No 31.

"I was at the left joystick and it was I who had to pilot first"— recalled Ben. So, here they are in their Bellanca, ready to go. Ben writes in the flight log: "June 29. Take off 5 o'clock from Harbour Grace for Warsaw, Poland."[8] Ben hands over the log to Joe. He sits more comfortably in the seat. He puts his left hand gently on the joystick and the right hand on the throttle. He is ready.

The takeoff was perilous. There was no real runway at

---

[8]Ben gave this time, 5:00 a.m., to Strumph-Wojtkiewicz. We don't know what he put in the log. We think that he took that time from his memory, not from the log and made an error. We have already established as the time of departure as 6:06 a.m., because this time appears in the majority of sources.

Harbour Grace. As we have said, the airstrip was simply a stretch of flat, natural terrain, barely cleared of bushes and boulders. "The manager, Mr. Simon, was kind enough to remove many stones. I thought that the runway was long enough for us, about 900 feet." But at its end were ponds and just beyond them rocks and hills. "If only I could get the machine in the air before these rocks! Later it would be easy."

He firmly pressed the brake pedal. He pushed forward the gas knob. The engine responded with an increasing roar. When the engine reached 1,900 revolutions per minute, Ben released the brakes. The rest was history:

> "The machine kicked forward and started to run. It was running faster and faster, but the dangerous rocks at the end of the strip were approaching with equally high speed. Finally, the airspeed indicator showed 105 mph. I pulled the joystick towards me and the machine painfully and slowly rose into the air. Yet, at the end of the runway we were only at the altitude of about 30 feet. The runway below ended and we were approaching the rocks ahead of us; rising as high as 150 feet. These rocks blocked the trajectory of the plane. I knew that I should not raise the nose too high, because the airplane might lose speed and stall, falling tail down. The other option was to turn, but it was equally dangerous because a too deep turn might have resulted in sliding to one side and, again, down. Even though this was dangerous, I chose the second option. I am not a coward but I clearly knew what was at risk. The plane, obeying the controls turned to the left and narrowly avoided the rocks. I aligned the machine back to the original flight path. It obeyed again and there we were in the air, high over the ground, flying towards the ocean."

They flew above the Atlantic, towards Poland, towards the great adventure. The American and Polish press published news items about their departure for the transatlantic crossing. A daily newspaper in Warsaw made a big deal of it, with a headline:

"The Adamowiczes Fly Happy!" Below, in a large font, the report confirmed that

"Brothers Benjamin and Joseph Adamowicz have departed from the airport at Harbour Grace on Newfoundland *en route* over the Atlantic to Poland. The departure took place at 6:30 a.m. local time in very favorable flight conditions.[9] The weather over the Atlantic is good. They have a supporting western wind from the back. If everything goes well they might accomplish the flight in 40 hours, and thus land in Warsaw on Sunday between 2:00 a.m. and 3:00 a.m. in the morning."[10]

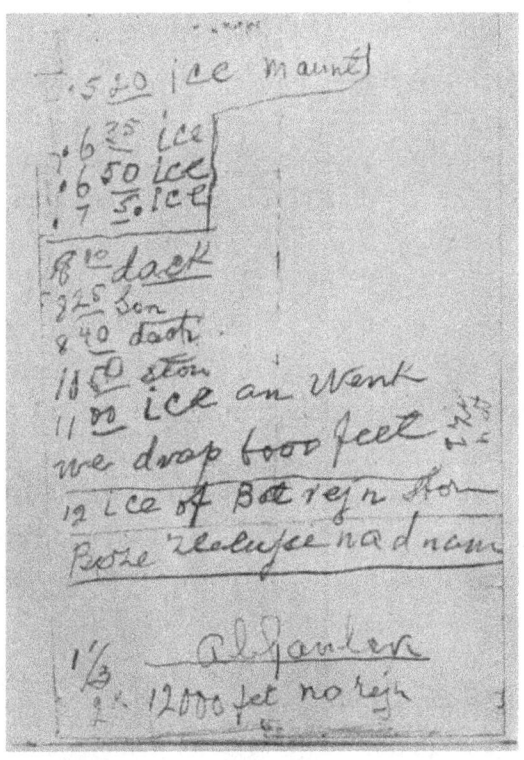

Figure 26: A note from the flight log, with a prayer "God, have mercy on us." From Adamowicz and Adamowicz, *Przez Atlantyk*, 1934.

---

[9] There are some discrepancies in the time of the departure given by different news organizations and sources. As stated above, we established that the most accurate time was 6:06 a.m..
[10]*Ilustrowany Kurier Codzienny*, 7/1, 1934.

They decided to fly high, because storms form usually close to the surface of the water. They were gradually gaining altitude and enjoying good weather. "In the beginning we clearly saw the ocean's surface with white combers. With the ascent the water was changing into a flat, immobile plain, increasingly dark."

They steered in turns, without a specific schedule. "Simply, from time to time we would give a rest to our fatigued muscles and replace each other at steering. My legs easily cramped even if we were both sitting quite comfortably on rubber pillows which a pharmacist from Brooklyn gave us"— recalled Ben. They did not speak. Their ears were filled with cotton, with pilots' helmets tightly fastened, and additionally fixed with the elastics of the goggles. They communicated with gestures or looks and only if necessarily they would shout out loudly. Sometimes, they would open a sliding side window to better see and assess the weather conditions.

After six hours of flight at the altitude of 10,000 feet they exchanged a few gestures indicating their joy and happiness. They had already covered about one fourth of the whole distance. It was an extraordinary sensation: a feeling of total freedom, ruling over the elements, fulfilling their dreams.

At the very moment of experiencing this outburst of happiness they were surprised by the sudden formation of ice danger: ice formed on the aircraft. At first, ice appeared on the front edges of the wings and on the windows — in front and on both sides. Joe wrote it down in the log: "5:20 — ice mount." It was 5:20 p.m. in the afternoon. Entries about the presence of ice kept appearing appeared in the log with increasing urgency and frequency:6:35 p.m. — ice, 6:50 p.m. — ice, 7:50 p.m. — ice, and so forth. The layer of ice on the whole machine was quickly growing. At 11:00 p.m. Joe wrote in larger and thicker letters: ICE. And just after this: "We are falling 6,000 feet."Ben remembered the ice very vividly:

"Suddenly I felt piercing cold. All the instruments and, in general, all metal parts began to grow an ice cover. It was impossible to touch any metal instruments or surfaces with a bare hand. The oil temperature fell from a normal 180 degrees to 150degrees [Fahrenheit]. The worst thing was that the plane began to refuse obeying the controls. At the same time the speedometer showed a dramatic increase. We were doing 160 mph instead of a normal speed of 110 mph. I understood that we were falling down, and falling very fast."

The situation must have been more than dramatic, because Joe, who was keeping the log in English, suddenly wrote a Polish prayer: "Boże, zlituj się nad nami" [God have mercy on us.] Ben commented on this later: "We got accustomed to writing in English. We kept our log in English. Yet, Joe recorded that thought in Polish. He could not explain why he did it." Death was very close, looking straight into their eyes.

It must have been terrible — that prolonged moment of falling down into an abyss, at the bottom of which waited the ocean. They must have both been filled with that awful, disgusting, feeling, dry throats, chills reaching to the very center of the spine: the sense of falling, combined with helplessness, despair, and dread. Their aircraft, overburdened by a thickening layer of ice on its wings, steering equipment, and fuselage was increasing its speed, nose-diving. The propeller was losing its driving force. The controls stopped responding. The ocean was approaching rapidly, with deep ravines opening between white-crested waves. The chasm was ready to swallow them and their plane, whole.

Ben imagined hearing the horrifying sound of a crash, which he had heard in the past at the moment of smashing into the ground or hitting an obstacle on the landing trajectory. In his tense neck and cramped legs, helplessly kicking the pedals, he almost felt the bone-breaking force of the crash.

Suddenly, the joystick in his hand budged. The pedals under his feet got loosened. At this moment, Ben delicately pulled the joystick towards himself. The stabilizer obeyed. The airplane hesitated for a moment and softly flew upwards.

It was the ice! At the lower attitude the air was warmer and the ice began to melt rapidly and fall in big chunks off the wings and the fuselage. The warmer air melted the ice and restored the Bellanca's steering ability. They were saved.

The wild plummeting down lasted for about five minutes. From the altitude of 10,000 feet they descended to 4,000 feet. Below, they spotted a few enormous icebergs floating in the water. They were certain that these icebergs were responsible for the sudden cooling of the air, which even under normal conditions is cooler at higher altitudes. This sudden drop of temperature resulted in the forming of ice on the aircraft. After that brush with death, the brothers were afraid that this phenomenon of icing may be repeated if they returned to a higher altitude. So they decided not to climb again as high as before and to keep their plane at a medium altitude of about 6,000 feet.

Everything would have been just fine for the rest of the flight, if not for a storm which suddenly attacked them from the front. They ran into complete darkness. They tried to penetrate it by relying on the instruments and flying blind. They were moving through walls of water. Bright flashes of lighting were bouncing all around them. They were afraid that they might be struck and electrocuted, or that the cables in the engine would get wet and the electricity would die out. Water was pouring into the cabin through all possible cracks. Ben piloted the aircraft using all his knowledge and experience gained from training in blind flights. His legs were wet and frozen. He had to take them intermittently from the pedals and bump them on the cabin's floor.

It was a very long span of blind flight into black matter. It was as if one storm was handing them over to the next one. After three hours Ben decided to fly at a higher altitude but it did no good. The lightning was raging up there, with even more frequent flashes of blinding and a deafening force. He changed his mind. He went lower, descending to the altitude of less than 500 feet over the surface of the water. At least, there it was not so dark, but the view of enormous waves below the plane was freighting.

Finally, the storms were over. Ben climbed to the altitude of 11,000 feet. He thought that they were going to have a smooth ride from then on. It was not so. Suddenly, Joe, whose job was to pump fuel from the main tank to a smaller one in the wing from where the fuel was going to the engine, screamed with utter anguish: "Ben, the main tank is empty!"

The main tank had the capacity of 380 gallons and this amount had sufficed for 15 hours of flight. They were in the air for only 11 hours. What happened? A leak? A higher than expected level of gas consumption?

At once, Ben decided to pour the gasoline from the canisters into the tank.

"We had 21 canisters, as I have said, five gallons each. I diminished the engine's speed to 1,200 revolutions per minute, so we would fly slower; this would have made the procedure easier. Joe, standing behind his seat, was opening canisters, pouring the gasoline into the main tank and throwing out the empty canisters through an open window. At the moment of each throw, I had to raise the machine's nose, so that the canister would not hit the tail; this would result in a disaster. This almost happened with the second canister. When Joe was throwing it out from the window, aiming at the water below, a handle broke and cut Joe's hand. The canister hit the fuselage and pierced it. Fortunately, the fabric cover was very strong and the tear did not extend far beyond the point of impact. While pouring gas from the canisters into the tank, Joe accidentally spilled some of it on our grilled chicken which we brought from Harbour Grace. The chicken had to go into the ocean.

Besides, we were not hungry and during the whole journey we only ate two oranges, nothing more."

The task of transferring gasoline from the canisters into the tank took about an hour and half. During this time, they slowed down and lost altitude. Now they were at 4,500 feet and they decided to stay at this level and not to climb up and excessively use their sparse supply of fuel. The sun was setting slowly and darkness enveloped them again. Soon, it was brightened by an enormous, red moon, low over the horizon. They spotted lights of a ship on the ocean below them – first one, then more – six ships all together. This encounter assured them that they were on the right course for Europe. Before long, the sun rose again; their watches, set to New York time, showed that it was only 2:00 a.m.

Looking down they spotted a small island. They were sure that Europe was near. In vain, they tried to find this island on the maps. They circled above it two times. There were some houses, fields, and meadows with cattle on them. They thought about landing to ask what this island was called, but there was no flat stretch of land that could have served as an impromptu runway. They continued eastward. Another piece of land appeared extending into the horizon. So, this was Europe!

Suddenly, a layer of clouds and fog covered the land and they were literally sucked into a very heavy rain. To escape bad weather, they climbed up to the altitude 10,000 feet, all the time relying solely on the instruments. This adventure took almost three hours. Even though they went higher, they found that the weather was still bad: clouds, rain, and occasionally even snow. They got lost. They did not know if they were over land or water. They thought that probably they were already over France or even Germany. Clouds still. Worried about running out of gasoline they decided to turn back. They turned around 180°.

Ben thus recalled this dramatic moment:

"We were flying blind for about an hour and half when suddenly we saw a hole in the clouds. Immediately, we went down! Land! But the ceiling of the fog was very low and I had to be careful not to hit a church tower — there were many churches there. Joe tried to find our position on the map. I shouted: 'The map is no use! We better look for a place to land!'"

They were searching for almost an hour. Their level of fuel was dangerously low. Finally they found a large meadow. They circled above it twice. It looked welcoming. They decided to land. The plane descended. When they reached a very low altitude, a herd of cows suddenly appeared in front of the propeller. The aircraft, steered by Ben, jumped over them and went down again, but the meadow was ending. They broke a small tree. The wheels touched the ground. The plane was hopping on an uneven terrain.

A fence popped up just in front of the aircraft. Ben pushed the brakes, but he had to stop breaking right away, because the tail went up, and the whole plane could flip over. The fence was near. Fortunately, it was low. The plane hit it between two posts. The fence fell down and the machine kept rolling. All of a sudden, the back wheel got stuck in a ditch and brought the aircraft to a halt. The Bellanca stopped. Ben switched off the engine. They opened the doors on both sides of the plane and jumped onto the grass. They ran towards the propeller. Thank God, it was not damaged! They looked at each other. Yes, they crossed Atlantic. They made it. "Let's thank God! It could have been worse" — said Joe. They prayed for a while, in silence.

It was 8:30 a.m. on Saturday, June 30, 1934, Newfoundland time. It was 2:30 p.m. Greenwich time in Europe. They were in the air for 26 hours and 24 minutes. They covered more than 2,500 miles. But where were they? Where was Warsaw? After a short while a man appeared. Then, a second. They spoke French.

There was no way to communicate with them. More people came, apparently thinking that an air crash occurred. Among the crowd, one woman spoke English. It turned out that she was a teacher in a local school. She told them where they were: on a pasture called Le Chessay, about a mile from the village of St. André de Messei, about five miles from the town Flers d'Orne, and about 50 miles from the city of Caen, in northern Normandy, France.

Figure27: Photo of the Brothers and onlookers before their departure from Chessay. From Adamowicz and Adamowicz, *Przez Atlantyk*, 1934.

When the people learned from the teacher that these aviators have just crossed Atlantic they burst with enthusiasm. The French police arrived. A Pole, Stefan Jamiołkowski, living nearby came and helped the two brothers. He sent cables about their landing to Paris and Warsaw. "The Adamowiczes Happily Crossed the Atlantic!" —"They Are in France!" — "Atlantic Conquered by the Adamowiczes!" — "Brave Brothers Connect New York with

France!" — such headlines popped up in all Polish newspapers.[11]

Mr. Jamiołkowski brought a mechanic to fix the rear gear and a truck with gasoline. Journalists, fellow pilots, a representative of the local administration, and dozens of others started to congregate around the brothers. They spent the rest of the day on the meadow, supervising the repairs, re-fueling the aircraft, signing autographs and giving interviews, as well as eating and drinking whatever the hospitable French farmers offered to them.

Mr. and Mrs. Lair, from a nearby estate invited them for dinner and to spend the night. Their neighbors filled the house with flowers. Ben and Joe went to bed. During the night the representatives of the French and Polish governments drove in from Paris: Captain Picard, Chief of Staff of the French Minister of Aviation, and Colonel Błeszyński, the Military Attaché at the Polish Embassy. In the morning, they officially welcomed the brothers, as guests on the French soil and as pilgrims to their homeland.

---

[11] For example: *Ilustrowany Kurier Codzienny*, July 2, 1934.

CHAPTER 15
IN EUROPE

After spending a comfortable night and having breakfast with their hospitable French hosts, on Sunday, July 1, 1934, the brothers went to the pasture where their airplane was parked, guarded by the police. "When French officials and Colonel Błeszyński saw our meadow, they vehemently tried to persuade us to not start from it. In their opinion a crash was inevitable" — recalled Ben. After a short conference with Joe, Ben decided to take off from there, anyway. They asked for an escort to show them the shortest way to Paris. Captain Picard made a call to a nearby airbase. A French Air Force plane soon appeared on the horizon and circled over the meadow. The Adamowiczes' Bellanca was light without much fuel left, so the takeoff was smooth, without any problems. They were in the air at 9:00 a.m.

At 10:37 a.m. they landed at Le Bourget civilian airport near Paris. They were greeted by the airport management and scores of Polish, French, and American journalists. Cables about the Adamowiczes' extraordinary achievement circulated all over the world. The Bellanca was moved to the nearby military airport. There, an official welcome ceremony took place with the participation of General Louis Houdemont, assisted by officers of the Fourth Air Brigade and Colonel Davet of the French Ministry of Aviation, the honor guard and a military band. The Ambassador Alfred Chłapowski with his entourage represented Poland.

At the ceremony, the Ambassador read a cable from the Polish Aero Club: "Congratulations and warm welcome to our brave compatriots who brought glory to Poland in the whole world." The pilots responded by becoming visibly moved and abashed. Again, scores of journalist and photographers swarmed around.

Figure 28: Bellanca in Paris. In front of the aircraft from the left: Polish Ambassador Alfred Chłapowski, Ben Adamowicz, Joseph Adamowicz. *Skrzydlata Polska* 6.

The brothers and their aircraft were photographed and filmed. Quickly, they shook off the initial shyness and enjoyed their sudden celebrity status. "They invited us for a banquet to the officer dining hall. We drank some champagne, but then we asked for beer" — as Ben recalled, in vivid detail. While the pilots were celebrating, French mechanics checked the Bellanca and discovered that there was a leak from the tank. This leak was responsible for the loss of fuel over the ocean.

"The repair would have taken too much time. I only asked to give us some fuel. They gave us just 200 gallons saying that it should be enough to reach Warsaw — only about a thousand miles away."

For the final portion of their transatlantic adventure, Ben

decided to take a route leading to Warsaw over Dresden, Berlin, Poznań, and Kalisz.

At 12:23 p.m. local time, on July 1, 1934, they started their last, as they thought, leg of the great journey. Warsaw was informed about their departure. "The weather was good. We climbed at once to 10,000 feet. We didn't want to waste any time and we planned to arrive in Warsaw before nightfall. The flight was fairly normal, we had rested well, and were very happy that soon we would land in our own country. I was checking the compass and Joe the maps. We were on the right course."

The brothers' arrival in Warsaw was expected around 6:30 p.m. local time, on Sunday, July 1, 1934. The radio and the press announced that momentous event. Large crowds poured into the newly opened Okęcie airport in Warsaw to "welcome the heroic conquerors of the Atlantic."[12] Polish and American flags decorated the airport. Officials, army commanders, and diplomats arrived ahead of time, including: the Mayor of Warsaw, Karol Ołpiński,[13] General Ludomir Rayski, the Head of the Department of Aviation in the Ministry of Military Affairs with his staff, Colonels Tomasz Turbiak, Julian Filipowicz, and Bogdan Kwieciński, the American Ambassador, John Cudahy, with the Military Attaché Gilmer, as well as a fellow pilot, Major Stanisław Skarżyński, who had flown over the South Atlantic.

The print press and radio journalists were there, along with photographers and film reporters. The airport was illuminated. Just in case, the other airport of Warsaw, Pola Mokotowskie ["the Mokotów Fields"], was illuminated as well. At 6:40 p.m. five military aircraft took off to welcome the Bellanca in the air, but they could not find it. They took off again at 8:15 p.m.— again, in vain. The large crowd waited with increasing worry. The Bellanca did not arrive. At 10:00 p.m. the lights were turned off

---

[12] *Kurier Warszawski*, July 2, 1934.
[13] Karol Ołpiński was Warsaw's "interim" Mayor.

and the airport was closed down. Everyone returned back to Warsaw deeply troubled. "There were speculations that the airmen got lost and landed in a location without communication."[14]

It was the right guess. The brothers had to land in Germany. At that time, Germany was in turmoil and disarray. A bloody internal strife shook up the ruling NSDAP (National Socialist German Workers' Party) of Adolf Hitler. The army and the administration were on "stand by." Conflicting orders were crossing the country in all directions. The report about the landing of a Polish-American plane was not immediately relayed to the proper authorities. Only at 11:00 p.m. a telegram about the Adamowiczes' landing in Germany reached Warsaw.

*

Figure 29: The plane and the onlookers after the landing in Nedlitz, Thiemenberg, Germany. Adamowicz and Adamowicz, *Przez Atlantyk*, 1934.

Indeed, while flying over Germany the brothers found that

---
[14]*Polska Zachodnia*, July 2, 1934.

their fuel was running out quicker than they had expected. They did not know how long their supply would have lasted, so, to avoid trouble, they decided to land. They descended when they saw the first, good-looking, flat piece of ground. They landed safely on a meadow near a forest. It turned out that they were in Brandenburg, in the vicinity of a town called Tschaudorf located about five miles away from Crossen an der Oder (presently this town is called Szczawno near Krosno Odrzańskie in Poland.)Some people appeared, including a German policeman. Again, as in France, it was hard to communicate because of the language barrier. Ben was repeatedly asking for a post office to inform Warsaw by a telegram about the interruption of the flight, but he was not understood. The Germans treated them with suspicion and hostility. A policeman searched Ben and did not allow Joe, who wanted to look for a post-office, to go anywhere. After quite a long struggle with languages, using gestures and maps, Ben was finally able to explain who they are, from where they came, and that they needed to send a telegram. The policeman ordered two locals to stay with Ben at the aircraft and went with Joe into town. Joe returned after an hour; he "was inventive enough to bring four bottles of beer. I was so thirsty that I drank three of them at once" — acknowledged Ben.

More people came, including an owner of a nearby estate, who invited them to spend the night. He was very cordial and hospitable, although they could not converse in any language. At 2:30 a.m. a phone call woke them up. It was the correspondent of the Polish Press Agency who called from Berlin and later published the following report:

"Both aviators told me that they were waiting with great joy for a moment when their airplane would finally fly over the Polish soil. They thanked me for our Agency's interest in their journey. They were happy that a Polish journalist was the first one who welcomed them in their native tongue at the gates of Poland."[15]

The Polish correspondent's report appeared on that very day, July 2, 1934, in Warsaw. In the same issue of the newspaper (and in extraordinary additions to all other papers), the readers could find the schedule of the expected welcome ceremony for the "Conquerors of the Atlantic." News-boys were running and shouting all over the Polish capital: "Adamowiczes Today in Warsaw!"

In the morning of July 2, 1934, a German truck brought 50 *liters* of gasoline, instead of the amount requested by Ben, that is 50 *gallons* — a result of an apparent miscommunication. Another unpleasant surprise was that the Germans, unlike the French, demanded payment for the gas. This incident is worth noting though, because it shows that the brothers *did* have some cash on them, contrary to previous complaints that they did not have any money at all when they left Harbour Grace. The Adamowiczes departed from Germany at 9:30 a.m. on Monday, July 2, 1934. They were sure that this time they were going to land in Warsaw.

Figure 30: Refueling of Bellanca at the Toruń airport, July 2, 1934.
Lotnictwo z Szachownicą No 31.

---

[15] *Kurjer Warszawski*, July 2, 1934.

CHAPTER 16

IN POLAND

After about half an hour into their flight, Joe, who was studying the map all the time, shouted into his brother's ear: "Ben! We are over Poland!"

What a spell! "It's hard for me to find words for what I felt, but I knew that this was the best moment a man can experience. Twenty three years ago I left the country as a young boy, not knowing what Poland really was. And now, along with my brother, I came so far from Brooklyn, to see this Old Country. The farms below were not as rich as in America or Germany, and there were fewer railroads. But everything looked so beautiful from the air!" During their whole stay in Poland, they spoke many times about their enchantment with the beauty of the Polish land.

When they saw a river and two large bridges they thought that it was Warsaw. They landed on an airfield near the river. Soon they learned that it was the Vistula river. But the city was not Warsaw. To their astonishment, they found themselves in a military airport near the city of Toruń — evidence that their navigational skills were far from perfect.

They were very warmly greeted in Toruń. Here is a press report on their arrival and visit to Toruń:

> "We were looking for a big city on a big river with bridges, therefore Warsaw on the Vistula' — the Adamowicz brothers told us. 'We are over Poland' — Joe called, obviously moved. 'And here is the Vistula and Warsaw with her bridges' — Ben triumphed a minute later. 'There! There! Do you see the runway? It's a Polish airport!' — Joe shouted again. They landed. It was July 2, 1934, about 11:00 a.m. The officer on duty at the 4th Air Wing in Toruń

was Lieutenant-pilot Barski. On a hot, summer day, an aircraft of a shape unknown to him appeared over the airport. It was a one-engine machine, covered with strange numbers and inscriptions. The airplane landed. The commandant of the airstrip showed it a parking place. Lieutenant Barski went to the airplane. The propeller stopped. Two short, corpulent men emerged from the cabin. Lieutenant Barski's thought that they certainly did not look like pilots. "'Hello, boy!' — shouted one of them. 'We are in Warsaw? Right?'

These two men were the Adamowicz brothers. The Commander of the 4th Air Wing, Colonel Heller, along with his officers welcomed them cordially and took good care of them. The brothers were invited to the Officers Club. Colonel Heller called the Polish Aero Club with information about the Adamowiczes' arrival and their intention to immediately continue on to Warsaw. Colonel Kwieciński, the general secretary of the Polish Aero Club, asked for a delay of this departure until 4:00 p.m. because Warsaw wanted to have more time to prepare a welcome ceremony.

While waiting in Toruń for the last segment of their trip, both guests were driven to the city center. In the meantime, news about their arrival in Toruń spread with lightning speed. Large crowd met them at the Old Town Square. They walked through the narrow streets of the medieval quarters of the city and were invited for a lunch in the best Toruń's restaurant, Dwór Artusa. At 3:30 p.m. a cavalcade of cars went back to the airport. Before the departure, Colonel Heller decorated the brothers with a badge of the 4th Air Wing. At 4:00 p.m., the Bellanca, escorted by a squadron of fighters took off from the Toruń airport. In the air above the fortress of Modlin another Polish air force squadron, from the 1st Warsaw's Air Wing, was waiting for the Bellanca and took over as the honorary guard, guiding the plane to Warsaw."[16]

In order to ensure that the brothers found their way from

---

[16] An account cited from: otoruniu.net/torun-etapem-rajdu-nowy-jork-%E2%8%93-warszawa

Toruń to Warsaw, Colonel Heller ordered Lieutenant-pilot Chrzanowski to fly with them, taking the seat of the second pilot in the Bellanca. Thus, Ben Adamowicz and Lt. Chrzanowski sat at the controls, while Joe Adamowicz crawled back into the fuselage, as he usually did before a landing. This time, he was lying on a mattress of flowers which the brothers received in Toruń. As it turned out, Lt. Chrzanowski's help was not much needed, since they were flying south following the course of the Vistula river[17] that glistened below in a perfect, sunny weather.

They arrived in Warsaw on July 2, 1934, at 5:00 p.m. Enthusiastic crowds greeted them at the Pola Mokotowskie airport.

Figure 31: Welcoming crowds at Warsaw's Pola Mokotowskie airport. *Polska Lotnicza,* 1937. http://pl.wikipedia.org/wiki/Bracia_Adamowiczowie

---

[17]The Vistula (Wisła) is the major Polish river. It runs across the whole Poland from the mountains in the south to the Baltic Sea in the north. Major cities — Kraków, Warsaw, Toruń, Bydgoszcz and Gdańsk — are situated on the banks of Vistula.

CHAPTER 17
IN WARSAW

In the 1930s, in Poland – as in the rest of the world – much attention was paid to aviation and the feats of intrepid pilots, breaking ever new records. The tremendous enthusiasm in Poland was fueled by the great successes of Polish pilots and aircraft manufacturers. Since 1930, modern RWD airplanes were designed and built by a company organized by Stanisław Rogalski (1904-1976), Stanisław Wigura (1903-1932), and Jerzy Drzewiecki (1902-1990). The name RWD was abbreviated from the first letters of the last names of the three men. Their planes were built in a factory at the Okęcie airport in Warsaw. In 1932, a Polish pilot, Franciszek Żwirko (1895-1932), flying an RWD plane with the engineer Wigura, won an international aviation competition -- the Challenge, held in Berlin. Emotions aroused by their success and the whole nation's focus on aviation were augmented when Żwirko and Wigura died in a crash of their RWD-6 plane just two weeks after their great victory.[18]

As the victor in the Challenge of 1932, Poland had a right to organize the next Challenge in 1934. A catchphrase, "The whole nation builds airplanes for the Challenge," was used to fundraise for the new machines and to enhance popular interest in aviation. During the Adamowiczes' visit in 1934, the Polish team, consisting of captain-pilot Jerzy Bajan (1901-1967) with mechanic Gustaw Pokrzywka won this international Challenge.[19] Poland was victorious, again. Another captain-pilot, Franciszek Hynek (1897-1958), with the navigator Zbigniew Burzyński, won

---
[18] The Challenge competition was held August 12-28, 1932. The winners, Żwirko and Wigura, perished in an air crash on September 11.
[19] The Challenge of 1934 was held in Warsaw, August 28-September 16.

an international balloon contest for the Gordon Bennett Aviation Trophy held in 1933 in the U.S. Poland repeated this triumph a year later: Hynek, this time flying with the navigator Władysław Pomaski, won, in the balloon category, the Gordon Bennett Trophy in 1934. Other Polish crews ended both races, the Challenge and the Gordon Bennett Trophy, in high positions. As we have already recalled, Captain Skarżyński conquered, as the first pilot flying solo, the South Atlantic in 1933, departing from Africa and landing in Brazil. Polish aviators glorified Poland. Polish technical thought, inventions, and technical solutions in aviation were respected and praised.

All this generated a very favorable climate for, and wide interest in, the transatlantic flight by the brothers Adamowicz. They were immediately inscribed into the myth of newly restored Polish independence. This myth, created by the elites and eagerly desired by the masses, showed Poland as a strong and vibrant European power, extending its political and cultural influences and aspirations far beyond its actual borders, embracing distant continents. The Polish Diaspora in America, with strong patriotic traditions, was a significant element of this spin myth. The Adamowiczes were perfect representatives of Polish Americans that loved the Old Country and were successful in the U.S.

All aspects of their successful crossing, from the flight itself, to the landing, to the crowd's enthusiastic reactions, to the subsequent welcoming ceremonies (one at the airport and one at the City Hall), to the triumphant parade through the city, to speeches given by both the hosts and the honorees – all these were recounted in great detail by the Polish press, under banner headlines. They were also proudly announced from the microphones of radio-reporters.[20]

---

[20] As an example let us quote a title from a newspaper article: "Incredible enthusiasm of Warsaw's population welcoming heroic flyers."*Ilustrowany Kurier Codzienny*, July 4, 1934.

The news reported the following narrative of triumphal arrival, based on multiple sources.[21] In all of them we see large crowds, thousands of people shoulder by shoulder, and police on horseback trying to no avail to keep order. We hear shouting and chanting of the heroes' names, exclamations of pride and joy. Press clippings from old newspapers feature many photographs of these scenes. In one of them the Bellanca's wings seem to be resting on people's heads. Short newsreels were also preserved.[22]

Enormous crowed gathers at the Pola Mokotowskie airport waiting for the brothers' arrival long before the expected time, 5:00 p.m.[23] The authorities decided at the last minute to welcome them not at the new Okęcie airport located a few miles from the city, as it was actually planned a day ago, but at the old airport, Pola Mokotowskie, which was almost in the center of the city and thus easier to access.

The Pola Mokotowskie hosted dignitaries, representatives of the administration, commanders of the armed forces, diplomats, and many other dignitaries. Among them were Warsaw's Mayor Ołpiński, the Chief of the Air Force, General Rayski, the American Ambassador John Cudahy, generals, government members, representatives of the Polish Aero Club and its branches from the whole country, and, of course, the journalists, press and radio reporters, photographers, as well as and a multitude of Warsaw residents. Viewing stands were erected for VIPs; crowds filled the airport meadows and surrounding streets.

---

[21] In the following paragraphs we combine in one composite narrative the reports taken from many sources, including: *Ilustrowany Kurier Polski*, July 4, 1934, *Kurjer Warszawski*, July 3, 1934, *Goniec Częstochowski*, July 2 and 4, 1934. We also use material based on the narrative by Strumph-Wojtkiewicz.

[22] The video is available on YouTube. Fox MovieTone news clips of the brothers in Warsaw also exist; in one of these clips, Ben is making a speech.

[23] The Pola Mokotowskie Airport (Lotnisko Mokotowskie) does not exist today. It was located in the vicinity of today's Park Piłsudskiego, in the area encompassed by Wawelska, Żwirki, i Wigury, Rostafińskich, and Batorego streets. Pola Mokotowskie was an airport, but its grounds were also used also for parades and large meetings.

"A squadron of 9 fighters PZL 11C of the 4th Warsaw's Wing appears on the skies from the north at 5:00 p.m. Just behind them the Bellanca. At the rear, three more fighters. They approach the airport and circle it. The escorting fighters fly away towards the Okęcie airport while the Bellanca lowers its trajectory and is ready to land. People shout, raise their hands, wave Polish flags, hats, and handkerchiefs."

Figure 32: Photo of a triumphant passage through Warsaw from the airport the City Hall. From Adamowicz and Adamowicz, *Przez Atlantyk*, 1934.

Joe Adamowicz remembered:
"Ben aimed at the main stand and a large moving crowd in front of it. We saw a virtual forest of risen hands. The machine touched the ground, rolled, and stopped. Time was 5:02 p.m. Suddenly, the crowd and a cluster of horseback police started to run towards us. They were quickly nearing. I shouted to Ben: 'Turn off the engine!' because the propeller could kill somebody. He shut the engine off at the last moment. The crowd was close. There were old and young, girls, soldiers, boys, and even Jews. Ben opened his door. We were surrounded by a dense swarm. The next moment

people yanked us from the airplane and carrying us on their shoulders took us to a car with an open roof. The car moved. An avalanche of flowers fell on us. 'Ben, what is this? Are you getting it? This is all for us!' My brother Ben — you should know him, how quiet, calm, and tough he is — said nothing. He only looked at me. And we understood each other. Only countrymen could give such a welcome to their own."

The brothers were driven to the main stand. A reporter described the events:

"A hurricane of applause, enthusiastic shouting, and waving of hats greet them. The wife of the Mayor Ołpiński, accompanied by General Rayski and Deputy Minister Bobkowski, give both aviators huge bouquets of white and red roses. The crowd, again, grabs them and carries them on their shoulders back and forth in front of the stands. All faces radiate. All people are ecstatic. It's sheer madness! Suddenly a group of men and women tries to stop them. It's the Polish family, the Adamowiczes. Enthusiasm mounts. People shout, throw hats and caps in the air, and flowers on the aviators.

The military orchestra plays marches. Excitement is so intense, and noise so loud that the welcoming speeches can't go on. Now people carry the heroes to a car adorned with roses. The car moves, followed by the whole motor-cavalcade with the officials and the press. They leave the airport and soon ride the streets of the center of Warsaw. Mounted police trots on both sides of the cars. A shower of bouquets drops from windows and balconies as well as from sidewalks. When a bouquet doesn't reach the open car of the brothers, paper-boys running alongside of the police dive under the horse's bellies, grab it and hand it to the car. At an instance, one of the boys is almost trampled. Joe sees that, gives a cry of fear, and wants to stop the car and help. Yet the boy gets up by himself, smiles and shouts: 'Long live our beloved brothers!' as he wipes tears of joy from his cheeks. A lady throws a bouquet and then her glove to the car. Ben catches it, puts in his pocket and yells: 'This will be my mascot.' On Marszałkowska Street even more people stand on the sidewalks, some run trying to match the speed of the cars. Still more flowers! One bouquet hits Joe in the head to which he responds with a smile. Drivers stop their cars and mount on the roofs. Hundreds of photo cameras click all the time. Shouting and clapping are moving as a sea wave with movement of the heroes' cars."

We have to be aware that Joe and Ben Adamowicz, two men from a provincial village, were in Warsaw, the capital of Poland, for the first time! Born and raised somewhere at the borderlands of the country, they knew only villages and small towns of their province. Once or twice, they may have visited the only large city in their area, Wilno (Vilnius). And now, suddenly, they dropped from the sky (literarily!) into the center of Warsaw, into the heart of Poland. Another journalist reported:

"The crowd gathered on the Plac Teatralny burst into a roar at 6:10 p.m. People clap and shout. Blocked by the police from two sides, a magnificent cortege rolls in. First, the troop of the police on motorcyclists, next a truck with a band of trumpeters, playing fanfares, just behind them the car of the Mayor of Warsaw and the car carrying the heroes of the day, the brothers Adamowicz, covered with flowers. A cavalcade of both official and private cars follows."

What happened next? According to Joe Adamowicz's continued account:

"We drive in the Plac Teatralny and through the gate into the courtyard of the City Hall. We get out of the car. On top of the staircase a lady is waiting and when we approach her, she welcomes us, very moved as we are, in the name of the Mayor; it later turned out that she was his wife. There are many people everywhere and everyone is shaking our hands, introducing themselves, and thanking us God knows for what. They lead us through some huge halls full of very important figures— generals, ministers, chairmen and others, who all the time introduce themselves to us and speak kind words. It looks like it is some kind of a festival — and it is all for us. The speeches, the welcomes, the greetings. All for us."

Among the welcoming crowds was General Andrzej Galica, known for his foul mouth. He shouted to them: "You are two damn fine Polish scoundrels! Let me hug you!" He hugs them and kisses on the cheeks. A group of elegant and refined ladies stops them and gives them flowers. Ben says: "Give these flowers only to Joe, ladies, he should marry in Poland. Don't let him go to America without a Polish wife!"

Figure 33: Ben and Joe with the American Ambassador John Cudahy at the Warsaw's City Hall just after their arrival.
Wikimedia Commons.

Everyone dressed up for the occasion and they were elegant, in suits, gowns, tuxedos, or gala uniforms with crosses and medals – but the two pilots were as they landed, straight from the aircraft. They only took of their pilot helmets, without even combing their hair, which is clearly visible on the photographs. They are in their brown jerseys, dirty and sweaty shirts, with poorly knotted ties, and stained, wrinkled pants. Joe is taller, heavily built, grayish. Ben, shorter than his brother, is stocky, with an oval and jovial face.

For the welcome ceremony, the grand chamber of the City Hall was decorated with Polish and American flags, as well as emblems of the Polish Aero Club and the League of Air and Gas Defense. At 6:25 p.m. the fanfares resounded. The brothers were led into the chamber of the City Hall. Again, they were greeted with never-ending exclamations "Long live!" and waves of applause. Finally, the official welcome ceremony began.

The Mayor of Warsaw, Karol Ołpiński, delivered the first speech:

> "As you conquered the ocean in one leap, so you instantly conquered Warsaw, the hearts and minds of all of us. I welcome you with great love, you, the fearless heroes, you, who have flown over the great waters and vast stretches of land, defeating all natural forces that were united against you. I also greet you as national heroes, who traced and established a new air connection between New York and Warsaw. We look at you with real and profound pride. You brought glory to Poland, to the Polish nation, to the Polish state and to its status as a world power. At the same time we are very grateful to you from the bottom of our hearts, for you have spread all over the world the glory of the name of Warsaw, giving your airplane the name of our beloved city.I want to share with you, dear sirs, my utter delight that an aircraft 'Warsaw' not only flew you safely over the Atlantic, but also connected all Polish-Americans with their Motherland, with a free and strong Poland."

After the Mayor's speech the orchestra performed the national anthem of the United States.

Next, the American Ambassador John Cudahy approached the microphones. He welcomed the brothers as fellow American citizens, congratulating them on their exceptional achievement. The Polish national anthem followed his speech. The speakers then included General Rayski and the Deputy President of the Senate, Dr. Bogucki. After each orator the orchestra performed military tunes. Then, Mayor Ołpiński took the microphone and announced that the City Board, in unanimous vote, decided to bestow on the Adamowiczes the Badge of Honor of the City of Warsaw. The chair of the Warsaw chapter of the League of Air and Gas Defense, Mr. Godlewski, gave the brothers a golden-framed picture of Marshal Józef Piłsudski — the first of the many gifts they were to receive in Poland. The Polish national anthem sounded again.

Mayor Ołpiński invited Joe and Ben to appear with him on the balcony of the City Hall. When their emergence was announced the crowd on the Plac Teatralny roared with enthusiasm. And here they came: the Mayor, the brothers, General Rayski, and Deputy Minister Bobkowski. The Mayor repeated his speech from the City chamber. Then, he pushed Joe to the microphone. The pilot, speaking in Polish with a heavy American accent, said:

"Here speaks to you Joe Adamowicz. Respectable Ladies and Gentlemen, we did all we could. We have beaten the Atlantic. We wanted to glorify Poland's name. We are happy that our victory is also a victory of all Polish-Americans. Our greatest joy and reward, however, is that our flight from New York to Warsaw contributed to the glory of Polish aviation. We are grateful to Poland, and especially to Warsaw, for the heartfelt enthusiasm that we have been experiencing since our arrival. Long live Poland! Long live the President of Poland! Long live Poland's leader, Marshal Józef Piłsudski!"

The crowd's enthusiasm reached its zenith. Joe shouted: "Thank you very much! Thanks to all of you!" People started to chant Joe's name: "Jó-zef — Jó-zef!" and "A-da-mo-wicz —A-da-mo-wicz!" And then: "Bo-lek — Bo-lek!"

They used Ben's Polish first name in its intimate, familial form. Ben approached the microphone and shouted:

"In the name of my brother and myself I thank you, my compatriots! I thank our dear Polonia in America! Our 'Warsaw' flew over the Atlantic and fulfilled the dream of our life. I will tell others in the United States about this magnificent reception you have given us in Poland. We are grateful for your cordial and warm welcome. I thank you all once more!"

The crowd responded with a storm of clapping and shouting his name. Again, let us listen to a reporter:

"After a glass of wine at the office of the Mayor and a brief encounter with the press, the Adamowiczes expressed a wish to go to the airport and retrieve their belongings from the aircraft. The wish was granted immediately. They were driven to Pola Mokotowskie. They took their luggage and they supervised the transfer of their Bellanca to in a hangar of the Polish Aero Club. Then they were driven to the Hotel Europejski where they will stay during their sojourn in Warsaw. They were treated to a sumptuous dinner — Polish soup 'borsch,' pork chops, and ice cream. They were offered wine, but they asked for beer. Together they drunk seven bottles of good Polish 'Żywiec.'"

The Hotel Europejski was one of the most luxurious hotels in Poland's capital and it is still in operation today. The city gave the brothers two separate suites, each with an entrance, living room, office area, bedroom, and bathroom. Long into the night a crowd stood in front of the hotel, while bell-boys delivered telegrams, letters and flowers, and the phones rang non-stop. Joe recalled:

"At last, about ten we were left alone. We were in my suite.

We sat for a while in silence. We were shocked and moved. I looked at my brother and saw that he was somehow morose too. I said: 'How is our Bellanca doing? What do you think? They did not allow us even to take care of it.' He smiled, but a bit sadly: 'It's in the hands of good mechanics. We'll see her tomorrow. I'm not worried about her. But...' — 'But what?' — 'Why they are separating us? Shouldn't we sleep in one room? As we've been living as one, flying as one...' We understood each other. Yet we decided that we had to stay in our suites for the first night. We didn't want to wake up the hotel staff. We planned to ask for one apartment for the two of us the following day. So, we said goodnight to each other. Ben went to his suite and I stayed in mine. He came to visit me two times during the night and I went to see him. Yet, it was hard to talk at the end of this day so full of emotions."

Accustomed to living in small, cramped quarters back at home in Janowszczyzna and in equally cramped apartments in Brooklyn, the brothers felt ill at ease in the spacious accommodations of the Hotel Europejski. They were uncomfortable. A whole suite of rooms just for one man? And a whole suite for the other man, too?

CHAPTER 18
A ROYAL RECEPTION

The next day the brothers got up late, about 9:30 a.m. Ben asked that breakfast be served in his suite only so the brothers could have breakfast together. They got scrambled eggs on ham, rolls with butter, coffee with milk. They asked for beer. The waiter, remembering that they drunk seven bottles the other day, brought them eight.

Two officers were appointed to care for Ben and Joe and to serve as guides, escorts, and chaperons — Captain Henryk Dąbrowski and Lieutenant Pilot Władysław Dzięciołowski. They appeared at the Hotel Europejski just when the brothers were about to end their breakfast. They informed them about the details of the proposed schedule of their stay in Warsaw.

A host of tailors, invited by the officers, appeared in the hotel suite, bringing several suits of different sizes for the brothers' fitting session. Those selected were immediately altered to fit. The orderlies of the two officers along with associates from the most elegant stores in Warsaw brought shirts, ties, belts, coats, hats, handkerchiefs, and underwear, as well as pajamas, robes and slippers. Everything was tried on and adjustments were made as needed. Suitcases, briefcases, and cosmetics appeared like magic. Bell boys brought armfuls of flowers and piles of newspapers with stories about their flight, the arrival and reception in Warsaw, as well as boxes with congratulatory telegrams. One of the telegrams was from General Italo Balbo, an Italian hero-pilot, who had led a fleet of 24 seaplanes from the Mediterranean Sea to Chicago World's Fair "A Century of Progress Exposition" in 1933. Many cables came from America — so many that the brothers could hardly browse through them.

Figure 34: Brothers Adamowicz received by the President of Poland Ignacy Mościcki. From the left: Capt. Henryk Dąbrowski (official chaperon of the brothers in Poland) Ben, Joseph, President Mościcki, and Ambassador John Cudahy. From Adamowicz and Adamowicz, *Przez Atlantyk*, 1934.

During the ensuing days, it seemed that a carousel series of visits, banquets, receptions, and meetings with state officials and military commanders, airmen, and business people started to spin. Every day was full of events, from morning till late at night. The brothers listened, looked, smiled, and tried to comprehend that all that activity was for them: the flowers, the greetings, the compliments, the toasts, the cheers, and the tears in the eyes of people addressing them. Tired and dazed, yet happy and joyful, the brothers inhaled Poland, assimilating images and sounds, learning history and culture, and, first of all, meeting many Polish people. They later said that they "saw Poland beautiful, great, and powerful."[24] They visited monuments in Warsaw, including the Royal Palace, the Cathedral and other churches, the Parliament, and the state buildings. In the evenings, they visited

---

[24] *Ilustrowany Kurier Codzienny*, August 2, 1934.

theaters and restaurants.

Here are the main points of the Adamowiczes' two-week visit to Warsaw, from the first day after the arrival to the departure from Warsaw — but not yet from Poland!

Tuesday, July 3rd, 1934. In the morning, the brothers, accompanied by their two chaperon-officers, went to the Royal Palace and put their names on the list for an audience with the President of Poland, Ignacy Mościcki (they were granted the audience the following week), and on the list of applicants for an audience in the "Belweder" Palace, the residence of Marshall Józef Piłsudski (who at that time was seriously ill and they did not get to see him.)

Next, they paid a courtesy visit to the American Ambassador John Cudahy, who received them as American citizens and was very proud of them. They also visited Mayor Ołpiński. Next, they went to the Ministry of Defense, where they were received by two Deputy Ministers, Generals Tadeusz Kasprzycki and Felicjan Sławoj-Składkowski. In the evening, they participated in the reception at the Polish Aero Club, hosted by its President, Prince Janusz Radziwiłł.

Late at night, at 11:00 p.m. they were driven to a revue-theatre "Rex" where passers-by at the entrance and the public in the auditorium greeted them with applause. Before the show, the popular actor, Kazimierz Krukowski, announced that they were both elected honorary members of the ensemble. Wild clapping followed, and Krukowski added: "Don't worry, Monsieurs, this honor does not oblige you to perform on stage."[25] We are guessing that this was the first time in their lives that Joe and Ben visited a theatre.

---

[25] "Kronika Warszawy," supplement to *Ilustrowany Kurjer Codzienny*, July 5, 1934.

Figure35: Joseph, Prince Janusz Radziwiłł (President of the Polish Aero Club), Ben, Ambassador John Cudahy, Major Stanisław Skarżyński (in the first row). From Adamowicz and Adamowicz,*Przez Atlantyk*, 1934.

<u>Wednesday, July 4th</u>. Escorted and assisted by their chaperons, who organized all events and served as drivers, the aviators undertook another series of visits: to the President of the Senate, Władysław Raczkiewicz, the Speaker of the House, Kazimierz Świtalski, the Minister of Transportation, Butkiewicz, the Ministry of Foreign Affairs, the Ministry of Internal Affairs, the League of National Air Defense, the Maritime and Colonial League, and the League of Air Defense, where its President General Gustaw Orlicz-Dreszer welcomed them especially warmly.

In the afternoon, at 2:30 p.m., they had an audience with the Prime Minister Leon Kozłowski. This dignitary was known for his simple and direct communication style. Seeing the aviators he said: "So, you two dear fellows, made a transatlantic flight as easily as anything, yes? Simply head-on, out and over the water? Two fools in the sky? Yes?" — "Yes! Just as you say, Mr. Prime Minister, two fools in the sky" — Ben replied straight away. A pleasant, friendly, and laughter-filled conversation followed.

The same day the brothers laid a wreath at the Monument of the Aviator. The military honor guard and officials of both the civil and the military aviation ministries were present. Soon after, the brothers went to the American Embassy for a reception celebrating American Independence — it was the Fourth of July! The reception was attended by the diplomatic corps, Polish VIPs guests and Americans working or studying in Poland. Later that day, the Polish Aero Club hosted a banquet in honor of the brothers at the Hotel Bristol. The elite of Polish fliers, as well as city, state, and military officials were present.

<u>Thursday, July 5th</u>. In the morning, the brothers were invited to the League of Air and Gas Defense, where they were welcomed by the League's Chairman, General Leon Berbecki, accompanied by members of the Board. The General informed the brothers that Poland, and his organization in particular, desired to buy the Bellanca and that a committee raising funds for the purchase had already been established. Ben mentioned the price: $22,000 — a large sum, but the hosts expected to raise enough money. Immediately after this meeting, the brothers went to the Powązki cemetery accompanied by many airmen, as well as state and military officials, where they laid wreaths on the graves of three brave aviators that perished in air crashes: Idzikowski, Żwirko, and Wigura.

For lunch they were invited by the Board of the Association of Poles Abroad, with its Chair, Stefan Lenartowicz. In the afternoon they toured Warsaw by car, and then were taken to dine with Polish civilian and military pilots at the "Oaza" Restaurant. In the evening they were hosted by Ambassador Cudahy in his private residence. Late at night they were driven to the Summer Theatre ("Teatr Letni") where the best seats in the house were reserved for them. They listened to a welcome speech by the Manager, Bolesław Górczyński, and then watched a play. But this was not the end of this day! From the theatre they headed to the studios of the Polish Radio. After being welcomed by the General Director, Zygmunt Chamiec, they made a live broadcast to American Polonia.

Figure 36: Ben and Joseph decorated with the Cavalier Cross of the Order of "Polonia Restituta" by the Minister of Transportation, Michał Butkiewicz (first from the left). From Adamowicz, *Przez Atlantyk*, 1934.

Figure 37: The brothers' Polish Air Force crosses, given to Lanny Kemmis; Photo by L. Kemmis sent to Maureen Mroczek Morris.

<u>Friday, July 6th</u>. In the morning the brothers watched news clips made by Fox Films of their departure from Paris. "We had a lot of fun, looking at ourselves and listening to Ben's speech, because everything was as it really happened" recalled Joe. The rest of the day was devoted to the Polish Air Force. In the company of tireless Captain Dąbrowski, the brothers went to the Okęcie airport and were guests of the 1st Air Division. They were greeted by the commander, Colonel Władysław Kalkus who, in front of distinguished guests and in the presence of the whole officers' core, decorated them with honorary medals usually reserved for distinguished Polish Pilots. The orchestra played the national anthem, while an entire division of the military marched by. Then Colonel Kalkus showed the brothers aircraft, hangars, sleeping quarters, and even the kitchen of the facility. In the modern kitchen they were served a typical soup from a soldiers' canteen, the precursor to a full banquet. Among the guests was Major Skarżyński, conqueror of the South Atlantic.

<u>Saturday, July 7th</u>. The first order of the day was a meeting with delegates of the Polish Touring Club who gave the brothers honorary medals with the insignia of their organization. Then it was off to Pola Mokotowskie airport to check on the Bellanca which they hadn't seen for almost a week. "We looked at her with pride and affection"[26] said Joe. "If not for her, we would have achieved nothing. Expert mechanics fixed the tank and the leaky gas line that gave us so much trouble" he added.

In the afternoon, in the movie-theater "Światowid" they watched a news reel of their departure from Paris. The public applauded and asked for autographs. At 6:00 p.m. they attended the opening of a revue *Two Victorious Adamowiczes*, staged especially in their honor in the Theatre "Mignon." The show was

---

[26] We refer to the Bellanca as "her" because in Polish, names ending with "a" signify the feminine gender. The Adamowiczes used the form "she" when referring to their plane, even though the Polish noun for "plane" is masculine.

performed twice daily for weeks afterwards. At 8:00 p.m. they enjoyed a concert of classical music by members of the Warsaw Philharmonic Orchestra in the main chamber of City Hall – probably their first such concert. At 10:00 p.m. they made a brief appearance at a dance at the Officers' Yacht Club on the Vistula. Again, the day was long; there remained a session of wine tasting at the winery of "Simon and Stecki."

<u>Sunday, July 8th</u>. Joe and Ben went to Mass at a nearby church, then met for the first time the writer and journalist Stanisław Strumph-Wojtkiewicz the man who penned their story; they had several more meetings with him in the days that followed. Later during the day they visited the notorious Cytadela Penal Complex, a place of imprisonment and execution of many Polish patriots at the hands of the Russians who occupied Warsaw in the 19th century. Then, it was off to an orphanage, where 200 cakes were distributed to the orphans. Next, they attended a picnic, a fundraiser for the Poles in Gdańsk. Polish-German conflicts in this port city had been escalating. The Polish minority was persecuted and subjected to unrelenting vexations, including job discrimination, disruption of the food supply, and sabotaged communication. Poles tried to help their compatriots in Gdańsk, and hence such fundraisers.

During the next week the brothers spent many hours talking to Strumph-Wojtkiewicz who was hastily scribbling their story for publication in a newspaper (later issued in book format). But the central event of that week was a visit with Poland's President, Professor Ignacy Mościcki. This took place in the Royal Castle, the residence and office of the President, on Tuesday, July 10th at 10:00 a.m. The Adamowiczes, as American citizens, were accompanied by the American Ambassador John Cudahy. The President allotted considerable time for them, conversing politely and warmly, asking many questions about their preparations for the flight and its course, as well as queries about the life of Poles in America. "He profoundly moved our hearts by his gentleness and intelligence" — reported Joe.

On Wednesday, July 11th, the brothers met with the Vice-Chair of the Polish-American Chamber of Commerce, Stanisław Arct. On Thursday, July 12th, besides giving hours of interviews to Strumph-Wojtkiewicz, Joe and Ben shopped for souvenirs, accompanied by their ever-present chaperons – Polish officers.

Figure 38: Bolesław (Ben) Adamowicz with wife Elizabeth before flying to Poland. From Adamowicz and Adamowicz, *Przez Atlantyk*, 1934.

On Friday, July 13th, the Minister of Transportation, Michał Butkiewicz, honored both brothers with a prestigious Polish distinction, a Cavalier Cross of the Order of Resurrected Poland (Polonia Restituta), Class IV. The ceremony took place at the Ministry and was attended by many high ranking government and military officials. Joe later told Strumph-Wojtkiewicz:

> "In his speech the Minister, who is also the chief of the Polish civilian aviation corps, spoke about our great merits. But we didn't feel that we had any special merits. Anybody who can set for themselves a purpose can achieve it by staying on course, making a good plan, and having a touch of luck."

The same day, the brothers visited the headquarters of the Polish Savings Bank (PKO). They were shown around by the Chief Executive Officer, Dr. Henryk Gruber. Joe already had an account in this bank with a balance of $1,700 (he deposited one of the gifts received in Warsaw). Dr. Gruber presented a checkbook to Ben with a matching sum, $1,700 [27] as a souvenir of their visit to the bank and wished them "constant growth of their savings." [28]

The last, pleasant touch to the brothers' stay in Warsaw was the arrival of Ben's wife, Elizabeth Mattke Adamowicz. She journeyed from New York on board of the American ship *Washington* to Le Havre in France. From there by train she reached Paris, and from Paris to Warsaw she travelled by a French passenger plane. In the following days she accompanied the brothers during their triumphant tour of Poland.

---

[27] *Ilustrowany Kurjer Codzienny*, July 15, 1934.
[28] *Gazeta Polska*, July 14, 1934.

CHAPTER 19
THE TOUR OF POLAND

From the very beginning of their visit, the brothers planned to visit several cities (Kraków, Lwów, and Wilno) as well as their birthplace, Janowszczyna, which at that time was under Soviet rule. They also planned to make pilgrimages to the shrines of the Virgin Mary in Częstochowa's Jasna Góra and in Wilno's Ostra Brama "to give thanks for a safe and happy journey."[1] The news about their planned trip to Częstochowa inspired impostors.

Two con artists and opportunists dressed in aviators' flying suites and at the shrine collected money, telling unsuspecting donors that the contributions were for Poland to purchase the Bellanca. Many naïve pilgrims were duped before police cut short the scam and arrested the impostors.

Figure 39: The brothers visiting the PKO Bank in Warsaw. From Adamowicz and Adamowicz, *Przez Atlantyk*, 1934.

Goniec Częstochowski, a newspaper that followed the brother's steps in Poland, in an article titled "The Adamowiczes fly around Poland: When will the heroic fliers

---
[1]*Ilustrowany Kurjer Codzienny*, July 6, 1934.

arrive in Częstochowa?"[2] included the brothers' travel itinerary:

> "Saturday, July 14th: In the morning the Adamowiczes will depart from Warsaw to start their tour of Poland. The Bellanca 'Warsaw' will leave Warsaw's Okęcie airport at 10:00 a.m., destination Inowrocław, where the Aero Club of Kujawy will organize an air show. Below, the readers will find a detailed itinerary of their scheduled arrival in other cities."

According to the article they planned to visit: Poznań, Łódź, Bydgoszcz, Gdynia, Grudziądz, Płock, Wilno, Lublin, Kraków, Katowice, and Częstochowa before their return to Warsaw. "The flight is organized and sponsored by the League of Air Defense and the Polish Aero Club. The brothers will be accompanied by Captain Dąbrowski and journalist Kupajło." The huge gas tank, installed in the Bellanca's fuselage for the transatlantic flight was removed and replaced by four additional seats, allowing seating for six.

This was the plan. But fate intervened. First, the Bellanca was damaged in Inowrocław, and, second, there was a massive flood in August of 1934 that was particularly destructive in the southern part of Poland; travelling there was impossible.

Inowrocław was the first planned stop. A three-day air show (July 14-16, 1934) at the newly-built civilian airport included a rally of planes from all over Poland, an air acrobatics show, a display of planes on the airfield for the public's pleasure, and an air race. Several dozen machines took part, including the famous RWDs. The brothers, with Mrs. Elizabeth Adamowicz, Captain Dąbrowski and M. Kupajło, arrived in Inowrocław from Warsaw in a three-engine passenger plane – a Fokker belonging to LOT Polish Airlines; the Bellanca was flown to Inowrocław by a professional pilot from the Polish Aero Club. Unfortunately, he

---

[2]*Goniec Częstochowski*, July 14, 1934.

damaged the landing gear of the Bellanca during the landing. The plane that had crossed the Atlantic could not participate in the air show and air race. But the Adamowicz brothers took up positions next to their grounded plane, greeting pilots and thousands of spectators, shaking hands, posing for photos, and signing autographs. People cheered and wildly applauded the "transatlantic heroes."

Figure 40: Bellanca before its takeoff from Warsaw to Inowrocław.

From Inowrocław, the Adamowicz party was flown by LOT's Fokker to Poznań while their Bellanca underwent repairs. There was an official welcome ceremony, a parade through the city by car, and a reception at City Hall. Afterwards, a famous globetrotter, Count Stanisław Mycielski, invited Joe and Ben to his palace in Mycielin, stopping en route in Gniezno, the first medieval capital of Poland in the 10th and 11th centuries. In the evening they returned to Poznań.

Because the Bellanca was not yet ready, the brothers were then flown from Poznań to Łódź. The attentive *Goniec Częstochowski* reported:

> "As announced, the heroic transatlantic fliers, brothers Joe and Ben Adamowicz, landed at the Lublinek airport near Łódź, July 17, at 11:30 a.m.. The awaiting crowd grabbed them at the doors of the airplane, carrying them on their shoulders to a hangar where a welcome ceremony took place. Colonel Rotarski, representing the Łódź Aero Club, and an official representing the city, delivered speeches and presented bouquets. They were taken by a flower-strewn car to City Hall, through the main streets of the city. In the ceremonial hall they were welcomed and asked to sign the City's memorial book. On the balcony of City Hall they spoke to an enthusiastic and adoring throng. Next, they had dinner, hosted by the Łódź Aero Club and soon after another banquet in the 'Tivoli' Restaurant. They spent the night at the Grand Hotel."[3]

Such scenarios of their visits, with only slight differences, were repeated in every city on their tour. Large, enthusiastic crowds, clusters of civilian and military officials, aviators, clergy, and children welcomed them, applauded and cheered. They were driven through cities in open cars decorated with flowers; bouquets were hurled at them. They were received by prominent civilian authorities of the cities and the local commanders of military garrisons and air squadrons. They were invited to dinners, banquets, and receptions. They listened to innumerable speeches and toasts praising their hard work, skill, courage, and patriotism. The brothers, still overwhelmed by all the attention, smiled, nodded, and responded in their broken, Americanized Polish with traces of the characteristic accent of the eastern provinces of Poland.

---

[3] *Goniec Częstochowski*, July 19, 1934.

Captain Dąbrowski and Editor Kupajło accompanied them on this part of their journey, and Ben's wife Elizabeth joined them for major events. Major Skarżyński was particularly attentive.

Figure 41: The Adamowicz brothers with Major Stanisław Skarżyński, the first Polish pilot to cross the Atlantic in a solo flight.
From *Polska Lotnicza*, 1937.

After the visit to Łódź, which concluded with a farewell ceremony at the airport, Joe and Ben were flown by charted plane (LOT Polish Airlines) to Bydgoszcz. "The Adamowicz Brothers arrived in Bydgoszcz at 2:45 p.m. At the moment the immense LOT Fokker landed, the multitude that had gathered at the airport heaved like an oceanic wave towards the plane, shouting and waving. The heroes appeared at the plane's door and were immediately greeted by three children (Krysia and Renia Słojewskie, and the son of deceased Captain Żwirko) who presented them with red and white roses.

The Mayor of Bydgoszcz, Mr. Barciszewski, delivered a moving speech, followed by the commander of Bydgoszcz's Air Division, Colonel Pomazański. Next spoke County Deputy Executive, Father Musiał on behalf of the clergy. Representatives of the local administration, the army, and fliers associations were present. Amidst endless shouting and clapping, the heroes were led to a hangar where they enjoyed lunch prepared by the local chapter of the Air Defense League."[4]

By this time, the Bellanca's landing gear had been repaired. A pilot from the Inowrocław Aero Club flew her to Bydgoszcz. Major Skarżyński arrived. After the tour of the city and a series of banquets, the Bellanca, piloted by Ben, with five passengers (Ben, Joe, Elizabeth, Major Skarżyński, Captain Dąbrowski, and Editor Kupajło) flew to Gdynia. They arrived at the airport of Rumia near Gdynia on July 19, at 11:30 a.m. The sojourn at the Polish seashore was to last until July 23.

Visits to tourist attractions and official events were planned. The guests were driven via a picturesque road through Karwia, Jastrzębia Góra and Jastarnia to the tip of the Hel peninsula, and back to Wejherowo, where they were greeted in the beautiful Kaszubian dialect characteristic of the region.

The official welcome ceremony took place in Gdańsk, a location with political significance: The "Free City of Gdańsk"[5]

---

[4] *Ilustrowany Kurjer Codzienny*, July 19, 1934.
[5] The "Free City of Gdańsk" existed from 1919 until 1939. It was created by the Versailles Peace Treaty. From the 10th until the 18th century Gdańsk was a Polish city, and later was under Prussian/German administration. In the 1930s the population was about 90% German and about 10% Polish. Since the election of the NSDAP (Hitler's

under German pressure, showed its defiance to foreign interference by an especially vociferous acknowledgment of the achievement of the *Polish*-born aviators.

From Gdańsk the visitors' party went to Gdynia, a newly-built Polish city and port. While there, Joe and Ben briefly boarded the Polish transatlantic ship *Puławski* which was about to set sail for New York. They gave the captain a letter to deliver to American Polonia, noting in their comments Poland's beauty, and expressing admiration for how quickly Poland shook off the yoke of foreign domination (Russia, Germany and Austria) and recovered from the devastation of the war (World War I). After a short visit on the deck of the *Puławski* the brothers boarded the navy ship *Gdańsk* and sailed to the Hel Peninsula.

Hel, a resort and naval base, prepared for them yet another warm welcome and bestowed on them honorary citizenship. The next stop was Puck, where they called upon the Navy Air Division and received Navy Pilots Medals. From Puck they went to Gdynia and from there they flew their Bellanca to Grudziądz, where again they were received enthusiastically. A photograph of their passage through the city of Gdańsk is typical of pictures of the Adamowiczes in Poland. We see an open car decorated with garlands and flowers. In the back seat are Ben, Elizabeth, and Joe. On both sides and in the background there is a huge crowd of cheering, smiling, and jubilant people crowding the sidewalks. From Grudziądz the Adamowicz brothers flew back to Warsaw.

On August 1st another dream was realized: Joe, Ben and Elizabeth travelled by train to Częstochowa to the shrine of the "Black Madonna" at Jasna Góra. They gave thanks to the Virgin, Queen of Poland, for their safe crossing of the Atlantic. After praying before the miraculous shrine, they visited the monastery complex guided by some of the Paulist priests in-residence there.

---

party) in 1933, German pressure on Gdańsk mounted steadily.

They were treated to a simple monks' dinner and in the evening they returned to Warsaw by train.

Figure 42: The brothers driven through the streets of Grudziądz. On the back seat – Ben, Elizabeth, and Joseph.

As mentioned above, a flood that ravaged Poland in 1934 changed the Adamowiczes' scheduled itinerary. Instead of heading immediately south, where the flood was most severe and the damage extensive, they flew north, to Wilno.

Press announcements of their visit claimed (inaccurately) that Wilno was "their birthplace and home city," that "Ben "went to primary school in Wilno, and Joe to high school there."[6] We don't know if the brothers deliberately embellished their story for the sake of the local media; but what we do know is that they characteristically varied their biographies when talking with both the American and Polish press. Did they think that it was more impressive to be born in Wilno than in Janowszczyzna? Or was it the Warsaw newsmen who exaggerated and embellished the facts? The Wilno reporters were not sticklers: "Do we need birth

---

[6] *Kurjer Warszawski*, July 6, 1934. This entry is far from the truth.

certificates to testify to their belonging to our land? Does their deed not speak for itself? They achieved their goal with the determination and tenacity of a Wilno native. That is enough. Without doubt they are blood from our blood, bone from our bone, and flesh from our flesh."[7] The heroes flew to Wilno not on their Bellanca but on a LOT passenger plane (the flight was delayed by fog).[8] Mrs. Adamowicz was with them, along with Lieutenant Dzięciołowski. At the Porubanek airport near Wilno, as many times before, a crowd was waiting. Among the hosts was General Lucjan Żeligowski, the most important political figure in the province of Wilno,[9] civilian and military dignitaries, clergymen, journalists, school children and ordinary people. Father Paczkowski, pastor of Olkowicze where the brothers were baptized, brought a box filled with soil from their home place as a memento of their visit.

General Żeligowski was first at the door to greet Joe and Ben in Wilno. There were speeches, shouts of "Long live the conquerors of the Atlantic," and showers of bouquets. A military band played. The motorcade stopped at the Ostra Brama Gate, home of the miraculous image of the Virgin Mary. The brothers got out of the car and walked through the gate. They knelt on the pavement and prayed for a long time. The Ostra Brama Gate is the entryway to a medieval fortification of the city with thick, double walls. A street passes through the gate. The image of the Blessed Virgin is in the chapel high over the gate. Escorted by the clergy, the brothers climbed the stairs to the chapel and

---

[7] *Kurjer Wileński*, July 25, 1934.
[8] In 1934 LOT Polish Airlines LOT had a network of both domestic and international connections.
[9] General Lucian Żeligowski, directed by Józef Piłsudski, incorporated Wilno and surrounding lands to Poland in 1920; until 1795 these territories belonged to the Republic of Both Nations (Poland and Lithuania.) In the 1920s General Żeligowski held various high posts in the army and government. In 1927, he retired, but still played an important role in politics, though behind the scenes.

prayed again. Then, they returned to the car and drove to the city center. They were lodged at the Hotel George.

After a short rest in the company of Mrs. Adamowicz and Lieutenant Dzięciołowski, there began a long series of official visits: at the Provincial ("Województwo") Government Office, at City Hall, and at the headquarters of the Wilno garrison. Later they were received by Archbishop Romuald Jabłrzykowski. In the afternoon and evening they enjoyed a quick lunch, dinner, and banquet. Again, there were dozens of speeches and toasts to the victorious Adamowicz brothers. A honored guest, Commander of the 5th Air Division, Colonel Wacław Iwaszkiewicz, said: "The Adamowicz brothers' triumph did a lot for Polish aviation. We have our own air fleet and air industry, and we wrote quite a few proud chapters in aviation history, but the transatlantic flight of these Polish airmen significantly enhanced the prestige of Polish aviation."[10]

It its quite clear that the highest Polish authorities, both civilian and military, wanted to exploit the Adamowiczes' achievement "to enhance the prestige of Polish aviation," and indeed Poland itself. This was the main reason that their visit was celebrated so lavishly and with such pomp – for political and economic gain. The Polish government, observing the public response to the brothers (massive crowds at the airports and on the streets; the expressions of love, admiration, and pride), was more than happy to accommodate. This was an unusual instance in the history of Poland when the government was truly responsive to the populace, and the population as a whole fully approved of the authorities' moves and decisions. The Adamowiczes were the catalysts of this phenomenon.

---

[10] Based on: Z. Kalicińska, "Impresje z obiadu i rozmowy z Adamowiczami" [Impressions from the dinner and a chat with the Adamowiczes.] *Kurjer Wileński*, July 26, 1934.

In the afternoon they were invited by the City Council for a reception, and in the evening they were hosted at the Theatre "Lutnia" where actor and manager Karol Wyrwicz-Wichrowski welcomed them before show time. The audience and actors applauded the brothers after the curtain dropped.

The next day, July 26, they were driven to a glider factory in Grzegorzewo. Warsaw, the Baltic Seashore, the central Poland fly-over with city-stops... these were already memories. Now the Wilno region and its attractions were showcased – beautiful scenery and landscapes at every turn in the road. When Joe and Ben returned from Grzegorzewo there was time for dinner followed by a banquet thrown by the Wilno Aero Club. Then it was back to Warsaw by express train in a luxury sleeping car.

After the flood waters subsided the brothers headed south to Kraków (September 10-12) and to Silesia — Katowice, Chorzów, Nikiszowiec — September 13-16). Repeated was the now familiar program: welcome ceremonies, car parades through city centers, applause from the crowds, official meetings, dinners, and banquets, speeches, interviews, and autograph sessions.

Figure 43: The brothers with their Bellanca. *Lotnictwo z Szachownicą,* 31.

CHAPTER 20

THE POLONIA CONGRESS IN WARSAW

The World Congress of Polonia (Poles and their descendants living abroad) took pace in Warsaw August 6-9, 1934.[11] Polonia is the Latin word for Poland. The term Polonia refers to Poles, Polish people, and Polish communities living abroad.

The timing of the Polonia Conference happened to coincide with the brothers' stay in Poland. Joe and Ben were invited to the Congress as honorary guests. It was attended by official delegations from 22 countries, and thousands of Poles traveled individually or in groups from all over the world to the conference. Additionally, a subsidiary of the Congress, the First World Rally of Polish Youth[12] convened at the same time, bringing to the Old Country students, workers, farmers, athletes, and Boy Scouts. About 10,000 Polonians visited Poland that summer.

Warsaw was decorated with flags, garlands, and banners. There were military parades and marching bands. Ancillary activities were sponsored by the Congress such as sports activities and special expositions, e.g., "Polish Life in the Arts," "Monuments of Polish Craft," and others. Both the Polish and foreign press wrote extensively about the convention.[13]

Several feature-length articles covered not only the meeting but delineated the centuries of contributions of Polonia to the construction and development of many countries. The names of

---

[11] The official Polish name of the Congress was "Ogólnoświatowy Zjazd Polaków z Zagranicy."
[12] In Polish: I Zlot Młodzieży Polskiej z Zagranicy.
[13] *New York Times*, August 11, 1934.

Poles living and working abroad were recalled, not only famous military men such as Tadeusz Kościuszko (1746-1817) and Kazimierz Pułaski (1745-1779), but also great scholars such as Ignacy Domeyko (1802-1889), geographer and geologist, and organizer of higher education in Chile, and Marie Skłodowska-Curie (1867-1934), chemist and physicist, two-time Nobel Prize winner. Mentioned as well were famous artists, such as Helena Modrzejewska (Modjeska, 1840-1909), Kraków's and Warsaw's internationally renowned tragedian, considered the best American actress in the 1880s; and engineers, such as Modjeska's son, Ralph Modjeski (1861-1940), railroad and bridge builder in America.

To provide some context for the Adamowicz brothers' reception in Poland, below is brief description of the Congress and some historical context. Joe and Ben's appearance at the conference dovetailed perfectly with the purposes of the Congress and the ambitions of the Polish government at that time.

The economic, political, and cultural situation of Poles living abroad provided many topics for discussion at the Congress. Presenters analyzed the relationship between Polonia and Poland, and the role of emigration and its impact on Poland.[14] There was considerable talk about Poland's status as a world power and about the intellectual and economic potential of émigrés with ties to their mother-county. Most attractive to Poland was America's Polonia — large and with considerable economic and political clout, as well as military might, as demonstrated during World War I. American Polonians were aware of their significance thanks to the organizational work and publications of its many

---

[14]Ks. B. Rosiński: "Zagadnienia emigracyjne w Ameryce Północnej," *Gazeta Polska*, August 5, 1934; R.K. [initials only]: "Przez wczoraj i dziś". *Gazeta Polska*, August 7, 1934; A. Janta-Połczyński, "Polacy zza granic Polski," *Gazeta Polska*, August 7, 1934.

activists, among them Mieczysław Haiman,[15] member and leader of the Polish Falcons.[16]

Polish Americans had been meticulously preserving memories of Poland, the homeland they left due to political persecution or unbearable poverty. In the 1890s, American Polonia toyed with the concept of a Polish homeland in the state of Illinois and to there declare a new and independent Poland – this because their native land was partitioned and under the yoke of foreigners – Russia, Prussia/Germany, and Austria. Land purchased in Illinois would be a "fourth Poland," a Poland free of bondage. This "fourth Poland" would preserve Polish traditions and values, give hope to Poles in the three partitions, support European Poles politically and economically, and help fettered Poles to free themselves. The idea of formally creating an independent Poland in America was a utopian one and, as we know, never realized.

Capitalizing on Polonians' love of homeland, Ignacy Paderewski (1860-1941), internationally recognized pianist and composer, spearheaded an endeavor during WWI to politically unify American Polonia. As its leader, Paderewski became advisor for Polish Affairs to President Woodrow Wilson; he

---

[15] Mieczysław Haiman (1888-1949),whose poem of 1928 is the motto to this book. He was an émigré from Poland to America where he arrived in 1913. He was the first historian of American Polonia, author of books and brochures about the history of Poles in North America, e.g., *Z przeszłości polskiej w Ameryce* [*From the Polish Past in America*](Buffalo 1927), *Polacy wśród pionierów Ameryki* [*Poles Among American Pioneers*](Chicago 1930), *Polacy w Ameryce. Historia wychodźtwa polskiego w Stanach Zjednoczonych* [*Poles in America. History of Polish Immigration to the United States*] (Chicago 1930.) Haiman was also publisher and editor of Polish newspapers and creator of the Polish museum in Chicago.

[16] "Sokół" [*Falcon*]— Związek Sokolstwa Polskiego was created in Lwów in 1867, and it quickly spread throughout Poland, in all three partitions, having both legal and illegal (underground) structures. Its mission was to free Poland from foreign rule. Since 1894, "Sokolonie" (units of "Sokół") started to spring up in the USA. They became a significant political force. They provided many recruits/volunteers to the Polish Kościuszko Army, organized in the 1910s. In English, known as Polish Falcons.

persuaded Wilson to plea for Poland's resurrection post WW I and for the establishment of just borders that would give Poland access to the sea. This was part of his Peace Plan, announced on January 8, 1918.[17]

Figure 44: Ben and Joe with their Bellanca in Warsaw, 1934.

Calling on the patriotism of American Polonia, Paderewski organized the "Kościuszko Army" in America. This force, 22,000 strong, sailed to the European theatre of war in May 1918. In August that same year, the Polish National Committee (Komitet Narodowy Polski), with Roman Dmowski at its helm and

---

[17] The famous Point 13 about Poland's independence.

Paderewski as the representative of American Polonia, appointed General Józef Haller as the commander. Later the Kościuszko Army was called "Haller's Army" (Armia Hallera) or the "Blue Army" (Armia Błękitna) because its soldiers wore blue French uniforms.

News about the arrival on the western front of this fighting force resulted in mass military desertions of ethnic Poles who had been conscripted from the Polish provinces to fight in the German and Austrian armies. Likewise, Poles who were prisoners of war of the Allies (because they were conscripted by their foreign overseers) clambered to join the "Kościuszko Army." Ultimately this Polish fighting force numbered 80,000 men; fought bravely on battlefields, and secured Poland's place at the WWI Victory Parade in 1918. However, the opposite occurred in 1945, when Great Britain and America appeased Stalin and betrayed Poland at the Yalta Conference; as a result, Poland, the most faithful ally of America in WWII, was denied its rightful place in the Victory Parade.

The Kościuszko Army in Poland played a decisive role in the Polish-Bolshevik war of 1920 – but this fact was subsequently underplayed because its role conflicted with the mythology of Piłsudski and his Legions, credited by the Marshal's followers with regaining Poland's independence. To make matters worse, the veterans of Paderewski's Polish army, as well as the families of deceased veterans, were unfairly treated by the Polish government which refused to pay them pensions under the pretext that they were American citizens or lived in America. This created a rift between the Polish government and Polish émigrés in America in the 1920s. As Piłsudski faded from the scene (he died in 1935), the government tried to mend the rift and ease friction between American Polonia and Poland, recognizing that American Polonia had great potential to enhance the status of

Poland. Building bridges between "Polonia" and Poland was loudly celebrated at the Polonia Congress, with the American delegation at its center. Harmonious relations were considered an investment in the future of Poland.

The Congress was held in the Polish Parliament building, a sign of its significance in the minds of the government. Members of the government, including Minister of Foreign Affairs, Józef Beck, heads of the Senate and the House (Sejm), as well as the Primate of the Catholic Church and the Patriarch of the Orthodox Church were on hand for the proceedings of the Congress. Also in attendance were luminaries of the world of culture and business. The President of Poland, Ignacy Mościcki visited the Congress on opening day. Marshal Piłsudski (gravely ill) sent a letter.

The Congress was chaired by Franciszek Świetlik from the USA to acknowledge the significance of American Polonia. At the working sessions, representatives of the Polish government and Polonia delegates spoke in turn. The main topic of the Congress was Polish unity, cooperation and mutual support in the domains of politics, economics, culture, and education.

Delegates from abroad vividly debated Polonia's relationship with the Polish government, i.e., should Polonians be dependent on the Polish government? The delegates, led by the American delegation, concurred in their conviction that Polonians should be fully loyal to their new countries and have no formal ties to the Polish government. At the same time, they should support and defend the interests of the Old Country.

Brothers Joseph and Benjamin Adamowicz epitomized this ideal in the views of many, because 1) they were of Polish-born; and 2) they were successful American citizens with Polish loyalties. Moreover, they were aviators, which placed them in an elite class. Their transatlantic flight from America to Poland demonstrated courage, industriousness, vision, and love of their motherland.

Both brothers spoke at the Congress and their addresses were welcomed with applause.

Figure 45: Greetings from the pilots to the Polish children, published in the Polish children's magazine *Płomyczek* [Little Flame], Warsaw, 9 July 1934.

CHAPTER 21

IN THEIR BIRTHPLACE

From the Polish perspective, "Bolshevia," as the Soviet Union was called, did not cease to be a major threat to Poland's independence even after it was defeated in the war of 1920, and before the Polish government and Polish citizens knew the scope of the crimes committed by Stalin and his terror apparatus. Poles were not aware at this time of Stalin's long-term plans to conquer Europe, "over Poland's cadaver" as Mikhail Tuchatchevsky put it when the Soviet forces attacked Poland in 1920. Few realized that Stalin's objective was to extend his rule over the whole of Europe and then over the whole globe. They did not foresee the dual Soviet-German aggression towards Poland in 1939, nor the post-war annexation of half of Polish territory, the Katyń massacre of thousands of Polish officers; the deportation of thousands to Siberia, and the complete subjugation of Poland to Communist rule from 1945 until 1989.

From the Soviet perspective Poland was an "imperialist" state with a "bourgeois" system. It was a "country of masters," while "impoverished masses" suffered injustice. For the Soviets, Poland was a "mortal enemy." The annihilation of Poland was the highest Soviet objective and had been planned for years. Revenge for the humiliating defeat of the Red Army by Polish forces in 1920 was a significant factor in Soviet foreign policy.

At the same time, in the early 1930s, the relationship on the surface between Poland and the Soviet Union was trending towards normalization in the political, diplomatic, economic and cultural spheres. A three-year non-aggression pact was signed in 1932. It was extended to ten years on May 9, 1934. Thus, it was binding until May 9, 1944. However, the Soviets attacked Poland on September 17, 1939.) In the summer of 1934, negotiations over the Soviet Union's acceptance into the League of Nations were finalized; the Soviets were accepted by this body on September 18, 1934. They were expelled after the aggression on Poland.

In this climate of "normalization," Poland and the Soviet Union had been exchanging official civilian and military delegations. For example, during the Adamowiczes' stay in Poland, a squadron of three Tupolev ANT-9 planes came to Warsaw on July 28, 1934. The ANT-9 was a very large four-engine transport machine, able to carry numerous troops. Commanders of the Polish Air Force with General Rayski and Soviet diplomats with Ambassador Davitian welcomed them. (As it turned out, the Soviets used occasions such as these to spy on Poland.) It is not surprising that in this apparently friendly climate the Adamowiczes' trip to their birthplace (in 1934, on Soviet territory) was possible. In mid-August the press announced: "Polish transatlantic flyers, the Adamowicz brothers, have been invited by the 'Inturist' Agency to the Soviet Union as guests of Soviet civilian aviation authorities. The Adamowicz brothers accepted the invitation and will depart for Moscow next week. [It was the week of August 20-26, 1934.] Today [August 13] at noon, the Adamowicz brothers were hosted at the Soviet embassy by Consul Podolski and his staff. The Adamowiczes will stay in the Soviet Union about two weeks [August 18 – Sept. 2, 1934]."[18]

From similar press notices we know that the brothers departed from Warsaw by train on August 18. They had a first-class compartment in a sleeping car. They travelled via Wilno to Moscow where they arrived on August 20, and stayed two days,

---

[18]*Polska Zachodnia*, August 13, 1934.

visiting the city. After that they went, also by train, to Mińsk. Beginning August 23, they were hosted by the Polish Consulate, which provided the brothers with a car and a driver to visit their birthplace, Janowszczyzna, Krajsk (where they attended school), and other towns in the region. We were not able to find any details about this leg of their travels. The brothers' Soviet sojourns were not highly publicized — either in Poland or in "Bolshevia."

We only can imagine how moved they must have been to see places and landscapes from their childhood. We can only speculate about what they talked about with their former neighbors who were now Soviet citizens. We can presume how unhappy the brothers were to see the devastation of villages and towns, and the poverty of the people. Whether the brothers were even allowed to speak with locals we cannot ascertain. They were at all times supervised and controlled by their Soviet hosts. We did not find any interviews or memoires of that visit. Perhaps the brothers had to sign a commitment, presented to them by the Soviets, to refrain from talking publicly. There may have been a political agreement between the governments of Poland and Russia. In any case, there is little record of this side-trip.

We do not know for certain what Joseph, Benjamin and Mrs. Adamowicz did in the first part of September, beyond visiting Kraków and Silesia. They remained guests of the Polish Aero Club and, when not traveling, stayed at the Europejski Hotel in Warsaw. Joseph might have looked for a Polish wife. Perhaps the brothers were contemplating a permanent move to Poland. In a report from their Wilno visit a journalist wrote that Joe "was thinking about marrying a Polish girl. He was dreaming about a girl from Wilno and about settling down in Wilno."[19] They might have been considering buying a country estate. They continued to negotiate the price of the Bellanca which they definitely wanted to sell in Poland. They told journalists that they wanted to return to America to put their business in order and then settle in Poland for good.

They maintained, more than once, that they came to Warsaw with only a few pennies in their pockets and that they had pawned their soda water factory to get money for the purchase of the Bellanca and the costs of the flight; these were habitual fabrications, as was the price they claimed they paid for the Bellanca — $22,000. Eventually, they signed a contract with the Polish League of Air and Gas Defense for that amount, giving them a nice profit. It was a lot of money and with it they could easily have purchased some real estate in Poland. However, they received only half the agreed-upon price; the other half was to be paid later. They took the down payment with them when they returned to America.

---

[19] Z. Kalicińska, "Impresje z obiadu i rozmowy z Adamowiczami," *Kuriej Wileński*, July 26, 1934.

CHAPTER 22

A "LITTLE MAN" ABOVE THE ATLANTIC

"Little man" is a descriptor frequently used in the 1920s and '30s to describe an average blue-collar, hardworking, down-to-earth man of goodwill and common sense. (The phrase is a double entendre, too, alluding to the short stature of Joe and Ben.) The "little man" ("Gray man,""szary człowiek" in Polish) was considered the salt of the earth and the backbone of society, and these words were used to contrast the "average Joe" with privileged elites, the wealthy and the powerful, and media celebrities. The Adamowicz brothers were routinely described as two "little guys," usually with admiration (but, also, with some not-so-subtle mockery). A novel by German author Hans Fallada (*Little Man, What Now?*)[20] paints the "little man" as brave, industrious, honest, and just. Fallada and others admired the "little man" for his power and dignity.

A Warsaw newspaper[21] published a fragment of an early interview with Ben. The writer perfectly captured Ben's way of talking and his curious vocabulary. It was a "Polish-Brooklyn tongue." (Ben did most of the talking and gave most of the interviews and speeches. Joe generally took a back seat.) Ben's distinctive accent marked him as a man from eastern Poland. Let's listen:

"How it was after the takeoff?"

"We went up and piloted in turns."

---

[20] Hans Fallada (born Rudolf Ditzen), *Little Man, What Now? (Kleiner Mann, was nun?)*, 1932.

[21] *Kurjer Warszawski*, July 3. No name of the interviewer. This interview was also used in other newspapers.

"Did you see any ships from above?"
"Six."
"Did they see you?"
"Who knows? After nineteen hours we saw an island. We went down to 2000 feet. Fog and more fog. We went five hours more. Suddenly a hole in the fog. We saw some farms. We looked for a bigger one and went down. At that time the sun was already shining on us.[22]
"Why did you land in Germany?"
"Gas was running away."
"How did the Germans react to your arrival?"
"At first surprised. Then fine."
"Are you going to return to America?"
"Possibly."
"By plane?"
"Sure!"
"Why did you come here?"
"Because we love Poland."
"What did you feel when you landed in Warsaw?"
"We felt very merry."
"What do you like to drink?"
"Beer."

From the moment these two men emerged from the cabin of their airplane and began to talk it was obvious that they were not highly educated or articulate. They were simple ordinary men, reckless dare-devils with ambition. What they said was direct and to the point. They were strong-willed, stubborn and sentimental about their home country.

---

[22] Ben uses an eastern Polish vernacular expression: „W ta pora słońce swieciwszy już w nas."

Crossing the Atlantic in a small one-engine plane was an extraordinary achievement for the mid 1930s, especially for amateurs. The brothers' feat touched the hearts of "little men" (and women) all over Poland and America and elsewhere. The brothers seduced the world press with their simplicity and quirkiness, especially in France where they arrived first, and in America, where they lived. Stories about their take off, in-flight adventures, mid-way landings, and arrival in Warsaw were published in nearly all American newspapers — from New York to California and everywhere in between.[23] Photographs of the two pilots and their machine were ubiquitous. Accounts of their tour of Poland, the incident involving the impersonators in Częstochowa, their visit to their birth place, the sale of the Bellanca, and their plans for the future were in myriad newspapers in both Poland and America.[24] To American reporters the brothers said what they knew would play well, i.e., that they planned to return to their soda factory, pay all their debts, and prepare for a follow-up flight to Poland (this time non-stop).

Stanisław Strumph-Wojtkiewicz wrote an article just after their arrival, stating: "Dear Adamowicz brothers. You are modest, hardworking people with common sense. You could have come to your beloved Old Country in a safe and comfortable fashion – on board a steam-ship. But you chose to fly for the greater glory of Poland. Your flight was rife with challenges. Your passion revealed a quiet heroism and now you are known the world over. We congratulate you and we write about you with admiration. Not only have you shown us the most direct route from America (home of the biggest center of Polish emigration) to your mother-

---

[23] 1934: *New York Times*, June 28; *El Paso Herald-Post*, June 28; *New York Times*, June 29; *Indiana Evening Gazette*, June 29; *New York Times*, July 1, July 2, July 3; *Brooklyn Daily Eagle*," July 2; *The Evening Gazette*, Xenia, Ohio, July 2

[24] *New York Times*, July 15, August 11, September 20

country, you have shown us the potential popularity of flying as a routine means of transportation. Most importantly, and what is of most value, you have shown us the heroism embedded in the hearts of simple, regular guys."[25] In another article, the same author posed a question: "How was this success possible?... By the sheer determination and stubbornness of two simple laborers with patriotic ambition."[26]

Figure 46: The Adamowicz brothers with their plane in Warsaw.

"Aviation did not know them. They did not attend any prestigious flying schools. They were not air force men or civilian professional pilots. They held no military rank. They did not have degrees or titles. They were small-businessmen. That's all. They flew planes in their spare time. They attended to their business and earned their living just like the rest of us. The Adamowiczes'

---

[25] S. Strumph-Wojtkiewicz, *Kurjer Warszawski*, July 3, 1934.
[26] S. Strumph-Wojtkiewicz, *Kartki z prywatnego archiwum 1921-1939*. Warszawa: Książka i Wiedza, 1967, page 191.

achievement has come just in time for Poland and for millions of Poles who have been dreaming about an air record, who have been hungry for a great success." The prevailing image of the Adamowicz brothers was that they were simple men with big dreams and a staunch love of Poland. All true.

So far, we have cited press reports bloated with superlatives: "heroes of the air," "heroic flyers," "true heroes," "quiet heroes," "knights of outer space," "conquerors of the Atlantic," "transatlantic flyers," "brave Polish hearts," and so on. In contrast, particularly in the American press, we encountered a range of pejorative descriptions: "chubby and portly boys," "ordinary men," "accidental flyers," "dilettantes," "amateurs," "duffers," or "bizarre Atlantic aviators."

The brothers, with all their contradictions, are well described in an article, "The Little Man Over the Atlantic."[27]

> "Polish people recognized in these two simply-clad men, in these two rubicund and smiling faces, in these two short and stocky figures — themselves. The saw their reflection in the hard working lives of the Adamowicz brothers. But what set them apart was their dream and their determination to make it a reality. They wanted to be at least half as brave as Lindbergh, Bird, and Kozietulski."[28]

The Adamowicz brothers appealed in a very special way to the feelings, emotions, and the imaginations of average Poles. They were "little men" too and they identified with Joe and Ben.

Because the Adamowiczes were pioneers they were heartily endorsed by a country striving for rapid modernization and

---

[27] *Kurjer Warszawski*, July 3, 1934. An article without a byline.

[28] Jan Kozietulski (1778-1821), Polish Colonel, who led the famous charge of the Polish lancers at the gorge of Somosierra in Spain, ordered by Napoleon Bonaparte; Poland was at that time allied with France, and Polish soldiers fought the "Napoleonic Wars" on the side of the French.

progress. The brothers were held up as role models not only by Poles in the Old Country, but also by Polish émigrés in the new country. The Adamowicz brothers gave Poland and Polonia a sense of national and ethnic pride. Their success was living proof that diligence, perseverance, and courage could pay off, and a reminder that everyone with a dream had a chance of seeing the dream come true. This was the gift bestowed by the Adamowicz brothers. In return, the brothers were rewarded – by ten weeks of celebrity, luxury, respect, admiration, and reverence.

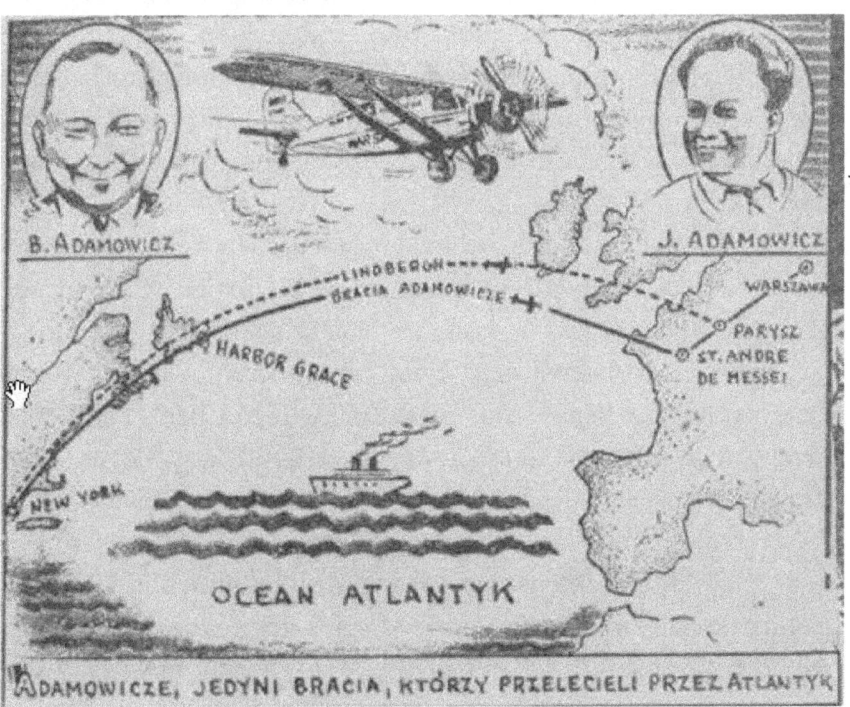

Figure 47: A Polish cartoon of "Adamowiczes, the only brothers that flew across the Atlantic."

CHAPTER 23
RETURN TO AMERICA

Joe, Ben and Elizabeth left Poland on board the passenger ship *Kościuszko* departing from Gdynia on September 17, 1934. Before they set sail a great farewell banquet was thrown by the city of Gdynia. The final three weeks of the Great Adventure (the voyage home) were the last happy days of their lives. They were seated at the Captain's table. They continued to be treated as celebrities, importuned for autographs and photographs. They lounged on the deck of the ship, sun-bathing. They made stops in Copenhagen and Halifax and toured these towns. They "flew high" for the last time in their lives.

The Bellanca was left behind in Poland. In September 1934, it was an attraction at the Air Fair in Katowice. Then it was moved to Świdnik and parked in a hangar at the local air base. It was remodeled to serve as a flying ambulance. Additional seats were installed and space was made for two stretchers. There were reports that after the alterations the aircraft was never really stable.

And what of the Bellanca's fate during the war?[29] There is a photograph on the Internet of a Bellanca that burned in a German air raid on Świdnik. But there is also testimony that the Bellanca landed in Brześć on September 7, 1939. It was reportedly shot but did not crash, falling sometime later into German hands. Some claim to have seen it in Romania. Others say that the Bellanca was seized by the Germans in Świdnik and was flown by them as far as Odessa on the Crimean peninsula in 1943 (at that time in Germans hands). In any case the Bellanca perished

---

[29]http://www.mysliwcy.pl/forum/watki/php?id=490&ustaw=sz&s=6

during the war. The poor, beautiful Bellanca, the pride and joy of the Adamowicz brothers, perished.

The Adamowiczes arrived in New York October 5, 1934. At the port they were welcomed by photo journalists, news reporters, cheering clapping crowds and... to their astonishment, the somber faces of their family. Why?

During their absence, precisely at 4:00 p.m. on September 18, while it was still dark, police and federal agents had raided the soda water factory on 111 Conselyea Street in Brooklyn. A huge alcohol still was uncovered. Who had tipped off the authorities? Prohibition was over, but the government expected its share of revenue for the production and sale of alcohol. The Adamowicz brothers never registered their still, nor paid a dime in taxes. In fact, they denied all knowledge of its very existence.

Thousands of illegal stills were sequestered all over America during Prohibition and doubtless some continued to operate without permits after Prohibition was lifted. Nonetheless, the vast majority of illegal stills produced alcohol on a relatively small scale. In contrast, the Adamowiczes' still was huge and produced alcohol on a commercial scale.

There are several versions of the events that unfolded in October. Some people in Brooklyn claim that the brothers themselves led the authorities to their still by their own reckless disregard and lack of imagination. The mash used for the production of vodka is made of potatoes. Large amounts of wet mash remain after the distillation process. Supposedly, Bruno, Joe and Ben disposed of large quantities of waste-mash by pouring it down the drains of the public sewers[30] in front of their own factory. The accumulation of large amounts of mash in the sewage system on Conselyea St. and its environs generated a strong, distinctive smell. The neighbors complained about the

---

[30] New York City's sewage system (Brooklyn included) was modernized in the 1890s.

odor and called the authorities. "Agents Thornton and Sarlo responded. They too sniffed. They opened the manhole cover of the sewer outside the bottling works, and the odor of alcohol mash nearly knocked them over."[31] The odor led them to the still in the soda factory.

Another story blames a snitch, or snitches, for the discovery of the still. Perhaps someone jealous of the brothers' financial success wanted to destroy their soda-water business. Perhaps there were resentments by bigots in other ethnic or religious groups – people who simply abhorred Poles and Catholics. Alternatively, the phenomenal aviation success of the Adamowicz brothers may have been too much for someone, perhaps even a jealous fellow Pole. After all, two simple laborers cum small businessmen outdid their competitors on a grand scale, achieving international acclaim. An unhappy competitor, a bigot or a jealous compatriot could have pointed the finger at them. Or maybe the "leak" was simply a case of loose lips. A drunken patron of the Speak Easy may have let slip some mention of the thriving business on the second floor of the factory.

Another possibility hints at Mafia involvement. Indeed, the whole illegal business of producing, distributing and selling alcohol likely involved a protection racket. Many, many people knew about the operation on Conselyea Street and someone may have talked out of turn. Perhaps there was an underworld turf war and someone squealed as an act of revenge.

One more hypothesis is that it was Bruno who was responsible for the downfall of the illegal alcohol business. Up until Joe and Ben's departure for Poland, everything had been going smoothly, without incident. Bruno was at the helm, overseeing the production of both soda and hooch, while Joe and Ben were abroad. Perhaps he lacked the expertise to deal

---

[31] *Hearst's International Combined with Cosmopolitan*, August 1935.

effectively with the Mafia. Or, maybe Bruno, hearing about Joe and Ben's kingly reception in Poland, proposed a deal to the Mafia that would bring in more profit – a deal that went sour.

Possibly, all these elements played some role. We will never know. In any case, it seems more than coincidental that Joe and Ben departed from Gdynia on September 17 and the raid at Conselyea Street occurred the next day. One cannot resist the temptation to conclude that someone precisely planned the timing of that raid. It was no secret that Joe and Ben were gone. An informer in Poland could well have sent a cable confirming when Joe and Ben had set sail for their voyage home. The search of the soda plant occurred while Joe and Ben were at sea and thus ignorant of the goings-on in Brooklyn.

The Adamowicz family in Brooklyn gave no forewarning. They could have cabled the brothers. But a telegram would have been received and read by the radio operator of the "Kościuszko" and subsequently the news would have gone public immediately. The relatives chose to not alert Joe and Ben that something was afoot. Perhaps they were warned by the authorities to keep mum. There were short notes in the Brooklyn press about the raid on the factory and the discovery of the illegal still, but at first this news did not make the international press, or most domestic newspapers. All hell broke loose soon after Joe and Ben arrived in New York.

The apparatus for alcohol distillation was found in the garage at the back of the soda factory on Conselyea Street. The capacity of the still was given differently by different sources — from 1,800 gallons to even 10,000 gallons. In any case it was huge. Additionally, there were barrels with fermenting mash on site. Theirs was an efficient large-scale liquor distillery.

The same morning the raid took place, Bruno was arrested when he arrived at work at 9:00 a.m.. Agents were waiting for him. They took him to the police station, interrogated him, and incarcerated him for two weeks. He was again interrogated on October 2, and later released on bail ($3,000). Several employees of the factory were also detained and interrogated, but soon released: Herman Sherman (a plumber, as well as a partner in the soda-water business), Zygmunt Majerowski, Harry Schwarz and Albert Murellas. A certain Mrs. Petronella Baukos, hearing about the raid, went to the police and claimed that the Adamowiczes owed her $2,900 for unpaid rent on her lot abutting the factory. Bruno maintained that he knew nothing about this.

The raid, the arrest of Bruno, and the interrogations had not yet been mentioned in local newspapers when Joe and Ben set foot in New York. They received a hero's welcome at the port and were driven to City Hall where they were feted by Mayor Fiorello La Guardia, a pilot himself. The press published laudatory reports of the event.[32] For a short while more, Joe and Ben were the darlings of New York and world heroes.[33]

Soon, however, news of their illegal still found its way into the headlines of leading newspapers. The heroes of the Atlantic were summoned for interrogation.

---

[32] *New York Times*, October 20, 1934.
[33] The Polish press also reported these events. *Polska Zachodnia*, October 22, 1934.

CHAPTER 24
FACING AMERICAN JUSTICE

The three Adamowicz brothers (Bruno, Joe and Ben) created *their* version of events. All three took the same line of defense: Two weeks before Joe and Ben's departure for Poland, they claimed to have rented part of their factory space to a man named Jack Schwartz, who wanted to produce condensed fruit juices of various flavors. The Adamowiczes needed juices for their flavored soda water and agreed to contract-out juice production to Schwartz. They would buy the juices from him and by keeping production under the same roof they would save money. So they accepted Schwartz's offer – so they said. They claimed total ignorance of *Schwartz's* production of alcohol.

The big problem was that they did not have Schwartz's address. They had no documentation of any rental agreement and no written contract. The space reputedly rented to Schwartz was large. It was a commercial garage at the back of the factory with an independent driveway and entrance from the backyard. To make matters worse for the brothers, the deputy Federal Persecutor Mr. Pearlman, announced that his office interviewed a contractor, John C. Semple, who informed them that months earlier (the press was not specific about the date), at the request of Bruno Adamowicz, Semple installed two steel beams to strengthen the walls and ceiling of the garage. Bruno explained that this was necessary for safety because above the garage was a dance hall and the ceiling was about to collapse. But some heavy parts of the still were suspended from this ceiling.

The prosecutors established that near the main entrance to the garage from the back of the lot there was a hidden entrance, access to which was controlled from the factory office. The door opened only after a bell, operated from the office, alerted occupants of the garage. Hidden electric wires for the door mechanism and the bell led to Bruno's desk. The switch was hidden under the table-top of the desk. A storage space for full and empty bottles of soda-water was on the second floor in the ballroom. This room was cut in half by a wall, hiding the storage area. The wall was masked by shelves and miscellaneous junk that covered the door to the storage space. A camouflaged 20-ton truck was discovered: in this truck the products for the production of alcohol were brought in, and empty bottles transported out. It looked like the other trucks in their fleet, but this particular truck was an empty shell with space inside for hauling crates of alcohol. The truck was found and confiscated by the authorities.

The press was intoxicated by the Adamowicz prosecution. More and more news articles appeared. Joe and Ben were often referred to as the "Polish Lindberghs"[34] — an allusion to Charles Lindbergh's transatlantic feat in 1927. The descriptor was used now with some mockery.

The press articles had a similar structure: praise followed by censure. Joe and Ben were introduced as Lindberg's successors but with a negative twist: The poor fools could not even find Poland even with maps; they had to land three times to reach their goal. Accounts of their triumphant reception in Poland and their statement that they flew "for the glory of Poland," were reported with derision. A note of *Schadenfreude* crept into news accounts. Their still was described as the biggest ever seized by the police. Specifications of this contraption were usually exaggerated, but it was indeed large, even if its capacity was only 2,000 gallons, not as quoted in some articles, 10,000. The value

---

[34] The Adamowiczs were often referred to as the "Polish Lindberghs" by the American press. See *Brooklyn New York Daily Eagle*, February 7, 1935.

of the Adamowiczes' property was estimated to be between $25,000 and $70,000 and the machinery was valued at about $20,000.

Their guilt seemed obvious. The constitutional amendment introducing Prohibition in 1919, during Woodrow Wilson's presidency, was rescinded by Congress in 1933, during President Roosevelt's administration. But operating a still without permits, and consequently, without paying taxes, was clearly illegal.

Prior to the trial, headlines were printed: "No Permit to Make Garage Into Still." "Adamowicz Denies Running a Still." "Fliers Indicted on Liquor Charge; Adamowicz Brothers Accused Over Still." "Fliers Indicted In Still Seizure." "Polish Fliers Tried As Still Operators." "Pop Soda Aviators Face Justice." "Polish Lindberghs Deny Still Charge."[35]

The threatened and terrified brothers hired and fired a series of lawyers. There was a whole parade of them: Milton Kropf, Louis Halle, Harry Bass, Morris Packer. This prolonged the legal process, certainly purposely, because every new attorney had the right to familiarize himself or herself with the trial documents, which took time. "So Many Adamowicz Lawyers Prosecutor Is Getting Dizzy" — commented one reporter.[36]

It is not clear how long the brothers operated the hidden still. There is no direct information about it. We can only guess that it was installed in the early 1920s; they had at their disposal space, bottles, and means of transport. Or, maybe the operation began in 1927 when Joe travelled to Poland and Czechoslovakia to buy equipment (the large still). The size and capacity of this contraption fascinated the press.

It is entirely possible that for some time the soda plant was a

---

[35] All the above quotes are from the American press, late 1934-early 1935; all can be found in online newspapers (http://www.fultonhistory.com/).
[36] Ibidem.

front camouflaging the production of alcohol. The statement that escaped from Ben's lips when he spoke to Strumph-Wojtkiewicz, about serving alcohol to the Italian ship captain, i.e., "We had as much alcohol as we wanted," seems to confirm this theory. As we have mentioned, Ben also said that they had "a permit for alcohol." No. They could not have had such a permit. It was 1927 and Prohibition was still strictly enforced. If they *did* have this permit, they would have produced evidence of this in court. They did not.

One can speculate further about the market for illegal alcohol; production was one thing, and sales another. A truck loaded with crates of booze-filled bottles left the premises regularly. Where did these bottles go? Who was unloading the truck? Who was storing the bottles? Who was buying? Who, if anyone, made arrangements with the producers to share in the profits?

Presumably for many years the alcohol business was the main source of income for the Adamowicz brothers and that this business financed Joe and Ben's aviation passion. Someone blew the whistle.

Precisely three months after the discovery of the illegal still, on December 18, 1934, in the Federal Court of Brooklyn, the three Adamowicz brothers were charged with possessing and operating an illegal still. All three entered pleas of "not guilty." Their trial was scheduled for January 4, 1935. The judge set bail at $2,500 for each of them. The family put up the bail.

CHAPTER 25
THE FIRST TRIAL

The defendants faced Judge Mortimer W. Byers on January 4, 1935. They were identified as Joseph Adamowicz, owner of the factory and Bruno Adamowicz, owner of the machinery and equipment. After a short delay it was also established that Benjamin Adamowicz was co-owner of the factory.

Before the transatlantic venture and also during their time in Poland, Joe and Ben hinted in interviews that they were no longer owners of the soda factory, having sold it to buy the Bellanca. During the trial this claim was not made. There persisted in Poland the belief that the brothers were penniless, having sold their factory to purchase the Bellanca (this they used as a bargaining chip when negotiating the sale of the Bellanca in Poland). The brothers acknowledged ownership of the soda-water business and were ready to bear the consequences of this admission.

All three testified in court, repeating their claim that before Joe and Ben's departure for Poland the garage at the back of the factory was rented to a fellow by the name of Jack Schwartz. They did not know, they said, that he was producing alcohol. Not at all! None of them knew it! They simply rented the garage and paid no attention to what went on there. Bruno claimed that he was waiting for Schwartz to set up his business and that no juices were ready for sale; hence no receipts.

But Bruno was unable to explain why the entrance to the garage from the factory was hidden, why its door could open by releasing a lever in the inside of his office, or why a warning bell was installed that rang in the garage when switched on in Bruno's office. He knew nothing.

Figure 48: Stamped mail envelope commemorating the flight, with American and Polish stamps. The brothers took with them several dozens of such envelopes on their flight to Warsaw. Maja Trochimczyk Collection. Used by Permission..

Several witnesses testified. The prosecutor's questions focused solely on the allegation of illegal alcohol production. The system for the distribution and sale of the alcohol was not even touched upon. It did not interest the court. No one else was accused or tried.

When the trial was still under way, on January 11, 1935 (thus before the verdict was rendered), the court issued a directive to confiscate the property of the Adamowicz brothers.[37] The final value of the factory was set at $25,000, and the value of the machinery at $20,000. We asked lawyers about this premature confiscation of property. Having limited documentation, they could only make educated guesses. All agreed, however, that seizure of the property before the verdict was delivered was unusual. Was someone in a hurry to ruin the brothers? To score

---

[37] "Government Grabs Flier's 'Soda' Plant. *"Brooklyn Daily Eagle*, May 23, 1935.

political points to enhance his or her career?

No effort was spared to pin the entire blame for the illicit business on the Adamowicz brothers. Again, no one else was indicted, though it was patently obvious that many people had to have been involved: employees, middle-men, buyers, and others. Curiously, the brothers did not defend themselves by fingering others (except for the fictitious Jack Schwartz). They did not give names of their contractors, dealers, or agents. Was there an "understanding" that if they shouldered the entire blame their sentence would be lighter? We'll never know.

The brothers opted for a jury trial. The evidence against them was overwhelming, but the brothers made a favorable impression on the jurors. They were quiet, modest and dignified. They spoke convincingly. And two of them were transatlantic airmen of international stature and fame. This mattered.

After two months of hearings the jurors listened to closing arguments and adjourned to deliberate. They were behind closed doors for seven hours. The jury was "hung;" they could not agree on guilt or innocence. The result was a mistrial and, by law, the case could be retried.

Immediately after the jury foreman announced the deadlock, Judge Byers resolved to retry the brothers. Certainly it was the wish of Byers to see the brothers behind bars. He set bail at $2,000 per person. The Adamowicz family ponied up. After the verdict the Adamowicz clan left the court as one unit. The brothers refused to give any statements to the press.

U.S. Department of Justice

Federal Bureau of Prisons

SEP 22 2009

Maureen Morris

Washington, D.C. 20534

For Further Inquiry Contact:
Federal Bureau of Prisons
320 First Street. N.W.
Room 841, HOLC Building
Washington, D.C. 20534
Attn: FOIA/Privacy Act Office

RE: Request for Information, FOIA Request No. 2009-09279

Dear Mr. Graybill:

This is in response to your recent Freedom of Information Act (FOIA) request for information regarding the Adamowicz brothers

In response to your request, a search was conducted by the Bureau of Prisons' Archivest. A Microfilm search revealed the below listed information concerning the three brothers. This is the only information available because the remainder of their inmate records have been destroyed.

Name: Benjamin Adamowicz
Reg#: 4301-NE
Age at time of incarceration: 38

Name: Bronislaw Adamowicz
Reg#: 4302-NE
Age at time of incarceration: 46

Name: Joseph Adamowicz
Reg#: 4303-NE
Age at time of incarceration: 43

All three had the same conviction information:

Offense: Conspiracy to Possess Unregistered Still
Sentence: 15 months
Federal Court: Eastern District of New York-Brooklyn
Sentencing Date: 4-1-36
Commitment Date: 5-27-36 to USP Lewisburg, PA
Conditional Release Date: 5-28-37
Discharged from Supervision: 8-26-37

If you have any questions or concerns please contact Wm E. Baumgartel, Senior Paralegal Specialist.

Sincerely,

Wanda M. Hunt
Chief, FOIA/PA Section

cc: File

Figure 49: Response from the U.S. Department of Justice to a query about the incarceration of the brothers Adamowicz: Benjamin, Bronisław and Joseph. Collection of Maureen Mroczek Morris.

CHAPTER 26

THE SECOND TRIAL

Given the publicity surrounding the first trial, it is probably safe to assume that the retrial was not without bias. The second trial of the Adamowicz brothers took place in Brooklyn, in the Eastern District of New York, in Federal Court, from March 19 to March 26, 1935. The presiding Judge was Grover M. Moskowitz.

The judicial system appeared bent on making an example out of the brothers, seemingly determined to send the brothers to jail. They were "small potatoes," easy targets. The retrial, as the first trial, focused exclusively on the three accused, failing to address the possibility of other co-conspirators.

Judge Moskowitz was at the time a Federal Judge.[38] He was known for his irascibility and an "attitude" towards Poles and appears to have selected jurors whose demeanor and responses indicated little sympathy for the defendants. During the hearing the judge conducted the proceedings very decisively and strictly, with obvious hostility and disdain for the brothers. He over-ruled many objections by the defense attorneys. He interrupted both the defendants and the witnesses many times.

The testimony of the defendants and witnesses did not vary from the first trial. Nobody else was accused, arraigned, or investigated. No new witnesses were called. Nothing new was revealed. No new questions were asked.

The basic facts were established as follows: The police and FBI agents discovered an illegal alcohol still at 111 Conselyea

---

[38] Nominated by President Calvin Coolidge and confirmed by the Senate in 1925.

Street, Brooklyn, New York on September 18, 1934; the still was not registered and had no permit to operate; taxes on it were not paid; a machine for alcohol production with a capacity of 2,000 gallons was found; several barrels of fermenting mash were found; the factory garage had a secret entrance/exit; a camouflaged truck was found; the still operated on the premises of a soda plant owned by the Adamowicz brothers; Joe and Ben owned the lot and the buildings on the premises, and Bruno owned the machinery and the equipment. Joseph and Benjamin Adamowicz testified that Jack Schwartz had rented space in their plant; all three brothers testified that they knew nothing about what Schwartz was doing on their premises.

There were witnesses who testified in favor of the brothers, among them two Polish priests from Brooklyn, Reverend Gervase Kubec and Reverend A. Jarka. They described the brothers as quiet and pious men who regularly donated to their parish; they were loved and respected by their neighbors. Neither priest ever saw them drunk or heard gossip about them producing or selling alcohol.

Judge Moskowitz's instructions implored the jurors to do their duty as upright citizens. He told them to carefully analyze the trustworthiness of the defendants' testimony, especially the bits about renting their space to a stranger, and to closely examine all technical aspects of the case, such as the location of the still on the premises, the capacity of the still, and the camouflage of the operation. These instructions revealed a clear bias. The judge concluded his presentation with a harsh warning: "There is no mercy for criminals and there is no mercy for fabricators."

This time, the jurors deliberated for only one hour and fifty minutes. They returned with a verdict. The foreman reported that on every count, for all defendants, the verdict was "guilty." Judge

Moskowitz congratulated the jury saying: "Many jurors have been fooled with fake leases in cases of this kind. But you, gentlemen, have put your stamp of disapproval against racketeers and others who break the law. There is no excuse now for bootleg liquor. Your verdict is absolutely just and is going to be very helpful to the administration of justice."[39]

The brothers vowed to appeal the verdict. The appeal was rejected within a few days and the brothers awaited sentencing. The judge set bail at $5,000 for each man — a lot of money. The family coughed up $10,000 (enough bail for two). Joe and Ben were released but Bruno was locked up. The following day, the family brought the outstanding $5,000 and Bruno was released. The brothers were sentenced on April 1, 1935.[40] Bruno, Joseph, and Benjamin Adamowicz were each remanded to 15 months in federal prison for operating an unregistered alcohol still. An appeal was filed the next day, April 2.

That a crime was committed was evident. The brothers could have been fined, given probation, ordered to pay outstanding taxes and asked to perform community service. But they were sentenced to jail. A hasty confiscation of their property and incarceration were sure to destroy the "conquerors of Atlantic." Aside from their business, the brothers had no accumulated wealth; they had no connections in the world of law, big business, politics, or aviation. They were simply hardworking men with a grand dream.

The American press announced: "2 Fliers Convicted in Still Plot Trial."[41] "Adamowicz Brothers Get 15-Month Terms"[42]

---

[39]*New York Times*, March 27, 1935. Judge Moskowitz's speech was quoted by many newspapers.
[40] In some newspapers the dates of the trial and sentencing vary slightly, but the differences are only a day or two.
[41]*New York Times*, March 27, 1935.
[42]*New York Post*, April 1, 1935; New York Times, April 2, 1935; *Schenectady Gazette*, May 25, 1936.

"Adamowiczes Jailed in Illicit Still Case." "Two Transatlantic Fliers and Brothers Get Fifteen Months in Federal Penitentiary."[43] "Soda Water Ocean Flyers Likely to Pop Into Prison" [*New York Post*, February 28, 1935].

The Polish press either wrote nothing or mentioned the trial with few details.[44] The brothers, who were the pride of Poland a short while earlier, were shamed and mocked. Not wanting to destroy the legend, Polish journalists said little about the crime and subsequent trial. Comments were made in euphemistic terms about the brothers' "problems with American justice." To avoid telling the story some authors wrote: "the Adamowicz brothers sunk into oblivion," "We don't know what happened to the Adamowicz brothers," or "The Adamowicz brothers vanished from New York."[45]

Harold Ross, a correspondent for the *New Yorker* published a lengthy article. It is marked by errors and is a bit sneering in tone but it is worth quoting for the mood it captures:

> "In a cubical, walk-up flat in Greenpoint, Brooklyn, after climbing two flights of stairs made of the same stone composition as the tops of soda fountains, and pushing baby carriages aside at both landings, you will find the only two brothers who ever flew the Atlantic together. They are the Adamowicz brothers, Joe and Ben, the Brooklyn soda-water bottlers who learned to fly in early middle age and popped to Warsaw from here last Summer, each earning a colonel's commission, just like Lindbergh, but in the Polish army.[46] You may not find them there long, for perhaps at the end of a fortnight the United Stated District Court will send them

---

[43] *New York Times*, April 2, 1935.
[44] See *Pałuczanin*, January 6 and 20, 1935; *Kurjer Bydgoski*, June 1, 1935.
[45] See: W. Rychter, *Skrzydlate wspomnienia*. Wydawnictwo Komunikcaji i Łaczności, Warszawa 1980, s. 238.
[46] An error: Actually the brothers did not get a military commission as "colonels". They each received a civilian decoration -- "Polonia Restituta" which was considered by an American journalist as equal to the military rank of colonel.

away to serve fifteen-month sentences for operating a still in their soda-water plant. They are out on $5,000 bail each."

As Ross admitted, he was more interested in the Adamowiczes brother than in any other transatlantic aviators. He was seeking a story of a dramatic contrast, a downfall of two men from the highs of success, socializing with John Cudahy, the US Ambassador to Poland, to the lows of being incarcerated in, as he claimed, the Atlanta Penitentiary.[47]

"Ben is short and plump, and interlaces his hands across his stomach when he talks. 'The District Attorney thought he'd get headlines by convicting transatlantic flyers,' said Joe, who is more angular, and whose smile is distinguishable from Ben's by the flash of a gold tooth. The third brother lives with them, Bronisław, affectionately known as Bronish [Broniś], but he bashfully remained in the kitchen while we were there. He did not fly to Europe. It is his fate to be left behind, apparently. When his brothers were released on bail, he was left in jail for a day while they raised his $5,000 bail. [...] Joe and Ben were the least ostentatious ocean fliers of all time. They bought a second-hand Bellanca, and asked Dr. Kimball whether it would be good flying weather. When he said pretty fair, they flew to Europe. They had a lot of trouble finding Warsaw after they got across, landing four times before reaching there.

The still was discovered while Joe and Ben were abroad. They testified that five days before they hopped off, they rented the rear of their plant to a man known as Jack Schwartz. The government claims he is fictitious. The brothers say he was a 'nice clean fellow

---

[47]This is an error. The Adamowiczs were not jailed in Atlanta. They served their time in Lewiston, Pennsylvania.

about five foot eight inches tall.' The plight grieves the brothers because they're pretty well strapped. For a while they were the only Polish-American soda-water bottlers and enjoyed a monopoly on pop at certain picnics, funerals, etc. During their excursion, rivals entered the field. This wouldn't bother them, what with their fame and invitations to every Polish club in this country, but they are out on bail and can't leave the state, and also the government has confiscated their bottling plant. They sold their plane to the Polish government for $25,000 [$22,000], but received only $12,000 in cash and 60,000 in złotys [Polish currency]. Just before their case went to the jury, the brothers received a formal-looking envelope from Warsaw and assumed that Poland was interceding for them, or at least paying the $13,000 balance owed them. The mailing turned out to be a suggestion from the War Minister that they forgive Poland the balance due for the Bellanca, $13,000."[48]

On May 28, 1935, the Court rejected the brothers' appeal and confirmed the 15-month jail sentence for all three Adamowicz brothers. The confiscation of the soda factory was also upheld.

The re-trial, sentencing hearing, and the legal appeal were widely covered in the American press. Jokes were part and parcel of printed stories. The Adamowiczes were no longer the heroic conquerors of the Atlantic but amateurs, simpletons, fatties, and so forth. The respectable motive for their flight, "for the greater glory of Poland" was ridiculed.

Their trajectory, from penniless immigrants, to wage earners, to small-business men, to entrepreneurs was the fulfillment of the American dream. They reached the zenith of their fame by successfully crossing the Atlantic by air and for that they enjoyed a kingly reception in Poland. After their conviction as criminals, they were figures of fun, bankrupt and morally defamed.

---

[48] Harold Ross, "The talk of the town. After the shouting." *The New Yorker*, April 10, 1935.

CHAPTER 27
IMPRISONMENT

The brothers were ordered to report to the police on May 27, 1936 to serve their 15-month sentence in federal prison. It must have been a difficult year for them.

They had $12,000 from Poland from the sale of the Bellanca and this sum was shared with the family. The balance of the money that Poland owed them was never paid as far as we know. The apartment house at 111 Conselyea Street had been confiscated, so Joe and Ben bunked with relatives and friends.[1]

Elizabeth left Ben. That she and Ben divorced is confirmed by the 1940 census (Benjamin's marital status is "D" for divorced). A relative of Elizabeth told us that "Lisa" remarried. This was confirmed in the 1940 census; Elizabeth was listed as married to John Kaczmarek. As Ben's wife, Elizabeth had the joy of being treated like a celebrity in Poland. At the side of the "heroic airman," she was kissed on the hand (according to an old Polish custom) by mayors of Polish cities, members of the government and generals. But life as the wife of a penniless convicted criminal was perhaps more than she could bear. All three brothers took odd jobs after their fall from grace. Ben worked as an associate in a store. We don't know what Joe and Bruno did during this time, but by 1940 they were apartment managers. We do know that the brothers did not fly. They no longer had a plane. They could not even show their faces at the airport. They, the conquerors of the Atlantic!

In the morning of May 17, 1936, they reported to the police

---

[1] This information is not confirmed since other sources claim that in 1940 they lived at 325 Manhattan, their usual address, and they were managing the apartment building.

station in Brooklyn. They were arrested, cuffed and shackled. Around noon they were led to a prison bus and chained to the seats; there were about 20 other prisoners with them. They were transported to a federal prison, the United States Federal Penitentiary in Lewisburg, Pennsylvania.

Lewisburg is situated almost exactly in the geographic center of Pennsylvania, about 60 miles north of Harrisburg, about 200 miles northwest of Philadelphia, and about 400 miles from New York. The penitentiary in Lewisburg was built in 1932, using cheap labor during the depression. It was the first and only high security prison on the east coast of the U.S. "High security" means that the facility had a unit of special guards on duty round the clock, at the ready to subdue violent inmates or to quell riots. The jail originally housed 1,000 inmates; presently — 1,500. At the Adamowiczes' time it was the primary incarceration facility for convicted Italian Mafia members, including Al Capone. One can guess that the brothers were sent there because they were considered rank and file Mafia members.

Today the jail houses terrorists, drug smugglers and dealers, and criminals with long-terms sentences. The penitentiary is located on top of a small hill in a gently undulating countryside. The main jail ground is a large square surrounded by a 20-foot, smooth, white wall with guard-towers planted every hundred feet. At the front, in the center, built in the wall, there is a guardhouse and a reception area. Inside the wall is the main jail complex of reddish bricks that includes the administration building and several blocks of cells, all connected by corridors. The whole structure is crowned by a high tower in the "Siena" style — an imitation of Italian Renaissance architecture.

(The jail was planned for the Italian Mafia — is it possible that the architects wanted to make their residents feel at home?) Inside, the jail is meticulously clean. Floors, presently tiled, were originally of the same brick as the walls. The entire Lewiston penitentiary is both depressing and oddly calming.

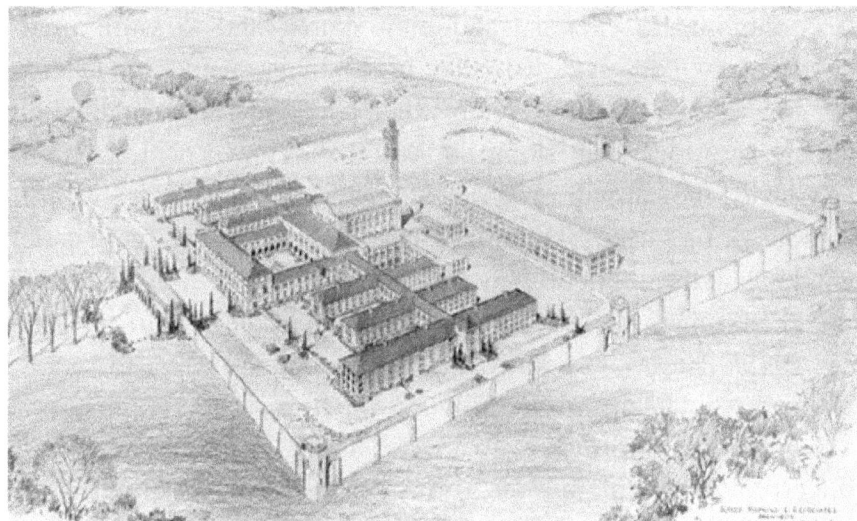

Figure 50: General view of the United States Federal Penitentiary, Lewisburg. Collection of Maureen Mroczek Morris.

Figure 51: Lewisburg Penitentiary with the "Siena" style tower. Collection of Maureen Mroczek Morris.

Besides the main jail complex, inside the perimeter other buildings were gradually erected, such as gyms, walking areas, and various sports fields, all encircled by high fences. Outside the wall there are shops including a furniture plant employing low-security inmates. The Adamowiczes belonged to that category.

Low-risk inmates have bigger cells with barred doors; this allows inmates to communicate; they are permitted to eat in a large cantina, to exercise and play sports, and to work in the prison plant. Today (in 2010) the prisoners are paid 22 cents/hour for their labor — in the 1930s it was 2 to 5 cents. More dangerous inmates are locked in small cells, and they have no recreational privileges; they are allowed out of their cells only in chains in the company of a guard. These prisoners receive food through small windows in the doors of their cells.[2]

The brothers arrived in Lewisburg late in the evening of May 27, 1935. They were admitted to the prison according to routine: stripped, subjected to a humiliating medical exam, supplied with a regulation uniform ("stripes"), registered, photographed, and fingerprinted. Benjamin received number 4301-NE, Bruno 4302-NE, and Joseph 3303 NE.[3] Afterward they were led to their cells.

The formal start-date of their term was May 27, 1936. Precisely a year and a day later, May 28, 1937, they were conditionally released. Their sentences were cut short by three months as a reward for "good conduct." They were under police supervision ("on probation") until August 26, 1937.[4]

---

[2] There is a documentary film, *Doing Time. Life in a Big House* about the Lewiston Penitentiary, directed by Allan and Susan Raymond, 1991.
[3] According to a document received from the U.S. Department of Justice, Federal Bureau of Prisons, September 22, 2009.
[4] *Ibidem.*

CHAPTER 28
BANKRUPTCY

After being released from prison the brothers faced a very difficult situation. The family's patience was wearing thin and money was tight. They could not make up for the total loss of business revenue, legal and illegal. The brothers' hard work since 1911 had gone down the drain.

The Adamowicz brothers tried to recover at least some of their losses. In the summer of 1938, Joe and Ben boarded the *Batory,* a Polish transoceanic ship and sailed to Poland. This time they kept a low profile. They were private travelers, they did not meet the press, did not give interviews, and did not pay official visits. They *did* visit the Polish Aero Club requesting the outstanding sum from the sale of the Bellanca, $10,000. We can imagine how humiliating that exercise must have been. We don't know if they actually received any money.

There is evidence of this trip: 1) Joe and Ben's applications for American passports, and 2) the passengers list of the *Batory* returning from Poland in the fall of 1938. They are on the list.

The American press paid virtually no attention to the Adamowicz brothers after their imprisonment. Purportedly they had "plans to make an air tour around the world" or "a flight from America over the North Pole to China."[5] These plans never materialized. There was no money, no aircraft, no energy, and no enthusiasm.

The brothers ran a small candy store in the late 1930s and early 1940s. Joe and Ben managed their former apartment house at 325 Manhattan Ave. from 1935-1940, according to the census

---

[5]*Brooklyn NY Daily Eagle*, December 20, 1938.

record for that year (they are listed as renters). The 1938 ship's manifest confirms their address, as well as Ben's passport application. Bruno, in 1940, was a "store manager for his own business." A certain "Joseph Adamowicz" is listed as filing for bankruptcy – in 1937 and 1940.[6] It is not clear if this is "our" Joseph; since 1936, Joe and his brothers had little to lose. Their sister Emilia (Emma Mathies) was forced to place a newspaper announcement stating that she was not responsible for her brothers' debts.[7]

In the 1940s, Joe and Ben worked at menial jobs for "Robaczynski Machine Corporation," 324 Ten Eyck Street, Brooklyn. The plant manufactured sewing machines, but during WW II it produced weapons. They were still employed there after the war. We don't know for how long — the press did not write about them. Joe and Ben lived together in a rented apartment, reminiscent of the early years of their American journey.

We found military registration cards for Joe and Ben for both WWI and WWII, but there are no records of active military service. In 1941, when America entered the war, Ben was 43 years old and Joe was 48. Ben married again in 1941 but that marriage was apparently short-lived.

After the war they lived in poverty or even penury.[8]

Joe and Ben and other family members applied for Social Security numbers; they could have been receiving Social Security benefits. Bruno's son Stanley applied for Social Security at the age of 38, claiming that he was unemployed. Was he ill? Disabled? Between jobs?

---

[6] *New York Times* article about Joseph's bankruptcy: May 27, 1937, and April 3, 1940. We don't know why this information appeared twice. The fact that all three Adamowicz brothers went bankrupt is undeniable.
[7] *Brooklyn Daily Eagle*, August 7, 1940.
[8] See F.Z. Wieremej with Ryszard Czarkowski, *Kierunki* 1974, no. 35, p. 9. This conversation contains many inaccuracies. The word "penury," however, seems to accurately describe the brothers' circumstances after the war.

Curiously, the brothers amassed means, post-incarceration, to acquire a summer house on Oak Hill Road in Parksville that they owned for about 10 years (approximately 1960-1970); this home they gave, shortly before their deaths, to Lanny and Nancy Kemmis. Ben gave Nancy Kemmis the brothers' aviation memorabilia (statues, medals, awards, photos and clippings) that were destined, reportedly, for the Smithsonian (Sunday Record, *Middletown Times Herald Record*, June 28, 1970). We learned that the Smithsonian Air and Space Museum (entrusted with the memorabilia for five years) never displayed the items. Most of the collection was returned to Mr. and Mrs. Kemmis who later sold the items at auction.

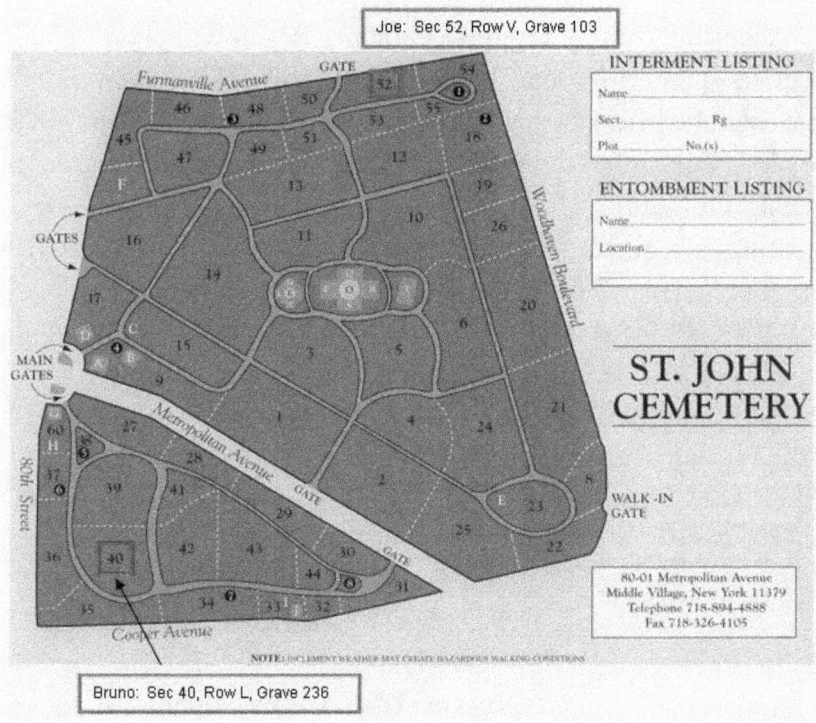

Figure 52: Map of St. John Cemetery in Brooklyn.

CHAPTER 29

THE ADAMOWICZ BROTHERS PASS AWAY

Bruno Adamowicz died on August 3, 1941. He was 54 years old; that is, relatively young. His Death Certificate, issued by the Kings County Hospital in Brooklyn, contains vital information.[9] He died of liver cancer, possibly exacerbated by heavy drinking. His wife Anna (maiden name Skrzetuska) signed his Death Certificate.

According to this Death Certificate, Bruno had been living in America since 1913, and his most recent employment was with Abrockler Brothers Sugar Refinery (the same plant where, years ago, he began his American journey, and where he placed his younger brothers).

Bruno's last address was 60-44 Cooper Avenue, Brooklyn, New York. [In 1936 he and his family were living at 578 Wythe Ave. Twenty years later, his daughter Anna was located at that address.] He is buried at St. John's Cemetery in Brooklyn.[10] The remains of his wife Anna (1888-1947) and son Stanley (1907-1982) are in the same plot. We found no obituary for Bruno.

The headstone for Bruno Adamowicz reads:

ADAMOWICZ
Son STANLEY (1907-1982)
Bruno (1888-1941)
Anna (1885-1974)

---

[9] Certificate of Death, Bureau of Records, Department of Health, Borough of Brooklyn. Certificate No. 17523, September 5, 1941. In this document Bronisław is listed as Bruno.
[10] Section 40, Row L, Grave 236.

Joseph Adamowicz died on November 26, 1970.[11] He was 80 years old and still living on 325 Manhattan Avenue at the time of his death. His "usual occupation" per his Death Certificate is "lathe operator" at a "machine shop." This document does not mention any wife. His marital status is "single." The informant was his sister Emma Mathies. Joe is buried at the same cemetery as Bruno.[12]

The headstone for Joseph Adamowicz reads:
ADAMOWICZ
Joseph (1893-1970)
Benjamin (1896-)

Figure 53:The Adamowicz brothers' tombstone: Joseph (1893-1970), and Benjamin (1896–). St. John Cemetery, Middle Village, New York. Photo by Adolfina Tymczyszyn.

---

[11] The City of New York, Vital Records, Death Certificate. Bureau of Records and Statistics, Department of Health, The City of New York. Certificate No. 156-70-323334.
[12] Section 52, Row V, Grave 103.

Together in life, the brothers expected to be buried together. Joe purchased the plot and likely ordered the inscriptions. However Ben was never buried with Joe. We found no obituary for Joseph. Ben Adamowicz died at Greenpoint Hospital in Brooklyn on June 1, 1979. His body was cremated on June 5 at the Garden State Crematory in North Bergen, New Jersey.

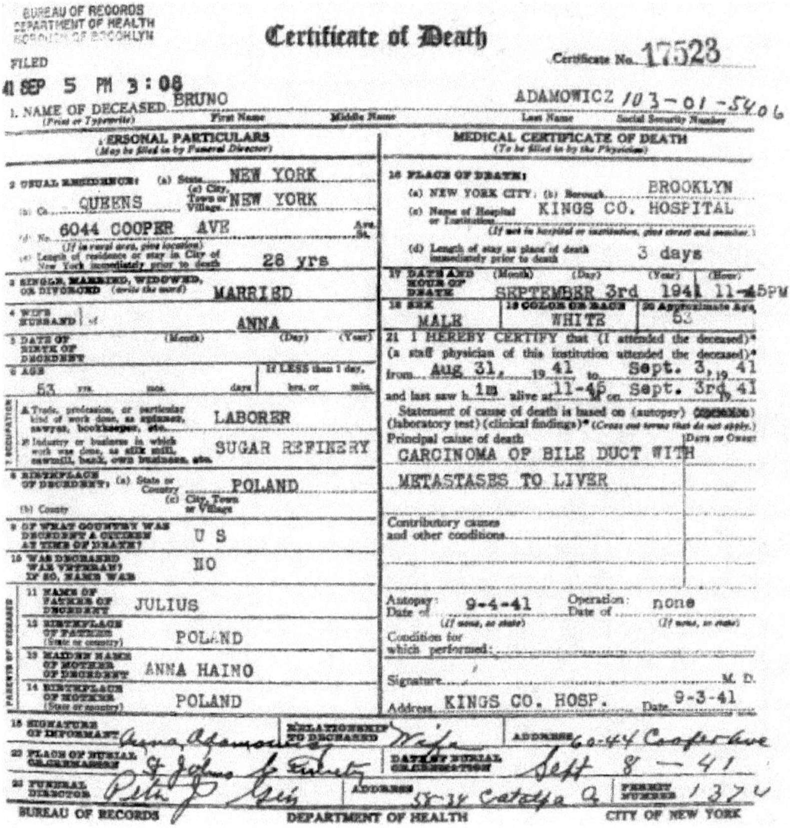

BUREAU OF RECORDS
DEPARTMENT OF HEALTH
BOROUGH OF BROOKLYN

Certificate of Death

Certificate No. 17523

FILED
41 SEP 5 PM 3:08

1. NAME OF DECEASED BRUNO ADAMOWICZ 103-01-5406
(Print or Typewrite) First Name Middle Name Last Name Social Security Number

PERSONAL PARTICULARS (May be filled in by Funeral Director) | MEDICAL CERTIFICATE OF DEATH (To be filled in by the Physician)

2 USUAL RESIDENCE: (a) State NEW YORK (c) City, Town or Village NEW YORK (b) Co. QUEENS (d) No. 6044 COOPER AVE
(e) Length of residence or stay in City of New York immediately prior to death 28 yrs

16 PLACE OF DEATH: (a) NEW YORK CITY: (b) Borough BROOKLYN
(c) Name of Hospital or Institution KINGS CO. HOSPITAL
(d) Length of stay at place of death immediately prior to death 3 days

3 SINGLE, MARRIED, WIDOWED, OR DIVORCED (write the word) MARRIED

17 DATE AND HOUR OF DEATH (Month) (Day) (Year) (Hour) SEPTEMBER 3rd 1941 11-45PM

4 WIFE/HUSBAND of ANNA

18 SEX MALE | 19 COLOR OR RACE WHITE | 20 Approximate Age 53

5 DATE OF BIRTH OF DECEDENT (Month) (Day) (Year)

6 AGE 53 yrs. mos. days | If LESS than 1 day, hrs. or min.

21 I HEREBY CERTIFY that (I attended the deceased)* (a staff physician of this institution attended the deceased)* from Aug 31, 1941 to Sept. 3, 1941 and last saw h 1m alive at 11-45 on Sept. 3rd 41
Statement of cause of death is based on (autopsy) (laboratory test) (clinical findings)* (Cross out terms that do not apply.)
Principal cause of death: CARCINOMA OF BILE DUCT WITH METASTASES TO LIVER | Date of Onset

7 OCCUPATION (a) Trade, profession, or particular kind of work done, as spinner, sawyer, bookkeeper, etc. LABORER
(b) Industry or business in which work was done, as silk mill, sawmill, bank, own business, etc. SUGAR REFINERY

8 BIRTHPLACE OF DECEDENT: (a) State or Country POLAND (b) County (c) City, Town or Village

9 OF WHAT COUNTRY WAS DECEDENT A CITIZEN AT TIME OF DEATH? U S

Contributory causes and other conditions

10 WAS DECEASED WAR VETERAN? IF SO, NAME WAR NO

11 NAME OF FATHER OF DECEDENT JULIUS
12 BIRTHPLACE OF FATHER (State or country) POLAND
13 MAIDEN NAME OF MOTHER OF DECEDENT ANNA HAINO
14 BIRTHPLACE OF MOTHER (State or country) POLAND

Autopsy: Date of 9-4-41 (If none, so state) | Operation: Date of none (If none, so state)
Condition for which performed:
Signature M. D.
Address KINGS CO. HOSP. Date 9-3-41

15 SIGNATURE OF INFORMANT Anna Adamowicz | RELATIONSHIP TO DECEASED Wife | ADDRESS 60-44 Cooper Ave
22 PLACE OF BURIAL OR CREMATION St Johns Cemetery | DATE OF BURIAL OR CREMATION Sept 8 - 41
23 FUNERAL DIRECTOR Peter J. Grey | ADDRESS 58-34 Catalpa A | PERMIT NUMBER 1374

BUREAU OF RECORDS DEPARTMENT OF HEALTH CITY OF NEW YORK

Figure 54a: Bruno Adamowicz Death Certificate. Courtesy of Bureau of Records, Department of Health, Borough of Brooklyn.

The fate of his ashes is uncertain but they may have been scattered by his sister Emma on the Parksville property (personal communication). Ben's Death Certificate,[13] with data provided by his nephew, James Gorman, states that he was approximately 86 years old, which would set his birth year around 1893.

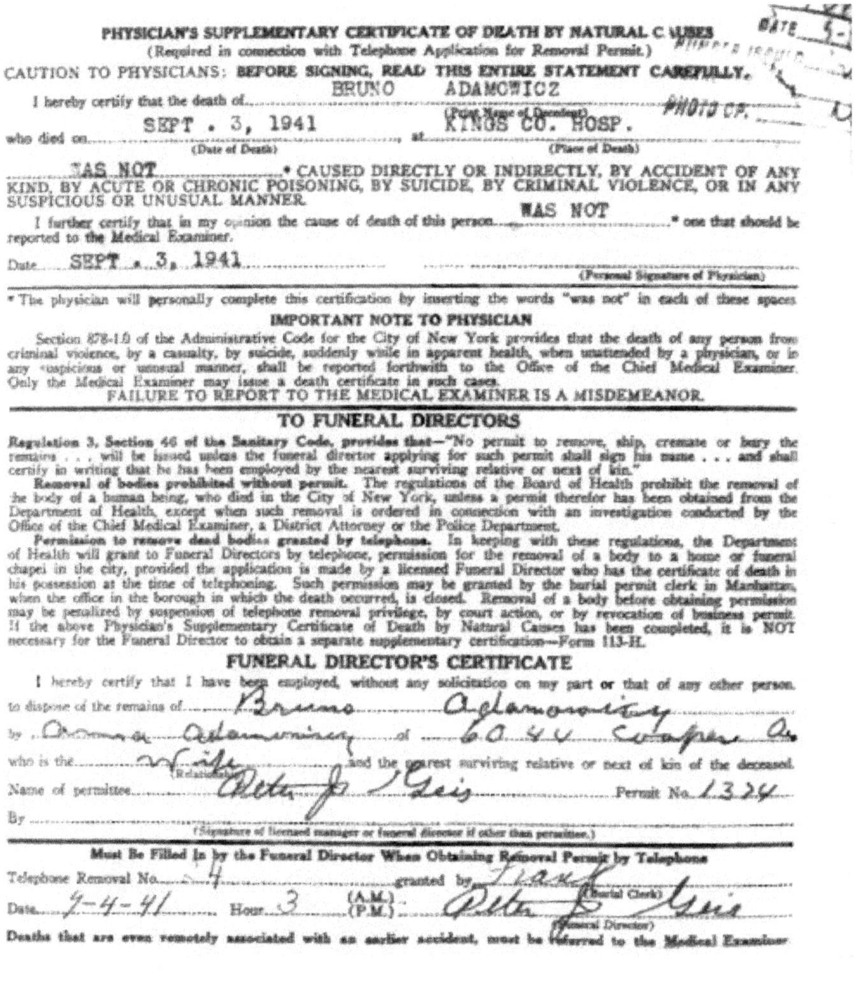

Figure 54 b: Bruno Adamowicz Death Certificate, cont. Courtesy of Bureau of Records, Department of Health, Borough of Brooklyn.

---

[13]Certificate of Death 156-79-308318, Division of Records, The City of New York.

On Joseph's headstone Ben's birth year is 1896. When arriving in New York in 1911, he declared that he was born in 1893, but his 1933 passport application lists his birth year as 1898. One last inconsistency. We found no obituary for Ben, but reportedly his passing was noted in the *Sullivan County Democrat*.

Rest in peace, brave aviators!

POSTSCRIPT

Two simple boys from eastern Poland, two Brooklyn laborers, two American businessmen, two transatlantic fliers, Joe and Ben Adamowicz. They accomplished in 1934 a feat which not many dared to attempt at that time. Among those who tried only a few achieved their goal. Many perished trying.

The Adamowicz brothers were hardworking, inventive and courageous. They were average men with an ambition, a grand spectacular ambition that they realized, and that makes them unusual. Though they squandered their financial fortune and spoiled their memory with reckless and unlawful acts, they belong in the annals of aviation history. Their aircraft, the Bellanca, also belongs to aviation history.

The Adamowiczes' story is in many ways typical of so many other immigrants. Their lives should *not* be summed up thusly "they flew over the Atlantic for the greater glory of Poland, with money from the illicit sale of alcohol." This is only *part* of the truth. Their lives are more complicated. Theirs is a story of mixed loyalties, the Polish experience in America, and a story of struggle, success and disgrace. For them, the road to the fulfillment of the "American dream" was twisty and led them down dark alleys.

The question remains... Why did the brothers flaunt Prohibition? Indeed it was a way to make money, quickly. They came from a culture where deception and outsmarting authorities was a way of life. They were risk takers – on the ground and in the air. They had the means at their disposal. They needed money to indulge their passion and to realize their dreams.

We can stipulate that the whole Polish nation, experiencing violence and injustice from invaders, dispossessed of their own land, deprived of their rights, straining to be free, considered it a virtue to break the law. Disdain for foreign laws and breaking them whenever possible were grounds for pride – a patriotic duty. Generation after generation of Poles have lived this way — during the decades of the partitions (1795-1918) as well as during both world wars (1914-1918, 1939-1945) and under Soviet-style totalitarian Communism (1945-1989). This mindset is partially responsible for the survival of the nation, but it has its downside.

Flouting the law and defiance were part and parcel of life for the Adamowicz brothers in their formative years. This was their mindset. Immigration to America did not change this. They were products of their upbringing. The brothers likely disregarded Prohibition because they saw it as one more law that was their duty to disregard; after all, they and their friends liked to drink, and perhaps they felt there was little harm in producing something that they and others wanted.

Prohibition (the XVIII Amendment to the Constitution) was imposed during the Presidency of Woodrow Wilson in response to intense pressure in 1919 by mostly Protestant zealots. Considered unconstitutional, it was revoked via the XXI Amendment in 1933, when Franklin Delano Roosevelt was President.

Prohibition was a godsend to the Mafia. If the Adamowiczes loosely associated with Mafia types — as some facts seem to suggest — they became Mafia victims, too. They "took the fall" for an illicit business that involved many people. They paid a price, not only in prison time, but also in the loss of prestige, their proper place in history, the loss of their material possessions and most importantly their good name. They did not rise from the ashes.

They flew high but in the end crashed. Nonetheless they deserve our attention and respect because theirs was an amazing accomplishment.

The three brave Adamowicz brothers have been mostly forgotten for years — for 75 years to be exact, until Grzegorz Braun rediscovered them and pushed us to write this book. Thank you, Grzegorz. Besides Grzegorz, there are many people who want to remember them.

One keen fan, Kazimierz Mazurek, built a beautiful and accurate model of their Bellanca, photographed it, and put it online. These efforts are worthy of gratitude and admiration.

Not only historians and hobbyists return to the history of the brothers. A Kraków newspaper *Dziennik Polski* in its "Kronika Nowohucka" (*Nowa Huta Chronicle*) printed the following on June 7, 2010:

> "The Council of the Town Czyżyny proposes that a new road at the settlement of Squadron 303,[14] which runs from the housing project on Włodarczyka Street No. 19 to No. 21c, will be named Adamowicz Brothers Street.' Jerzy Woźniakiewicz, Mayor of the town explained: 'We want the streets around the historic airfield Czyżyny to bear the names of people connected with the history of aviation. The Adamowicz Brothers are representatives of American Polonia, amateur flyers, who became famous for their successful crossing of the Atlantic by airplane in 1934.'"[15]

We hope that the ceremony of bestowing the name of the Adamowicz brothers on that street becomes a good opportunity to recall them. When this street will indeed bear that name, we will proudly walk that road in their memory.

---

[14] Squadron 303 was the famous Polish air fighters unit in Great Britain during War World II. It distinguished itself in August and September 1940, in the "Battle of Britain." See Arkady Fiedler, *303 Squadron: The Legendary Battle of Britain Fighter Squadron*. Los Angeles: Aquila Polonica, 2010.
[15] *Dziennik Polski*, June 7, 2010.

THE END

SELECTED BIBLIOGRAPHY

Adamowicz, Bolesław and Adamowicz,Józef. *Przez Atlantyk.* Spisał z relacji lotników i opracował Stanisław Strumph-Wojtkiewicz. „Pod egidą Aeroklubu R.P."[Acrossthe the Atlantic. Written down from the reports of flyers and edited by Stanislaw Strumph Wojtkiewicz. Under the aegis of the Aero Club of the Republic of Poland]. Warszaw: Wydawnictwo M. Arcta, 1934.

Arct, Bohdan.*Rycerze biało-czerwonej szachownicy*[The knights of the red-and-white chessboard].Radom: Polwen – Polskie Wydawnictwo Encyklopedyczne, 2003, pp. 75-85, 93.

Berkowicz, Magdalena.*Stefania Wojtulanis-Karpińska. „Aviomama". O kobiecie, która kochała latać.*[Stefania Wojtulanis-/Karpinska. „Avio-mom." About a Woman who Loved to Fly]. Warsaw: ZP Grupa, 2009.

Bryson, Bill. *One Summer: America, 1927.* New York: Doubleday, 2013.

Bukowczyk, John, J., ed. *Polish Americans and Their History: Community, Culture and Politics.* University of Pittsburgh Press; 2006.

Bukowczyk, John, J. *A History of the Polish Americans.* Transaction Publishers, 2007.

Crouch, Tom D. *Wings: A History of Aviation from Kites to the Space Age.* New York:W.W. Norton & Company, 2004.

Czarkowski, Ryszard.„Co się dzieje z braćmiAdamowiczami? Bohaterowie lotu z przed 40 lat."[What's up with the Adamowicz brothers? The heroes of a flight from 40 years ago]. *Kierunki,* 1974, no. 30, p. 9.

Czyż, Adam.*Wielka przygoda braci Adamowiczów.* [A Great Adventure of the Adamowicz Brothers]. *Kierunki* 1974, no. 35, p. 8.

Dziadulewicz, Stanisław. *Herbarz rodzin tatarskich w Polsce* [The armorial of Tartar families in Poland]. Wilno, 1929.

Ellis, F.H. and Ellis E.M., *Atlantic Air Conquest. The complete story of all North Atlantic flights and attempts during the pioneer years from 1910 to 1940.* William Kimbel, London, 1963.

Erdmans, Mary Patrice. *Opposite Poles: Immigrants and Ethnics in Polish Chicago, 1976-1990.* University Park, Pa.: Pennsylvania State University Press, 1998.

Fiedler, Arkady.*Dywizjon 303.* London: M.I. Kolin, 1943.

Fiedler, Arkady. *303 Squadron: The Legendary Battle of Britain Fighter Squadron.* Los Angeles: Aquila Polonica, 2010.

Gajl, Tadeusz.*Herbarz polski od średniowiecza do XX wieku,* [Armorial of the Polish coats of arms from the Middle Ages to the 20th century], Gdańsk: L & L, 2007.

Galush, William J. *For More Than Bread: Community and Identity in American Polonia, 1880-1940.* Boulder, Co.: East European Monographs; New York : Distributed by Columbia University Press, 2006.

Glass, Andrzej. „50-lecie przelotu Adamowiczów przez Atlantyk na samolocie Bellanca."[The 50th anniversary of the Adamowicz's flight across the Atlantic on the plane Bellanca]*Technika Lotnicza i Astronautyczna,* 1964, no. 6, pp. 30-32.

Grant, R.G. *100 Years of Aviation.* Penguin Australia, 2007.

Haiman, Mieczysław.*Z przeszłości polskiej w Ameryce.* [From the Polish past in America]. Buffalo, 1927.

Haiman, Mieczysław.*Polacy wśród pionierów Ameryki,* [Poles among the Pioneers of America].Chicago, 1930.

Haiman, Mieczysław.*Polacy w Ameryce. Historia wychodźtwa Polskiego w Stanach Zjednoczonych* [Poles in America. A History of Polish Exile in the United States]. Chicago, 1930.

Jackson, Robert.*Historia lotnictwa*[A history of aviation]. Ożarów Mazowiecki: Wydawnictwo Oleksiejuk, 2010.

Kaczorowska, Teresa.*Herodot Polonii amerykańskiej Mieczysław Haiman.* [Herodot of American Polonia, Mieczysław Haiman]. Warsaw: Muzeum Wychodźtwa Polskiego, Łazienki Królewskie, 2008.

Goska, Danusha V.*Bieganski: The Brute Polak Stereotype, Its Role in Polish-Jewish Relations and American Popular Culture.* Boston: Academic Studies Press, 2010.

Anna Jaroszyńska-Kirchmann, *The Exile Mission: The Polish Political Diaspora and Polish Americans, 1939-1956* (Athens: Ohio University Press, 2004).

Kessener,Thomas. *The Flight of the Century: Charles Lindbergh and the Rise of American Aviation (Pivotal Moments in American History).*Oxford, London and New York: Oxford University Press, 2010.

Kędzierski, Janusz.*Pod niebem własnym i obcym.* [Under our own and foreign sky]. Warsaw:Wydawnictwo Ministerstwa Obrony Narodowej, 1978.

Kojałowicz, Wojciech Wiiuk. *Herbarz szlachty Wielkiego Księstwa Litewskiego, zwany Nomenclator* [Armorial of the Nobility of the Grand Duchy of Lithuania, known as Nomenclator]. 1658. Reprinted in Kraków, 1905.

Koliński, Izydor. *Wojsko Polskie : krótki informator historyczny o Wojsku Polskim w latach II wojny światowej. 9, Regularne jednostki Wojska Polskiego (lotnictwo), formowanie, działania bojowe, organizacja, uzbrojenie, metryki jednostek lotniczych.* Warszawa: Wydawnictwo Ministerstwa Obrony Narodowej, 1978.

Kurowski, Adam.*Kraksy i wzloty. Wspomnienia lotnika.* [Crashes and Flights. Memories of a Flyer]. Warsaw: Wydawanictwo MON,1965.

Łukaszewicz, Janusz.*Szarża przez Atlantyk.* [A charge across the Atlantic]. *Skrzydlata Polska*, 2004, no. 6, pp. 52-53.

Majewski, Karen.*Traitors and True Poles: Narrating a Polish-American Identity, 1880-1939.* Athens: Ohio University Press, 2003.

Mielcarek, Adam Janusz, *Podziały terytorialno - administracyjne II Rzeczypospolitej w zakresie administracji zespolonej.* [Territorial-administrative divisions of the Second Republic in the domain of unified administration]. Warszawa: Wydawnictwo Neriton, 2008.

Niccoli, Ricardo.*Historia lotnictwa. Od maszyny latającej Leonarda da Vinci do podboju kosmosu.* [The History of Airflights. From Leonardo da Vinci's flying machine to the conquest of cosmos]. Warsaw: Carta Blanca, 2008.

Przedpelski, Adam.*Przez wielką wodę.* [Across the great waters]. *Wiraże*, 2004, no. 10. pp. 20, 21, 24.

Pula, James S. ed., *The Polish American Encyclopedia*. Jefferson, NC: McFarland, 2011.

Rychter, Witold.*Skrzydlate wspomnienia*. [Winged memories]. Warsaw: Wydawnictwa Komunikacji i Łączności, 1980.

Simons, David, and Withington Thomas.*Historia lotnictwa. Od pierwszych dwupłatowców po podbój kosmosu.*[The history of air flights. From the first two-plane airplanes to the conquest of cosmos]. Łódź: Wydawnictwo Parragon, 2007.

Sobol, Wacław.,,Lotnicy z Bożej Łaski,"inMarian Romeyko, ed., *Polska lotnicza*. [Flyer's Poland]. Warsaw, 1937, pp. 281-286.

Strumph-Wojtkiewicz, Stanisław, ed. *Przez Atlantyk*. See: Adamowicz.

Strumph-Wojtkiewicz, Stanisław.*O własnych siłach. Kartki z prywatnego archiwum 1921-1939*. [By my own strength. Pages from a private archive, 1921-1939]. Warsaw: Książka i Wiedza, 1967.

Tyszkiewicz, Jan. *Z dziejów Tatarów polskich: 1794-1944.* [From the history of Polish Tartars]. Pułtusk, 2002.

Wasilewski, Tadeusz. "Kim był Skrzetuski," *Mówią wieki*, 1964, no. 9. Reprinted on the website of the Royal Palace Museum in Wilanów, http://www.wilanow-palac.pl/kim_byl_skrzetuski.html, accessed on February 14, 2011.

Wieroch, Jan, *Od braci Wright do braci Rutan*. [From Brothers Wright to Brothers Rutan]. Warsaw: Egros, 1998.

Will, Gavin. *The Great Atlantic Air Race*. O'Brien Press, 2011.

Wright Orville, Wright Wilburn, Claxton William.*A History of Early Aviation.*St. Petersburg, Florida: Red and Black Publishers, 2009.

Wyka, Kazimierz.*Stara szuflada i inne szkice z lat 1932-1939.*[An old drawer and new sketches from the years 1932-1939]. Kraków: Wydawnictwo Literackie, 2000.

ABOUT THE AUTHORS

Zofia Reklewska-Braun is literature and theatre historian, journalist, and educator. She studied Polish Literature at the Warsaw University, earning Master of Letters degree. She worked as editor at the State Scholarly Publishing House in Warsaw and as literary manager at the Osterwa Theatre in Lublin. She was teaching polish language and literature in Polish and American high schools, Buffalo State College, and University at Buffalo. She wrote a book, *How It Really Was* (about the martial law in Poland) and co-authored, with her husband Kazimierz Braun, a monograph, *Director Teofil Trzciński* and a historical book *Good Priests.* With theatre scholar and critic, Konstanty Puzyna she wrote a study *Jacques Copeau's "Bare Stage."* She published several articles in literary, religious, sociological, and theatre journals in Poland, and she collaborated with *Nowe Życie* in Wrocław, *White Eagle* in

Boston, *Am-Pol Eagle* in Buffalo, and *New Daily* in New York, as well as with Polish radio stations in Chicago, New Jersey, and New York. She was active as an Instructor of Girl Scouts in Poland and as an adviser in various organizations and Roman Catholic parishes in Poland and the USA. Her memoires *I Was Born in Between*, (Norbertinum, Lublin, 2009) was a bestselling book in Poland. For her merits and achievements in teaching and promoting Polish history, literature, and language she was decorated with the Cavalier Cross of the Order of Merit of the Polish Republic by President Lech Kaczyński.

Photo by Zygmunt Malinowski

Kazimierz Braun is director, writer, and scholar. He received his Ph. D. in Letters and Ph. D. in Theatre at the Poznań University, Poland, as well as M.F.A. and Ph.D. in Directing at the National School of Drama in Warsaw. He holds the Professor's title in both Poland and the USA. He was artistic director and general manager of professional theaters in Poland, including The Contemporary Theater in Wrocław.

He directed more than 150 productions, both professionally and academically, in Poland, the United States, Canada, Germany, Ireland, and other countries. He taught both at Polish and at American universities, including Wrocław University, Poznań

University, New York University, City University of New York, Notre Dame University, University of California Santa Cruz, and University at Buffalo. He published more than 50 books in Polish, English, and Czech languages, including scholarly works, novels, and plays, which were produced in Poland, Canada, the United States, Ireland, and Russia. He also published extensively in Polish and American literary and theatre journals, as well as in encyclopedias. He received several prizes for theater, literature, and scholarship, including the awards of the Guggenheim, the Fulbright, the Turzańskis, and the Japanese Foundations. He is member of the International PEN Club, International Theater Institute, Polish Writers Association, and Polish Actors Union.

Zofia Reklewska and Kazimierz Braun married in 1962. They have three children: Monika, Grzegorz and Justyna, as well as five granddaughters: Anna, Joanna, Aniela, Zofia and Elżbieta.

INDEX

Abrockler Brothers – 12, 22, 194,
Adamowicz Anne (Anna, daughter of Bruno) – 13, 19
Adamowicz, Ben, Benjamin (Bolesław) – 3, 4, 5, 9. 10, 11, 14, 15, 16, 17, 18, 22, 23, 24, 25, 26, 27, 28, 30, 31, 32, 33, 38, 40, 41, 42, 44-50, 58, 59, 61, 62, 64, 65, 69, 70-74, 76-8, 80, 85-7, 89-100, 102-107,109-111, 114-116, 118, 121-135, 137-9, 142-8, 151, 161, 163, 166, 168-174, 176-7, 182-5, 187, 191, 192, 193, 196, 198, 199
Adamowicz brothers –1, 3, 5, 8, 13, 14, 20, 21, 27, 30, 39, 43, 51, 56, 59, 64, 70, 72, 74, 78, 79, 81, 84, 97, 98, 116, 117, 142, 144, 146, 149, 150, 159, 162, 164-7
    accident, car – 40, 41
    accident, plane – 24, 48-52, 56, 60, 76-7, 85, 110, 119, 134, 168
    bankruptcy – 25. 190-191
    bicycle – 23, 25
    court – 25, 176-186
    death and death certificates – 193-197
    medals – 125, 136, 139, 146, 185, 193, Polonia Restituta 135
    passport – 12, 14, 36-37, 70, 76, 89, 191, 192, 198
    prison – 24, 87, 137, 183, 184, 187-190, 200
    trial – 42, 43, 73, 86, 175, 176-186
Adamowicz, Bruno (Bronislaw) – 3, 5, 10-19, 22-7, 30-34, 47, 50, 80, 85, 86, 93, 169, 170-3, 177, 182-3, 187, 190, 192, 194, 195-7
Adamowicz Joe, Jozef – 3, 5, 9, 10, 14-18, 22-28, 30-3, 36, 38, 40, 43-8, 50, 61-4, 70, 72, 76, 79, 85-7, 90-4, 98, 99, 102-5, 107, 109-111, 114, 116, 118, 122-9, 130, 132, 136-9, 142-8, 150-2, 154, 160, 162, 166, 168, 169, 170-7, 182-7, 191-2,195, 196, 199
Adamowicz Julian – 3, 4
Adamowicz Łukasz – 3, 4
Adamowicz Emma – see Mathies, Emma (Emilia)
Adamowicz, Stella (Stanislawa, married Gorman) – 3, 31
Adamowicz, Stanley (Stanislaw, son of Bruno) – 13, 19, 192
Aero Club – 71, 141,160, 204; division in Łódź – 143, Inowrocław – 145, Wilno – 150
airplane – 24, 44, 49, 51, 52, 59, 67, 69-70, 78-80, 89-90, 93. 100, 104, 110, 114, 117, 119, 123, 126, 143, 163
Akron (airship) – 51
Alcock, John William – 53, 57
America (airship) – 51
alcohol – 39-43, 59, 65, 92, 93, 169-173, 176-8, 181-83, 199
Annapolis - 69
Assmann, William – 51
Atlantic Ocean – 19, 24, 26, 44, 51-62, 64, 70-2, 74, 76, 88, 90, 92-109, 112, 115, 120, 126-8, 133, 136, 141-2, 144, 146, 148, 156, 159, 162, 164, 166, 167, 172, 174, 178, 183-7, 191, 194, 196, 197, 201-206
Australia – 52, 53, 205
Austria – 4, 20, 21, 82, 146, 153, 155

Bajan, Jerzy, pilot - 119
Balbo, Italo, General – 58, 130
Baldwin, Thomas Scott – 51
balloon flight – 58, 120

Balomain (Guinea-Bissau) – 54
Baltic Sea – 118, 150
Barski, Lieutenant-pilot – 117
Bass, Harry – 175
Batory (oceanliner) – 191
Bellanca, Augusto – 69
Bellanca (airplane) – 54, 58-75, 77, 78, 80, 85-7, 89, 90, 92-99, 104, 107, 110-12, 115, 117, 118, 121, 122, 128-9, 134, 136, 140-3, 145-6, 148, 150, 154, 161, 164, 168-9, 177, 185-7, 191, 199, 201, 204
Bellanca, Giuseppe Mario – 65-68
Belweder – 132
Berbecki, Leon, General – 134
Blanchard, Jean Pierre – 51
Bellonte, Maurice – 57
Belarus, Belarussian – 3,5, 8, 13, 31
Bleszczyński, Colonel – 108, 109
Bolshevik, Bolshevia – 3, 4, 31, 155
Bobkowski, Deputy Minister – 123, 127
Brandenburg – 114
Bremen – 11
Bridgeport – 52
Bronson, Charles – 8
Brooklyn – 40-5, 59, 64, 65, 70, 76, 85, 89, 93, 102, 116, 129, 164, 169, 171, 174, 176, 178, 181, 182, 184, 188, 191, 192, 193, 194, 196, 197, 199
Burgin, Emile „Eddie" – 77, 78, 79 94
Butkiewicz, Michał, General – 133, 139
Burzyński, Zbigniew – 119
Bydgoszcz – 55, 118, 141, 144, 145

Cadillac – 44
Campbell, Dr. – 88, 96
Castilho, Jorge de – 54
Catholic (Roman) – 20, 24, 82, 156, 170, 209
Chamberlin, Clarence D. – 54, 65
Chamiec, Zygmunt, General Director – 135
Chicago – 51, 82, 88, 130, 153, 205
Chłapowski, Alfred, Ambassador – 110, 111
Chrzanowski, Lieutenant-pilot – 118
Conselyea Street – 27, 28, 30, 42, 43, 58, 59, 93, 169, 170, 171, 181, 187,
Copenhagen – 19, 31, 70, 168,
Corren, Cecil – 48
Costes, Dieudonne – 56
Cudahy, John, Ambassador – 112, 121, 125, 127, 131, 132, 134, 137, 185
Czechoslovakia – 38, 39, 40, 43, 175
Częstochowa – 24, 140, 141, 146, 164

Darius, Steponas – 60
Davitian, Ambassador - 159
Dąbrowski, Henryk, Captain – 130, 131, 136, 141, 145
Distillation (of alcohol) – 38, 40, 169, 171
Dresden – 112

Detroit – 46, 47
Domeyko, Igancy – 152
Dzięciołowski, Władysław, Lieutenant – 130, 148, 149

Earhart, Amelia – 60
Ellis Island – 12, 16, 17, 82
Europe – 4, 9, 16, 25, 54, 56, 60, 65, 78, 82, 83, 97, 106, 107, 110, 120, 128, 129, 139, 153, 158, 160, 185, 204

F. Hass Motors – 32
Fallada, H ans – 162
Fatina, Jadwiga – 39, 40
Father Jarka – 30, 182
FBI, agents Thornton and Sarlo – 170, 181
Filipowicz, Julian, Colonel – 112
Finland (oceanliner) – 14, 16, 18
Floyd Bennet Airport – 61, 62, 80, 81, 92, 93, 120
Fokker (airplane) – 60, 141, 142, 144
France – 106, 108, 109, 114, 139, 164, 166
Frederik VIII (oceanliner) – 19

Galica, Andrzej, general - 125
Garden City – 47, 67
Gdańsk – 7, 118, 137, 145
Gdynia – 39, 141, 145, 146, 168, 171
Germany – 11, 20, 54, 56, 60, 65, 82, 106, 113-6, 146, 153, 163, 208
Girenas, Stasys – 60
glider – 51, 52, 150
Gorman, Stella (Stanisława, born Adamowicz) – 3, 31
Gorman, James – 197
Górczyński, Bolesław – 134
Gruber, Henryk – 139
Grzegorzewo – 150

Haiman, Mieczysław – 153, 205
Halifax – 24, 59, 80, 168
Halle, Louis – 175
Haller, Józef, General – 155
Harbour Grace – 62, 65, 70, 77, 78, 79, 85, 92, 94-99, 100-1, 105, 115
Hausner, Stanislaus L. – 59, 60, 65
Hawker, Harry – 52
Hel, penninsula – 145, 146
Heller, Colonel – 117, 118
Heyno, Anna (Adamowicz) – 3, 31
Hilling, Otto – 57, 61, 65, 70, 71, 72, 94
Hitler, Adolf – 113, 146
Hodur, Franciszek, Bishop - 83
Hoiriis, Holger – 57, 65, 70, 71, 94, 97
Holland (The Netherlands) – 12
Hotel Europejski – 110, 128, 129, 130, 160
Houdemont, Louis, General – 110
Hudson Avenue – 17, 18 32

Huntington, Huber – 86
Hynek, Franciszek – 119, 120

Idzikowski, Ludwik – 56, 57, 58, 134
Inowrocław – 141, 142, 145
Irish, Ireland – 60, 78, 83
Italy – 65, 69
Italian – 18, 29, 41, 43, 45, 51, 57, 58, 78,
Iwaszkiewicz, Wacław, Colonel – 149

Jamaica Bay – 62
Jablrzykowski, Romuald, Archbishop – 149
Jamiołkowski, Stefan – 108, 109
Jankowski, Jan – 32
Janowszczyzna – 3, 5, 8, 14, 15, 31, 129, 140, 147, 160,
Japan, Japanese – 11, 209
Jasna Góra – 140, 146
Jastarnia – 145

Kaczmarek, Jan – 187
Kasprzycki, Tadeusz, General – 132
Katowice – 73, 141, 150, 168
Kelly, Major – 81, 81
Kemmis, Lanny and Nancy – 135, 193
J.F. Kennedy Airport – 62
Kitty Hawk – 52
Kościuszko (oceanliner) – 158, 171
Kościuszko Army – 153-156
Kościuszko Tadeusz – 152
Kozietulski, Jan – 166
Kozłowski, Leon, Prime Minister – 133
Kraków – 118, 140, 141, 160, 201, 205, 206
Kropf, Milton – 175
Krukowski, Kazimierz – 132
Kubala, Kazimierz – 56, 57
Kupajlo, journalist – 141, 144, 145
Kwieciński, Bogdan, Colonel – 112, 117
Krajsk – 3, 4, 5, 11, 14, 15, 87, 160

La Guardia, Fiorello – 67, 172
Lair, Mr. and Mrs. – 109
Le Bourget Airport – 53, 109
League of Air Defense – 133, 141
Leliwa, coat of arms – 6, 7
Leska, Anna – 61
Leroux, Charles – 51
Levine, Charles – 54, 65, 70, 185
Lewisburg Penitentiary – 188-190
Lindbergh, Charles – 46, 53, 54, 57, 61, 67, 69, 70, 166, 174, 176, 184, 185, 205
Lipka Tartars – 7, 8
Lithuania – 3, 5, -9, 13, 16, 17, 20, 60, 81, 148, 205
LOT Polish Airlines – 148

Lublin – 141, 208, 209

Mackenzie-Grieve, Kenneth – 52
Mafia – 43, 170-171, 188, 200
Mathies, Emma (Emilia, b. Adamowicz) – 3, 18, 19, 185, 196
Mattke, Elizabeth (Adamowicz), Ben's wife – 50, 138, 139, 144-147, 168, 185, 187,
Manifest of Alien Passengers – 11, 16
Marchlewski, Consul – 98
Milan – 67
Muslim – 7
Manhattan –17, 28, 50, 67, 187, 191, 195
Mińsk Mazowiecki – 7
Miss Liberty (airplane) – 71, 74
Modlibowska, Wanda – 61
Modlin – 117
Modjeski, Ralph – 152
Modrzejewska (Modjeska), Helena – 152
Moscow – 159
Moskovitz, Grover M., Judge – 181-183
Mościcki, Igancy, President of Poland – 131, 132, 137, 156
Motorcycle – 25, 27, 30, 44, 50, 124
Mussolini, Benito – 58, 69
Mycielski, Stanisław, Count – 142

Napoleon, Napoleonic – 166
National Air and Space Museum – 46
Naturalization – 18, 33-35
National Socialist German Workers' Party (NSDAP) – 113, 146
Newfoundland – 24, 52, 55, 60, 62, 65, 71, 76, 79, 80, 81, 85, 92, 95, 98, 99, 101, 107
New York – 4, 11, 12, 13, 17, 18, 19, 25, 27, 39, 4o-1, 47, 50, 53-4, 56-62, 65, 67, 71, 74, 77, 79, 80, 82, 83, 89, 91-8, 106, 108, 126, 127, 139, 146, 151, 164, 169, 171, 172, 174, 181-4, 186, 188, 192, 194, 195, 197, 198, 203, 204, 205, 208
Newspaper – 32, 39, 40, 83, 89, 90, 100, 115, 120, 121, 130, 137, 140, 153, 162-3, 171, 172, 175, 183, 192, 201
Nitry Henry – 47
Nobel Prize – 8, 152
Normandy – 24, 108

Obituary – 194, 196, 198
Odessa – 166
Ogniem i Mieczem, a novel – 13
Oldsmobile (car) – 44
Ołpiński, Karol, Mayor of Warsaw – 112, 121, 123, 126, 127, 132
Orchard Lake – 83
Orlicz-Dreser, Gustaw, General – 133
Orteig, Raymond – 53
Ospalska Stanisława – 18
Ostra Brama (Marian shrine in Wilno) – 24, 140, 148
Ottoman Empire – 7
Old Country – 21, 25, 31, 43, 116, 120, 151, 156, 164, 167
Olkowicze – 4,5, 12, 19, 31, 148

Ożarów – 7

Packer, Morris – 175
Paderewski, Ignacy Jan – 153, 154, 155, 156
Paris – 3, 6, 7, 108, -111, 136, 139
Parksville – 193, 196
Piłsudski, Marszałek (plane) – 55, 56, 57,
Piłsudski, Józef, Marshal – 56, 127, 132, 148, 155, 156
Picard, Captain – 108, 109, 110
Plymouth – 52
Pokrzywka, Gustaw – 119
Pola Mokotowskie (airport in Warsaw) – 89, 112, 118, 121, 128, 136
Polish diaspora – 25, 80, 120, 206
Polish Aero Club – 71, 86, 110, 117, 121, 126, 128, 132, 134, 141, 160, 191
Polish-Lithuanian Commonwealth – 3, 5, 6, 8, 13, 16, 20, 81
Polish-National Catholic Church – 83
Polonia – 82, 128, 135, 139, 146, 150-156, 167, 184, 201, 204
Portugal – 59
Poznań – 112, 141, 142, 143, 209
President Wilson (ship) – 41, 45
Prohibition – 3, 8, 40-1, 59, 92, 169, 175, 176, 199, 200
Prussia – 4, 20, 22, 50, 145, 153
Przemyśl – 7
Puck – 146
Pułaski (oceanliner) – 39, 43, 146,
Pułaski, Kazimerz – 152

Queens – 40

Raczkiewicz, Władysław – 133
Radziwiłł, Janusz, Prince – 132, 133
yski, Ludomir, General – 112, 121, 123, 127, 159
Riga – 31
Robaczynski Machine Corporation – 192
Rogalski, Stanislaw – 119
Romania – 168
Roosevelt Field, airport – 47, 53
Roosevelt, Franklin Delano, President – 8, 175, 200
Ross, Harold – 185, 186
Rotterdam – 12
Russia – 3- 4, 9, 10, 11, 14, 16- 18, 20, 21, 41, 82, 137, 146, 153, 209
RWD Planes – 55, 119, 141
Ryan Company – 53, 67

San Diego – 67, 70
Sarmento de Beires, Jose – 54
Savings Bank – 22, 90, 139
Savinos' Quality Pasta – 29, 93
Savoia Marchetti (seaplane) – 58
Schwartz, Jack – 171, 177, 179, 182, 185
Semple, John C. – 173
Senegal – 56

Seyfang, Frank George – 51
Siemiatycze – 7
Sienkiewicz, Henryk – 8
Silesia – 150, 160
Skarżyński, Stanisław – 55, 56, 112, 120, 133, 136, 144, 145
Skłodowska-Curie, Maria – 152
Skrzetuska, Anna (married to Adamowicz) – 12, 13, 18, 19, 31,61, 194
Skrzetuski, Jan – 13, 206
Skrzetuski, Mikołaj – 13
Sławoj-Składkowski, Felicjan – 132
Sobieski, King Jan III – 13
Soviet Union – 3, 4, 8, 31, 140, 158-160, 200
Speak Easy (speakeasy) – 39-43, 59
Spirit of St. Louis, The (airplane) – 46, 53, 67, 69, 70
St. John's Cemetery in Brooklyn – 193-195
St. Stanislaus Kostka Parish (Roman Catholic church) – 24
Suwałki – 17
Stalin, Josef – 8, 155, 158
Strumph-Wojtkiewicz, Stanisław – 4, 41, 58, 71, 76, 98, 99, 121, 137,-9, 164, 165, 166, 176, 203, 206
Studebaker (car) – 44
Stultz, Wilmer – 60
Szczecińska Zofia – 61

Świetlik, Franciszek – 156
Świdnik – 168

Tarnowski family – 8
Tartar names: Aksan, Aksanow, Adamowicz, Abramowicz, Musicz, Illasiewicz and Smolski – 8
Teutonic Knights – 7
Toruń – 75, 115, 116, 117, 118
Triaca, Albert C. – 51
Tschaudorf – 114
Turk, Turkish – 6,7
Turbiak, Tomasz, Colonel – 112
Tyszkiewicz – 8 (Jan), 10 (countess), 207 (Jan)

Vienna – 7
Vilnius (see also Wilno) – 5, 60, 124
Vistula (Wisła), a river – 116, 118, 137

Warszawa – 9, 24, 39, 56, 58, 59, 61, 62, 71, 74, 75, 76, 78, 79, 89, 90, 92, 95,96, 97, 98, 99, 100, 101, 107, 108, 11, 112-128, 131-2, 134, 139, 140-2, 146-7, 150-2, 157, 159, 160-5, 178, 184-6, 203, 205, 206,
Warsaw (airplane) – 74
Washington, D.C. – 46, 87, 90
Washington (oceanliner) – 139
Wehmhoefer brothers (Wehmhoeffer) – 28
Wigura, Stanisław – 119, 134
White Eagle (airplane) – 50, 58, 74, 79, 89, 90, 208
Whitehead, Gustave – 51

Whitten-Brown, Arthur – 53, 57
Wilno (see also Vilnius) – 3, 5, 8, 14, 124, 140, 141, 147-151, 160, 161, 203
Wilson, Woodrow, Presiden – 153, 154, 175, 200
Wingfoot Air Express (airship) – 51
World War I – 3-5, 8, 25, 31, 45, 52, 53, 55, 61, 67, 146, 152, 153, 155
World War II – 5, 8, 21, 25, 155, 192
Wojtulanis, Stefania – 61, 204
Wright, Orville and Wilbur – 52, 207
Wright's engine – 50, 69, 72
Wyrwicz-Wichrowski, Karol – 150

Yalta Conference – 8, 155

Zeligowski, Lucjan, General – 148

Żwirko, Franciszek – 119, 134, 145

www.ingramcontent.com/pod-product-compliance
Lightning Source LLC
Chambersburg PA
CBHW031140160426
43193CB00008B/202